GALLIPOLI TO THE SOMME

Gallipoli to the Somme

RECOLLECTIONS OF A
NEW ZEALAND INFANTRYMAN

By
Alexander Aitken
8/2524 N.Z.E.F.

Edited and Introduced By
Alex Calder

AUCKLAND
UNIVERSITY
PRESS

First published 1963 by Oxford University Press

This edition published 2018
Reprinted 2018
Auckland University Press
University of Auckland
Private Bag 92019
Auckland 1142
New Zealand
www.press.auckland.ac.nz

Introduction and notes © Alex Calder, 2018

ISBN 978 186940 881 7

A catalogue record for this book is available from
the National Library of New Zealand.

Cover image: George Edmund Butler, *At the Alert, Gas Zone* (detail), c.1918.
Oil on board, 450 x 350mm. Archives New Zealand Te Rua
Mahara o te Kāwanatanga, AAAC 898 NCWA Q458.

Book design by Katrina Duncan
Cover design by Carolyn Lewis

This book was printed on FSC® certified paper

Printed by Ligare Ltd, Auckland

Contents

Editor's Introduction

O N 14 JULY 1916, AT ARMENTIÈRES, THE 4TH COMPANY OF THE 1ST Otago Infantry Battalion made a disastrous night raid on the trenches opposite. Of the 181 men who blackened their faces and clambered over the parapet, 163 would be killed or wounded. Sergeant Alexander Aitken, of 10th Company, had been picked to lead a section of his former platoon in a supporting position on the left flank. The platoon wriggled through the wire in advance of the main assault and dug into shell holes in the middle of no-man's-land. A tremendous artillery barrage went overhead, crashing into the German trenches. Aitken checked his watch: zero hour, the raiders would be on their way. Suddenly, bright flares shot up from the enemy lines, illuminating the men of 4th Company as they fell to machine-gun fire and crumpled under shrapnel bursts. Out on the flank, the supporting party themselves came under fire. Aitken had earlier noticed that men from another section of the platoon were dug in rather too close to a row of trees—a natural ranging target for German mortar crews. Few would survive the night's long bombardment. Come daylight, having helped carry in the wounded, Aitken returned exhausted to his own lines.

He was in a bad way, suffering—he thought later—from minor shell shock. Captain James Hargest gently guided him back to Company HQ and suggested he try to catch some sleep. Whenever Aitken closed his eyes, he 'heard again . . . the whistle of the falling mortar bombs', he saw his dead and dying comrades, he saw that line of trees. He gradually became aware of a conversation continuing around him, and that it involved his former platoon's roll book, presumed missing along with the sergeant in whose pocket it had been inadvertently taken into action. The details it contained were now urgently needed. In a semi-trance, Aitken dictated the full name, the regimental number, the name of next of kin, and the address of next of kin, for every member of his old platoon—a total of fifty-six men.[1]

Those who were killed that day are buried in the Cité Bonjean military cemetery just out of town. It contains a total of 453 individual New Zealand graves, along with a 'Memorial to the Missing' listing the names of a further 47 known to have been killed in this sector but whose bodies were never recovered. In one corner of a manicured lawn stands a monument with the inscription: 'THEIR NAME LIVETH FOR EVERMORE'. For a visitor like me, that cannot be true. I do not remember any of 'the fallen': the names are mere names, alphabetised into anonymity. A battlefield tourist following in Aitken's footsteps can drive in not much more than an hour from Armentières, where the New Zealand Division was introduced to the Western Front in May 1916, to the necropolis of the Somme, where another 'Memorial to the Missing' at Caterpillar Valley lists the names of 1,205 New Zealanders whose remains were unidentifiable or never found—an astonishing half of those killed here in September and October 1916, yet the merest fraction of the 72,194 names inscribed on the nearby British 'Memorial to the Missing of the Somme' at Thiepval. That total is so unfathomably large it seems impossible they can all be there; yet every name is present and correct and locatable by a relative making a pilgrimage.

I made my own visit to the Thiepval Memorial in September 2016, during the hundredth anniversary of the Battle of the Somme. Naturally, I looked first for my own name. I could see Calder after

Calder in the Highland Regiments, but who was to say any of them were 'mine'? Lacking a known personal connection, the mind struggles to take in the magnitude of this towering monument to loss. But an information panel helps the visitor size up this edifice in mathematical terms. There are 72,194 names—so many per square foot on a site of so many square feet. How did the architect fit them all in? Sir Edward Lutyens found a geometrically elegant solution: by basing his design on a stack of interlocking arches, he was able to maximise the surface available for inscription.

While I was pondering dimensions, our battlefield tour-guide had retired to change his clothes, emerging in a suit and bowler hat to MC a brief ceremony of remembrance. There was to be one of these for each of the 141 days of the Somme. Huddled family groups mounted the steps to lay a wreath. People spoke. There was a minute's silence, followed by a Last Post—someone pressed play on a boom-box—that was nonetheless moving in this setting. Not so the closing Exhortation:

> They shall grow not old, as we that are left grow old:
> Age shall not weary them, nor the years condemn.
> At the going down of the sun and in the morning,
> We will remember them.

Familiar words, yet I recoiled from them. There is a gap between names that are recorded and people who are remembered—and I felt it open like a chasm in the air between the arches of the missing at Thiepval.

Yet my encounter with these 'intolerably nameless names'[2] is offset by a story about one of them, carried from the war as a letter from the comrades of a lost Irishman, killed that very day a hundred years ago, to his widow. The grandson explained that the letter had little to say, except to acknowledge an act of kindness recently performed by the dead man, and to assure his wife that while her husband's body had not been recovered, they had had time to arrange his limbs, that he had not died uncared for. All modern war stories need to find a way between these two extremes. There is a human scale—individual, singular, ordinary—on which our sympathies are engaged. Set against this world of particulars and singularities is everything that is too big or too much for ready comprehension. This forms the least communicable part of a soldier's experience. We see it in the way diaries written at the time so often need words for a lack of words: 'I can't say', 'you had to be there'. Perhaps something similar happens when we read about war. To learn that 19,240 British soldiers were killed on the first day of the Somme gives one measure of grief and suffering, yet all such numbers, to paraphrase Stalin, are merely statistics. So while friends and relatives may feel the loss of a single soldier's life as a tragedy, that focus is less available to anyone trying to explain what it was like to be a soldier in the Great War. Aitken at one point explains that grief for a school-friend would be felt later, but in the pitch of battle, his strongest impression is of casualties occurring everywhere around him. The true theme of the war memoir is not the single death, but death in numbers, death over and over, even though those numbers numb the mind.

Yet Aitken's restoration of the missing roll-book works the other way. No-one really believes the names on these war monuments live 'for evermore': there is no human memory that could encompass them. But, like so much else in this volume, Aitken's hypermnesic recollection of impersonal military records has a particularizing, and humanizing, force. Against the odds, fifty-six names, along with their connections, have been remembered. Rolls of the dead make the mind glaze over, but on this occasion we feel wonder. It is not surprising the episode soon grew into legend. Some soldiers said Aitken knew the numbers of their rifles too, and he was himself put out when, in the 1930s, the episode returned in an even more unlikely form: a lubberly newspaper reporter had mistaken his platoon for a battalion. Like all good stories, this one went around the world. And so, one afternoon, on his quiet walk home from the university, Professor Aitken noticed newspaper billboards with the headline, EDINBURGH WIZARD. Much to his dismay, on opening the evening paper, he discovered the wizard was himself.[3]

The man with the enchanted memory was born in Dunedin on
1 April 1895, the eldest of the seven children of Elizabeth and William
Aitken, a grocer's assistant. William's parents ran a small leasehold
farm on the Otago Peninsula at Seal Point. The grandchildren were
frequent visitors there, as well as to the farm of their Auntie Jeanie,
on the coast north of the city at Waitati. In 1945, Aitken recalled those
childhood holidays in a letter to his aunt that is interesting not only for
the flavour it gives of his early years, but also for the highly imagistic
quality of the recollections, and for his habit of listing one impression
after another, making a slideshow out of his long, semicolon-heavy
sentences. He also intertwines these vividly recollected images with
a reflexive commentary on how his memory is functioning. His war
experiences would be remembered in this way too.

I always remembered with greatest clearness my visits to, and stays at
Waitati. How I used to hear the trains at night come round the cliffs,
away over across the bay, from Purakaunui, and then quite a time after,
rumble by the creamery; . . . the washing and polishing of the cream-
separator, the two-handed sawing of wood with Uncle George; you and
Mrs Pullor going off to paint; the Rev. A. M. Finlayson looking hard at
me when I said 'to commiserate with' instead of 'to commiserate'; . . . .
the pig-hunting expedition, . . . no wild boar, but an unforgettable memory
of the pure clear water of the Waikouaiti River in its upper reaches,
purling over golden shingle as we emerged upon it from the bush in the
early morning . . . I could if I liked add detail to detail, a little here and
a little there, and recapture the whole picture of some thirty years ago.
And I can do the same for an earlier time, the old days down Seal Point
at Grandpa's; even the earliest, enormously far back in time, yet vivid;
going to holidays in the cart, our mother in it, we in shelter under cover,
leaving behind us Dunedin and Otago Harbour, and reaching that high
point by Highcliff where suddenly the outer Pacific is seen, the Gull Rock
and that other rock, the tongue of cape stretching out toward it from
Sandymount, and away down, the tiny farm-houses of Seal Point in their
clumps of trees . . .[4]

As a child, Aitken's horizons were not to be encompassed by any classroom. 'Can you spell cat?' asked the infant mistress on his first day; he preferred to spell words like 'Invercargill'.[5] Others in the family had been precocious. An uncle had shown an early gift for mental calculation, but there was no money in the family for education. Aitken's father also had a pronounced facility with figures, mentally totting up the pounds, shillings and pence in the grocery account books, and requiring his eldest boy to do the same. That was putting a talent to use. One feels there would have been no great sorrow had Alec also been obliged to leave school early; fortunately, he obtained a scholarship to Otago Boys' High School, but his wife Winifred would later recall that it was 'touch-and-go whether he wasn't taken from school at 13'.[6]

On his first day of high school, Aitken was dubbed 'Swotty' after memorising a Latin vocabulary at a glance. It takes a certain milieu to produce a nickname like that, but it stuck with some affection and went with him to the trenches. Aitken seems only to have minded that the label was so misapplied: 'Few pupils at OBHS have ever worked less', he insisted. 'I played an inordinate amount of fives, I took some part in athletics, and used to leave preparing my lessons until just before classes, walking up the three hills of London Street.'[7] Nonetheless, in his final year, he took first place overall in the National University Scholarship Examinations by a considerable margin, having come first in Latin, third in both English and Mathematics, and fourth in French.[8]

But the most important points of growth for Aitken in his teenage years were extracurricular. Winifred recalls his introduction to the violin:

When my husband was 18, his father produced an old fiddle, an execrable instrument, & said that if he liked to teach himself to play it, he could have it. He had one term's tuition from an old and nearly blind fiddler, who couldn't even see the position of the fingers on the strings properly, & everything since then has been done by himself, by almost superhuman efforts.[9]

The musician we meet in these pages has only had three years with his instrument, yet he is already proficient enough to attempt Bach's 'Chaconne' when confined to quarters at Estaires. Later in life, Aitken became the leader of the Edinburgh University Musical Society Orchestra and performed much of the repertoire for string quartet to a high amateur standard. He often said he gave far more thought to music than to mathematics.[10] One is bound to wonder how someone so intellectually gifted could spend most of his war, not as an officer with all the advantages rank might offer a diffident young man, but as a regular N.C.O., rubbing along with the labourers and farm-workers and tradesmen of the Regiment. The violin is the strongest clue: as Sarah Shieff points out, 'this incongruous piece of contraband' is passed hand-to-hand on long route marches only because the men judge it worth carrying. As she goes on to suggest, it represents moments of community, of the fragility of precious things, and for Aitken himself, in his solo practice sessions, a way of structuring time that runs counter to an inhuman military order.[11]

The discovery that mathematics opened a door to memory came at the age of fifteen. Until then, school arithmetic was a bore, but algebra, when introduced by a gifted teacher, came as a revelation. Simple formulae could be short-cuts to large calculations and Aitken soon made a game out of squaring three-digit numbers. 'I then began to feel I might develop a real power', he recalled, 'and for some years ... practiced mental calculations and memory like a Brahmin Yogi.'[12] He also noticed an increasing ease:

> I found that gains were cumulative and, so to speak, stratified, in the sense that they formed a deposit sinking deeper and deeper into the subconscious and forming a kind of potential which, in certain states, I make drafts at extraordinary speed. I discovered, too, that the more I used *relaxation,* not concentration as ordinarily understood; for concentration, the dinning in by force, is the surest way to put a clamp on your brain, to stop its easy functioning and to lose all your gain. Memory naturally played a great part, and reciprocally memory itself was strengthened

in all other departments of acquired learning as well. For example poetry, especially Latin poetry, and music became easier to learn at a few readings.[13]

Aitken seems to have been a tenacious improver in any field that took his interest. He had no special flair for athletics, but pushed himself as a jumper, setting higher and higher bars on a frame made from saplings in a bush clearing, and took pride in reaching a reasonably competitive level at school and, later, inter-university games.[14]

When war broke out in 1914, Aitken was nineteen years old and in his second year at university. He wanted to join up immediately along with fellow students like his friend George Pilling, but his father would not give the necessary permission. Alec had to wait until April 1915, when he was of an age to enlist without parental consent. Unusually for a war memoirist, Aitken's narrative begins not with these events, but with his embarkation for Egypt with the Sixth Reinforcements on 14 August 1915. He tells us nothing about his motives for going; nor is there a single anecdote about his induction into military life, or the months of training and drill-bashing at Trentham military camp. So far as telling a war story is concerned, this is a significant omission. As Paul Fussell points out: 'Every war is ironic because every war is worse than expected. . . . But the Great War was more ironic than any before or since.'[15] The irony, at its simplest, is of a war that would be over by Christmas dragging into four years of deadlock; or of General Sir Douglas Haig, writing to his wife on the eve of the Somme, 'I feel that every step of my plan has been taken with the Divine help', and confiding to his diary, 'the wire had never been so well cut nor the artillery preparation so thorough'.[16] Irony is what we are left with when events conspicuously prove otherwise. But by forgoing the 'before' of a 'before-and-after' narrative, Aitken's memoir cannot so easily follow the familiar contours of a story in which an innocent and optimistic young soldier is confronted by human savagery on an unprecedented scale. Nor can his memoir follow the archetypal story of a journey and return home common in war narratives from the *Odyssey* to *The Lord of the Rings*. As a writer, he would need to find other points of contrast and subtler tones and effects. His memory helped him in at least two ways. The clear, postcard-like images he could summon to mind work hand in hand with the power of the telling detail to suggest more than themselves. And we see his memory develop a more intimate relation to irony in the way it picks out events from the ambient horror: it is nothing to jump into a trench littered with dead bodies, but when a man drops into a trench to find his brother, not seen since Gallipoli, lying dead at his feet—that is bound to be memorable.[17] As Aitken himself puts it: 'The Somme seemed to predispose such abstract and inhuman coincidences as these.'

Despite his decision to focus only on his period of active service overseas, there can be little mystery about Aitken's motives for enlisting. His idealism is legible between the lines of his narrative, and there is no reason to suppose he would have felt differently from fellow Otago students, like Pilling, whose personal diary reveals that he volunteered out of loyalty to the Empire in its time of need, and that he felt a duty to defend civilised values against the militarism of the Central Powers. Had Aitken's father allowed him to leave with the Main Body, he may, of course, not have returned with a story to tell. And had he survived the disasters of the April landings on Gallipoli or the Sari Bair offensive of August 1915, he would perhaps have been among the remnant evacuated to Lemnos, men so hollowed out by sickness and exhaustion, they seemed ghosts of themselves to the fit and unbloodied reinforcements. Shaken to be meeting so few survivors, Aitken introduces a quasi-mathematical calculation: 'the sixteen companies in the four infantry battalions . . . had been reduced in almost the same proportion', and itemises his own North Otagos as an instance. They number only eighteen men, have no officers, no senior N.C.O.s, only two lance-corporals, and even with the influx of fresh troops, the company is less than a third its full strength. One senses the kind of applied maths question that might invite an examinee to compute the full strength of the Expeditionary Force and its casualties suffered to date, but there is no calculation to perform. He might have provided an actual figure from published histories of the campaign, but has instead portrayed himself trying to take in the situation mathematically. Aitken served at Gallipoli for five weeks prior to the evacuation, and we often see him coming to terms with his experience in this mathematical way. Troubled one night by the thought of having possibly killed someone—he and another soldier had fired simultaneously at an incautious Turk—his mind turns to a probability table, but he finds 'to become analytical might lead to doubt the cause for which we were fighting'—which was awkward, since 'he was far from such doubt then'. On one of several occasions in which he escapes death by a whisker, he remarks, again with a mathematician's objectivity, that since survival and death in these circumstances are equally matters of chance, there is no comfort to be found in the fatalism of those who speak of their 'number being up' or of a shell with someone's name on it.

The Anzacs had been mauled by Gallipoli, but worse was to follow on the Western Front. More detailed explanations of historical and military context are best left to the editorial notes, but it is worth reminding the reader that in May 1916 the New Zealand Division arrived at a front that had been locked in stalemate since the so-called 'Race to the Sea' of 1914, a series of attempted and countered flanking movements that left in its wake lines of opposing trenches running from the Belgian coast to the Swiss Alps. On the whole, the German Army had the better position: they were drier, on higher ground, and had the great advantage of perfecting well-prepared defensive positions while the British and French, if the war was to be won, were obliged to push back the invaders. Allied attacks in the summer of 1915 had cost 200,000 casualties to no effect. The problem, it seemed then, was ineffective artillery support for the infantry and deadly retaliation from enemy guns; moreover, because the infantry had attacked on a narrow front, it was difficult to bring in reserves in support of any advantage gained, yet counterattacks could be tightly focused. For six months, Haig and his generals prepared countermeasures and formulated new plans for a major summer offensive that would annihilate the German Army.

Meanwhile, the Germans attacked the French at Verdun. Unlike the British, they expected no quick, decisive victory. The plan was to attack at a place the French were committed to defend and grind them down through attrition. When the Anzacs reached the front in May 1916, Verdun was already a pressure point, and the so-called 'nursery sector' around Armentières was proving to be no kindergarten. The Germans had to be prevented from reinforcing at Verdun and along the Somme. The raid of the 4th Otagos on 14 July may have been prompted by such considerations, but, as Aitken suggests, its catastrophic result cannot be sheeted home to Haig and his most senior generals only. Night raids were usually the work of twenty or thirty men who had a definite and limited objective, such as capturing prisoners for interrogation. 'Who was to blame for its failure, that is to say, for the plan itself?' Aitken asks. 'Probably Division or Brigade, having chosen so large a unit as a company to go over—but surely Battalion also, for drafting so unimaginative a scheme.'

Two weeks earlier, on 1 July, after a week-long artillery bombardment in which a million and a half shells were fired, the Allies attacked along a broad thirteen-mile front at the Somme. At 7.30 a.m., as the British guns increased their range and began to pummel more distant targets, some 110,000 troops began to walk towards the German front lines. They were expecting cut wire and little opposition. At 7.31 or thereabouts, the German troops emerged like angered wasps from their deep dug-outs, and within moments were deploying machine-guns. As a child reader of the war comics of the 1960s, I have found it difficult to entirely lose the impression that machine-gun 'nests', with their inevitable 'rat-a-tat', are positioned not far in front of advancing troops, their pinging bullets nimbly side-stepped by a rushing attacker or passing harmlessly over the head of the commando wriggling towards the enemy, grenade in hand. In fact, the effective range of machine-guns in the Great War was two and a half kilometres. They could be fired en masse on an upwards trajectory to land as a carpeting bombardment or, more deadly still, positioned at an angle to attacking troops, so that the hail of bullets arrived in enfilade, which closed up the gap between individual targets. The geometry is important: a pair of machine-guns positioned squarely in front of those Otago men making a dash of a hundred yards or so might account for around two-thirds of them before they themselves were overrun. But if the same pair of guns were placed at an angle of 45 degrees to the direction of the attack, the entire attacking force might be killed or wounded in less than a minute. Separate the pair, and the cross-fire becomes more lethal still.

Having lost 60,000 casualties on the first day of the Somme, Haig proposed a second push for mid-July, and, having once again made only small gains at enormous cost, a third for mid-September. With Aitken's story, we follow the New Zealand Division as they assiduously practise the new tactics: close cooperation with air support and an attack timed to the moving curtain provided by a creeping artillery barrage, which (if it worked) meant the first wave would be on the enemy before they had time to reorganize. There was also a surprise weapon, the tank—a 'rhomboid' to a mathematician—introduced for the first time alongside the New Zealanders in their attack on Flers. But despite early successes and incremental gains in September and into October, one could never say the Allies had overcome the essential disadvantage of attacking positions defended by wire and machine-guns and supported by mobile, long-range artillery. Moreover, the Germans were now using a more a flexible system of defence. Trenches were an obvious target for artillery. Rather than garrison those, they began to defend the zones before and behind them, in which ruined farm buildings, blasted woods, and even the shell-holes of no-man's land provided cover for machine-gun ambushes.

As Aitken's narrative slows in tempo to focus on a week, then a day, then the hours and minutes of a day, we discover that some of the New Zealand Division's finest moments on the Western Front occurred in close proximity to many of their worst. On 25 September, Aitken found himself leading the first wave of an attack supported by a creeping barrage. He had to set the exact pace—counting 'nought abc, one abc'—to bring the Company onto the German line at the precise moment the barrage lifted. That day, everything went like clockwork. Our troops have been accused of regularly killing German soldiers who were attempting to surrender on the Western Front.[18] Whatever the merits of the charge, Aitken and his platoon are a humane counter-example. On reaching the enemy trench, they jumped in with fixed bayonets but ignored the grisly incitements of their training. Looking at the young faces, Aitken 'felt a compunction'. His men bandaged the German wounded and sent the remainder back as prisoners. When their badly wounded commanding officer, 'deathly white and in grievous pain', thanked him in French, Aitken realized, 'I could have no quarrel with such a man.'

Two days later, attacking along the same communication trench, Goose Alley, three companies of the 1st Otagos were almost annihilated—the machine-gun bullets, again in enfilade, sweeping the Otagos' unprotected left flank from the ruins of Eaucourt l'Abbaye. Aitken was hit in the upper arm and, seconds later, in the ankle. He crawled to a shell-hole as German artillery ranged the battlefield. After some time, and in the midst of all that cacophony, Aitken thought he could detect 'a regularity, a periodicity, in a particular type of explosion'. He concentrated more carefully and, sure enough, it sounded like shells from a howitzer were 'coming closer every two minutes, apparently in a straight line'. When he first noticed the pattern, the explosions were 500 yards away. 'I visualized the German gunners lowering their howitzers by a fraction of an angle each time; I reckoned that in about ten minutes one of these shells would fall near my crater, possibly on it'. And so he made the decision to risk crawling to a safer position. A howitzer bombardment has no thought for individual human targets; it is a systematic, calculated, impersonal technique. Under that kind of fire, I suspect most of us would nonetheless feel ourselves to be the quivering epicentre of all the hostile forces arrayed against us—and would have stayed curled up like a hedgehog in our shell-hole. Aitken's capacity for pattern-recognition promoted an unusual objectivity. He could see himself as an impersonal coordinate in space; in a sense, mathematics had saved his life.

Many extraordinary mathematical minds went through the Great War—Ludwig Wittgenstein with the Germans, André Bloch with the French—but I doubt anyone had a memory to match Aitken's. It was as if his brain, like the arches at Thiepval, had somehow maximised the surface available for inscription. After the war, he would perform astonishing mental calculations with lightning accuracy: the result of a nine-digit by nine-digit multiplication was available to him in seconds. When asked on BBC Radio to convert twenty-three forty-sevenths into a decimal, he began reciting 0.489361 and continued to crank out numbers like a ticker-tape until, at forty-six decimal places, he found the point at which the sequence repeats. Everything he saw, he could remember. And yet his memory was not strictly photographic: it was stranger than that, preternatural in its reach and in what it could recover. Given a sequence of five digits from anywhere in the first thousand places of *pi*, Aitken could resume a rhythmic chant of the series as unerringly as he could, if thrown a passage of the *Aeneid* or *Paradise Lost,* pick up and continue the verse.

A memory so prodigious attracted scientific examination. One of the more common tests involves asking the subject to give back a random list of twenty-five words. Many of us might manage one or two more than five. Someone trained to recall haphazard lists might produce all twenty-five, perhaps by relating each word to a detail in a mental walk through a landscape. Aitken did not use those tricks. It took three turns before he could repeat the entire sequence, but he was then able to recall the sequence the next day, the next week, and again three months later. A psychologist doing similar tests with Aitken in 1960 was interested in that earlier test—Aitken laughed, said he remembered the occasion well, and went on to recover all the words from the test card of twenty-seven years before.[19]

Compared to his military service, Aitken's subsequent academic career, distinguished as it was, must seem uneventful. He entered Otago University in 1912 and took courses in Latin, French, and Mathematics, the latter poorly taught, and on his return from the war, not taught at all. He was tutored by his old high-school teacher. Final exams for an MA with double honours in Mathematics and in Languages and Literature were marked in England: he achieved first-class honours for his French and Latin, but—thanks to questions on post-war research in aeronautics that bore no relation to the stated curriculum—graduated with only second-class honours in Mathematics. A future seemed laid out before him: he would teach French and Latin at Otago Boys', and did so from 1920 to 1923. His classroom was said to be rowdy: in a caning school, he never caned a boy.[20] But he got to know a real mathematician when, in 1920, Professor R. J. T. Bell from Glasgow was appointed to the university. With Bell's encouragement, Aitken applied for, and was awarded, a postgraduate scholarship to the University of Edinburgh, where he came under the guidance of Professor Sir Edmund Whittaker. Winifred Betts, the musically gifted botanist whom he married in 1920, accompanied him to Scotland a few months later. Neither would return to New Zealand. A brilliant doctoral thesis earned Aitken the higher degree of D.Sc., and with a lecturing position in statistics and actuarial mathematics falling vacant in a timely manner, he began his long professional association with the University of Edinburgh, rising through the ranks, publishing regularly, and replacing Whittaker as Senior Professor and Head of Department in 1946—a position he held for nineteen years. One could say without reservation that Alexander Aitken was a leading mathematician who made significant contributions in statistics, numerical analysis, and algebra, but one could say much the same of a hundred other professors of his day. He had a genius of a mathematical sort, but its quirks and applications did not become those of a mathematician of towering accomplishment.

For those of us for whom matrices might as well be mattresses, the most intriguing thing about Aitken's subsequent academic career is that it was interrupted once again by war. According to a revised entry in the *Oxford Dictionary of National Biography*, Aitken was one of the Bletchley Park code-breakers, working in Hut 6.[21] Since he was bound by the Official Secrets Act, Aitken no doubt kept the information to himself. But I must strike a note of caution: the *ODNB's* reference to Hut 6 is unverified. Only one of the many histories of Bletchley Park

I have consulted has a mention of him—again without further reference.[22] It makes sense that someone of his abilities would be drawn into this secret mathematical world, possibly for a brief period, but a nervous breakdown in 1941, along with documented evidence of his continued presence in Edinburgh, suggests the bulk of his war work may have been, as he told his brother, in the less glamourous field of agricultural statistics.[23]

Gallipoli to the Somme was published in 1963, when the soldiers of the Great War were in their seventies, happier now to talk, and to make possible the more intimate television documentaries and oral histories that would follow. Aitken's memoir is of this time, as well as the earlier times of its composition. In many ways, it is exactly what it seems to be: a vivid account of recent personal experience, written from memory over the six months in which he was an outpatient undergoing daily treatment for his wounds at Dunedin Hospital in 1917. (Several excerpts were published anonymously the following year in the *Otago University Review* as 'Scraps From A Diary, 1915–16' and are reprinted as an appendix to this volume). In 1930, stimulated by the example of Blunden, Graves, and Sassoon, Aitken 'disinterred' his old typescript and turned it into a chaptered book. In reflecting on his experience, in trying to understand how and why such terrible things happened, the author, like his contemporaries, has no time for patriotic lies or militaristic euphemisms: he communicates the cost of war. Later still, as his wife Winifred recalled, 'whenever he had one of his nervy spells, the old manuscript was dug out & worked on, as at such times his war experiences recurred—I've seen him at such a time yelling to his men to lie flat in the trench'.[24] The manuscript reached an almost-finished form in 1961 when Aitken wrote it all out carefully by hand, in three little black notebooks, with the title: 'An Anzac Remembers'.[25] There were no definite plans for publication.

Aitken was severely ill by this stage—incapacitated by insomnia, depression, and arteriosclerosis. Winifred did all the work of seeing the book through the press, and in November 1962 explained its fortuitous road to publication to their friend, the mathematician Arthur Erdélyi:

Well, in August of last year, Prof. T. B. Smith (Civil Law) a close friend of Alec's, called here to see him, & the typescript was lying on the table. So we told him about it, & he asked whether he could take it away to read. In a couple of days he rang up & said he had found it intensely moving, & asked if he might send it to his old Brigadier of the 2nd World War (Brigadier Bernard Fergusson, now Sir Bernard Fergusson, Governor General of New Zealand). The latter read it (shortly before he left for N.Z.) & was so impressed by it that he asked Alec if he might send it to his literary agents & get their opinion of it. Then a little later, the latter wrote saying O.U.P. would like to publish it. Sir Bernard Fergusson very kindly offered to contribute a foreword. So the book, more or less the result of accident, has come out, & has had most gratifying reviews.[26]

In fact, the literary agents, Curtis Brown, doubted whether the market would stand another book on the war, and it wasn't until Fergusson himself made a personal approach to another New Zealand soldier and writer, Dan Davin, a senior editor at Oxford University Press, that the book's future was assured.[27]

The reviews were, as Winifred said, both extensive and 'most gratifying'. Many took the line that a new classic had been added to the literature of the war. The historian, A. J. P. Taylor, commenting on his personal selection of the year's best books for the *Observer*, thought it 'eclipsed all others as a book both true and moving'.[28] The reviewer for the *Daily Telegraph* wrote: 'I have seldom read anything which moved me more . . . much of the prose is purest poetry.'[29] Aitken had been a Fellow of the Royal Society since the 1930s—one of the rarer accolades was his election to the Royal Society of Literature on the strength of this single work.

Aitken's enduring achievement is *Gallipoli to the Somme*. Had the book appeared in the early 1930s, it might well have joined the distinguished body of poetry and memoir that still defines the war. Appearing in 1963, it arrived after that canon had taken shape and too late to join it. It has been remembered by people with Otago connections, and by a small phalanx of military, mathematical, and literary specialists, but has more generally faded from view. It perhaps needs to be said that this is unquestionably the most distinguished writing we in New Zealand have from the Great War. Not that it is the only such writing to claim our attention: Robin Hyde's documentary novel, *Passport to Hell,* focused on a larrikin soldier known to Aitken, is of permanent interest, as are the histories by a soldier in the Auckland Regiment, Ormond Burton, the author of *The Silent Division* (1935), as well as the two late-life memoirs of another university professor, Cecil Malthus, who served with the Canterbury Infantry Regiment. The latter says of *Gallipoli to the Somme* 'it stands in a class apart'.[30] I think he is right, not only because the writing is of a superior order, and with a tone you will find nowhere else—restrained, erudite, precise, compassionate—but also for what it says about memory and the ongoing significance of the war.

The reader will notice that when Aitken refers in passing to a fellow soldier, he often supplies regimental numbers and dates and places of death. These little acts of memory, mostly but not always accurate, were recorded without reference to external sources. L. S. Jennings, killed at Flers, 15 September 1916; T. Wilson, killed at Armentières 28 May 1916; K. C. Finlayson 8/918, [killed] in the first battle of the Somme; Sergeant Carruthers, killed Passchendaele, 12 October 1917; or Private William J. Clarke, 8/1432, who threw himself on a defective grenade in the days before the raid at Armentières. Of the latter, Aitken comments: 'for me, it is enough in pride, however undeserving, to be permitted to describe his last act with precision and to associate it with his name'. That, in essence, is what 8/2524 has to say about 8/1432— and all the counted and remembered dead. It is in a spirit of precise commemoration that numbers that would otherwise make a tally are recollected as numbers that truly name.

As for the book's significance to our memory of the First World War more generally, I note that *Gallipoli to the Somme* shares its year of publication with the popular anti-war musical *Oh, What a Lovely War!,* in which the British generals are portrayed as callous buffoons. 1963 was also the year of the first collected edition of Wilfred Owen's poetry. The BBC's 26-episode documentary, *The Great War,* came out the following year. Its indelible title sequence pans down a photograph of a trench wall to rest on the horrific remains of a decomposing corpse sinking into its uniform. Works like these have made Gallipoli and the Somme bywords for waste, suffering, and military incompetence. More recently, a revisionist line emerged from researchers with a detailed technical interest in the military history of the Western Front. They not unreasonably argue that, when a country finds itself at war, the point is to win it. For them, Haig and his senior staff were intelligently going about the formidable task of pushing the Germans back. Casualties were indeed high, but not unacceptable give the large numbers of personnel involved. And so, as the blurb to one new history of the Somme has it: 'a positive interpretation of the battle emerges. Not only did the battle form a crucial part of the learning process, which helped the British generals eventually adopt winning tactics, but it also ripped the heart out of the German Army.'[31] General Russell, commanding the New Zealand Division, would have enjoyed that assessment. In his foreword to the *Official History of the Otago Regiment,* he says: 'Fate . . . seemed to take a sinister pleasure in placing the Otago Regiment in the hottest corners of the fight.' And after noting the serial catastrophes of 'Pope's Hill, May 2nd 1915, the raid at Armentières July 13–14 1916, and Goose Alley on September 27th of that same year', he concludes: 'they were hard days, but each experience only served to put a finer edge on their steel'.[32] I am not qualified to argue the nuts and bolts of military history, but against these distasteful euphemisms, I reach for *Gallipoli to the Somme.* How can one talk of 'Fate' and 'finer edges' or even 'the learning process' when, as every front-line soldier knew:

The enormous casualties of the Somme . . . were due to the combination of uncut wire and unsilenced machine-guns, especially those which, firing from either flank, sent the deadliest kind of all, the intersecting streams of cross-fire. The losses incurred from these causes at the Somme, at Arras, and Passchendaele later, were incalculable. They made nonsense of the theory of attrition; what was produced was a disproportionate detrition of our manpower.

That is a mathematician using words precisely. Elsewhere, he decon-
structs the euphemisms of war: 'brisk fighting', a 'sharp retaliation'—all
likely to mean that some company had lost 50 per cent or more of its
effective strength. Moreover, 'one might almost suppose that those
shells and bullets were an unexpected meteorological phenomenon, instead of having been foreseen hours before by everyone who
took part'. Against the official language of the war, we have become
accustomed to the deployment of scorn, irony, and black humour in the
prose of Graves or Sassoon—or, more pungently still, in the tragicomedy
of *Blackadder.* Aitken introduces an altogether different note. Perhaps
our cover image captures something of it: a painting of a sergeant (not
Aitken himself but a generic New Zealand soldier) on gas-alert duty
somewhere in France. Something terrible might be about to unfold.
Yet we see this figure not in mud but in sunshine and in foliage—and his
expression is pensive. He might almost be thinking of music. A reviewer
expressed the underlying tone of Aitken's prose in these words: 'if here
and there an undercurrent of criticism is perceptible, yet there is no
bitterness, no rancour, no self-pity; and the narrative, faultless in its
prose style and vivid in its powers of description is the more moving
because it is at once so sensitive and so objective'.[33] Another put it this
way: 'Even his sadness has the balance of an equation, the symmetry of
a Bach fugue. The gods have been kind to Professor Aitken.'[34]

The latter sentence might have brought a wry smile. Aitken's great
memory was not acquired without cost. 'There is much to be said for
leaving memory alone, for letting the faculty of forgetting perform its
natural diffusive function', he told an interviewer. 'There are dangers
in an intensive discipline of memory training, and I should not advise
anyone to try it. It is not the brain, but the whole personality, even to
the remotest parts of the physical and nervous system, that participates;
and if "Brother Ass" is ridden too hard, the rider risks a severe fall.'[35]
It took Aitken almost a year to recover physically from his wounds,
but for him, the war would never become a distant blur. From time
to time, he would feel his ordinary perception of the world shift in its
foundations. Clouds and trees might take on a strange and ominous

aura. During his breakdown of 1941 he told a colleague: 'I was seeing everything through distorted glasses; landscapes, for example, rocked and toppled as if I were in an uncontrolled aeroplane.'[36] In 1950, the symptoms were back, and the same colleague wrote a letter of concern. Aitken replied:

> What a nice letter! You have no idea how it heartened me in this state of smashed nerves in which I am, the pavement, or floor, rising or falling under me like the deck of a ship in a swell. . . . These breakdowns, Sidney, are a legacy of the war, esp. Sept. 27 1916, when we were thrown against a fourth line defended by barbed wire; dash of 1000 yards, under all the machine gun fire, shrapnel, and high explosive in Christendom! I got further than most, 500 + yards; of the 400 or so who started, 387, say, lay on the ground at halfway; 12 and 1 officer got into the trench—to find it empty! The Germans had vacated to shoot at us the better from their support line. This was 2.25 pm. I waited, badly shot in arm and foot, until 8 pm, and crawled 500 yards (4 hours) to our lines. To this I attribute the smashes of 1927, 1929, 1934, 1941, 1948, and now this. This last has not been so bad; 1927 was perhaps worst, 62 days of almost complete insomnia; 1929, 42 days; 1941, 21 days of complete insomnia. In such states the mind works at 100 times (more) normal speed; and my desk is littered with pencilled stuff written at 1 am, 2.30 am etc.[37]

I have walked across those fields near Goose Alley, where the ground heaved on 27 September 1917, and a slight camber of ditch offered just enough protection from the perforating machine-guns, keeping Aitken safe until he could begin that long, slow-sidling crawl to safety. He once said he felt his memory had become 'stratified', the older deposits lying under, but still accessible, especially when unsought. On this quiet field between Factory Corner and Eaucourt l'Abbaye, the potato crop had just been ploughed over, uncovering marble-sized balls of lead in the rich grey soil—shrapnel from a hundred years ago. In less than five minutes, each of us had a handful.

Alex Calder

A Note on the Text

This edition reproduces the first edition of *Gallipoli to the Somme,* published by Oxford University Press in 1963. The book was reprinted later the same year, with some corrections. These errors, as well as others, have been silently corrected in this edition. The OUP edition was set from a typescript derived from a 1961 manuscript that survives in three notebook volumes. In making this edition, I have compared MS-1961 with the published text. Minor revisions to syntax and vocabulary are passed over in silence, but where the changes are significant, I draw attention to them in the endnotes. MS-1961 has a foreword that was replaced by the Author's Note and Epilogue. The original foreword adds significant detail to the account of the compositional history of the text provided in the published version.

These recollections of a year of infantry service, 26 September 1915 to 28 September 1916, were written from memory, aided by few maps, in 1917. I was for three months in 2nd London General Hospital, St Mark's College, Chelsea; for part of the time on crutches from foot injuries, and almost incapacitated from writing by the arm injury. I was invalided home to New Zealand, reaching Dunedin in March 1917. Until 30 September I was a daily outpatient at Dunedin Hospital. During these six months I jotted down in pencil, in the form of a long discursive letter to no one in particular, and with no regard for literary style (which I imagined would put a false gloss on the facts), a tolerably full and accurate record of my service; for I remembered all incidents, regimental numbers of men, voyages and journeys and even dates; in the main correct, I believe, except that in a few cases, as during the twelve indescribable days at the first battle of the Somme, they may be in error, but by no more than a day.

In 1920 memory had recovered some more details, which I incorporated in a revised version, seen and certified by two friends, C. Parr and F. K. Tucker, mentioned in the account. In 1930, by that time having come to live permanently in Edinburgh, I read Mr Blunden's *Undertones of War* and Mr Sassoon's *Memoirs of an Infantry Officer*, and was induced to disinter my old manuscript and to rewrite it with rather more care, and in chaptered form.

In 1961, I excised some trivialities and corrected the syntax a little and had a final typescript made, to be put among my papers.

MS-1961 also includes several pages of 'Notes for Recollection Only'. Where these are of interest, I have incorporated them into the endnotes. This edition also includes as an appendix the earliest extant version of the text, 'Scraps from a Diary, 1915–1916', which was published anonymously in the *Otago University Review* in 1918. In this edition, all footnotes are by the author; all editorial notes and comments appear as endnotes.

Acknowledgements

I am grateful to the University of Auckland for periods of research and study leave and the grant of a 'Summer Scholarship' which enabled me to employ the talents of a student, Max Ashmore, in the early phases of preparing this edition. Max digitized the original text, found maps and other resources, and made timelines that have proved helpful. I am grateful to staff at a number of libraries and archives holding Aitken material and for their permission to reproduce materials: the University of Edinburgh Library, the Hocken Collections, Uare Taoka o Hakena, University of Otago, and the archives of Oxford University Press. I am grateful to the following for permission to reproduce images: The William Ready Division of Archives and Research Collections, McMaster University Library, The Imperial War Museum, The Australian War Memorial, The Museum of New Zealand Te Papa Tongarewa (Wellington), Otago Boys' High School (Dunedin) and Archives New Zealand Tu Rua Mahara o te Kāwana-tanga. I have consulted many helpful works of military history in the course of preparing this edition, but my chief lodestones have been Christopher Pugsley's *Gallipoli: The New Zealand Story* and Andrew Macdonald's *On My Way to the Somme.* I am especially grateful to both authors, as well as to battlefield guides by John Gray and Peter Pederson that helped me make sense of the ground. For information on Aitken, Peter Fenton's biographical introduction to Aitken's posthumously published memoir, *To Catch the Spirit,* has been a helpful pathfinder, and I have been fortunate to have the benefit of a family view from Aitken's niece, Bev Abernethy. A word of thanks, too, must go to Professor Don Smith who introduced me to *Gallipoli to Somme* and to Dr. Sidney Smith who helped me with French translations. I would also like to acknowledge the professionalism and support of everyone at Auckland University Press who has helped with the commissioning and preparation of this edition, especially Sam Elworthy, Katharina Bauer, Katrina Duncan, Louisa Kasza, Andy Long, copyeditor Damian Love and proofreader Sarah Ell. My largest personal thanks are to my wife, Sarah Shieff, who accompanied me to the Somme battlefields, as well as to my daughter, Octavia Calder-Dawe. My final thanks must be to Alexander Aitken himself—a man as humane as he was extraordinary.

Chronology

1895	1 April: ACA born in Dunedin.
1901	Attends Albany Street School, Dunedin.
1908	Scholarship to Otago Boys' High School.
1910	Death of mother.
1912	ACA is taught mathematics by W. J. Martyn who opens his eyes to the subject. He is dux at OBHS and gains the highest aggregate marks in National Scholarship exams.
1913	Enters Otago University, studying French, Latin, and Mathematics.
1914	8 June: Assassination of Archduke Ferdinand at Sarajevo.
	4 August: Britain declares war on Germany; New Zealand follows suit a day later.
	8 August: British Expeditionary Force arrives in France.
	23–24 August: Battle of Mons, BEF begins retreat.
	29 August: Advance party of NZEF captures German Samoa.
	7–10 September: Battle of the Marne.
	16 October: Main Body NZEF sails from Wellington.
	5 November: Britain and France declare war on Turkey.
	19–22 November: First Battle of Ypres (Western Front).
	3 December: Main Body disembarks at Alexandria.
	8 December 1914: NZEF combines with Australian forces to form Australian and NZ Army Corps (ANZAC).
1915	1 April: ACA turns 20, enlists with the 6th Infantry Reinforcements, joining the 1st Otago Infantry Battalion (1st OIB).
	April–August: Training at Trentham. ACA becomes a corporal in the draft of reinforcements.
	25 April 1915: Anzac landings at Gallipoli.
	5–8 May: Second Battle of Krithia (Gallipoli).
	22–25 May: Second Battle of Ypres (Western Front).
	6 August: Sari Bair campaign begins (Gallipoli).
	8–10 August: New Zealand troops capture and briefly hold Chunuk Bair.

14 August: ACA embarks with the 6th Reinforcements on the *Willochra* for Egypt.

21, 27, 28 August: attacks on Hill 60 (Gallipoli).

15 September: Remnant of Main Body and reinforcements to date move to Lemnos for recuperation.

19 September: 6th Reinforcements arrive at Zeitoun camp (Egypt).

25 September–15 October: Battle of Loos (Western Front).

29 September: 6th Reinforcements arrive at Lemnos, ACA reverts to ranks and joins 10th Company.

9 November: New Zealand troops leave Lemnos for Gallipoli.

10 November: ACA at Otago Gully.

17 November: ACA at the Apex.

27–28 November: 'the great blizzard' (Gallipoli).

14 December: ACA evacuated from Gallipoli.

20 December: Evacuation of Anzac Cove completed.

23 December: 1st OIB leaves Lemnos for Ismailia.

1916   2 January: ACA promoted to Corporal.

1 March: New Zealand Division formed.

8 April: 1st OIB leaves Moaskar Camp.

13 April: ACA arrives at Marseilles.

15 April: ACA arrives at Hazebrouck.

16 April: ACA arrives at Steenbecque.

21 May: 1st OIB in front line at Armentières.

5 June: ACA promoted to lance-sergeant.

19–26 June: ACA at Grenade School at Terdeghem.

1 July: First day of the Battle of the Somme. ACA promoted to sergeant.

14 July: Raid of the 4th Otagos. ACA reconstructs platoon book; temporarily reassigned to be orderly room sergeant.

21 July: ACA back in the line (Armentières).

19–20 July: Australians attack at Fromelles.

15 July–3 September: Battle for Delville Wood (Somme).

20–25 July: Attacks at High Wood (Somme).

23 July–3 September: Battle of Pozieres (Somme).

c.10 August: 1st OIB withdrawn to Wardrecques, beginning their move from Flanders to Picardy and the Somme.

17 August: 1st OIB detrains at Abbeville.

18 August: 1st OIB arrives at Citernes.

29 August: ACA promoted to second lieutenant and is transferred from 10th to 4th Company.

31 August: ACA takes command of 1st Platoon.

3–6 September: Battles for Guillemont and Ginchy (Somme).

11 September: 1st OIB arrives at Fricourt.

15–22 September: Battle of Flers-Courcelette (Somme).

15 September: New Zealand Division makes a successful advance near Flers.

25–28 September: Battle of Morval (Somme).

25 September: ACA in vanguard of successful attack on Goose Alley.

27 September: ACA wounded in unsuccessful attack on Gird Trench.

9 October: ACA moved from field hospital to British Red Cross Hospital at Le Touquet.

18 October: ACA admitted to Second London General Hospital, Chelsea.

18 November: End of the Somme offensive.

1917   13 January: ACA embarks on hospital ship *Marama* for New Zealand.

10 March 1917: *Marama* arrives in Port Chalmers. ACA begins writing his war memoir as an outpatient in the waiting rooms of Otago Hospital.

14 March: Germans begin retreat to the Hindenburg Line.

7–9 June: Battle of Messines.

21 June 1917: ACA discharged from the Army.

31 July–10 November: Third Battle of Ypres.

4 October: New Zealand Division attacks Gravenstafel Spur (Passchendaele).

12 October: 3,700 New Zealand casualties in attack on Bellevue Spur (Passchendaele).

1918   ACA resumes as a student at University of Otago and becomes heavily involved in the activities of the Students' Association.

March: German Spring offensive, Allies in retreat.

Late April: German offensive stalls.

	August: Allied counter-offensive, Battle of Amiens.
	29 September–5 October: New Zealand troops help break through the Hindenburg Line.
	4 November 1918: New Zealand troops capture Le Quesnoy.
	11 November: Armistice Day.
1919	ACA completes MA in Mathematics and Languages.
1920	ACA begins teaching at OHBS.
	Marries Winifred Betts.
	Prof. R. J. T. Bell appointed to Chair of Mathematics and employs ACA as a part-time tutor.
1923	Awarded University of New Zealand Postgraduate Scholarship to Edinburgh University. In August travels to Europe via Panama Canal, New York, and Boston. Winifred follows in November.
1925	Appointed lecturer in actuarial mathematics at Edinburgh University.
1926	Awarded D.Sc.
1927	Suffers first severe breakdown.
1936	Appointed reader in statistics at Edinburgh University.
1945	Made a Fellow of the Royal Society.
1946	Becomes Chair of Mathematics at Edinburgh University.
1961	Completes three manuscript notebooks, entitled 'An Anzac Remembers'.
1963	*Gallipoli to the Somme* published by Oxford University Press.
1965	Retires from university.
1967	3 November: ACA dies at home.

Gallipoli to the Somme

Introduction

O F THE MANY BOOKS ABOUT THE FIRST WORLD WAR, THREE MOVED ME more than the rest. Two were about Gallipoli: *The Secret Battle*, by A. P. Herbert, and *The Path of Glory*, by George Blake. The third concerned the Western Front: Edmund Blunden's *Undertones of War*.

Gallipoli to the Somme covers both these theatres, and has a strong affinity with Professor Blunden's classic. When I first read it in type-script, thanks to the good offices of a friend, I found it deeply moving. I have found it no less so at a second reading.

Professor Aitken was born in Dunedin, New Zealand, in 1895. He is Professor of Mathematics in Edinburgh University, one of the leading mathematicians of the day, and a Fellow of the Royal Society. He was only twenty when, in company with many of his former schoolfellows from Otago Boys' High School, he went to Gallipoli as a private soldier. Having first risen to sergeant and then been commissioned, he was still only twenty-one when two wounds sustained in the Somme fighting put him out of the hunt. It is forty-six years since he wrote the first draft of the book. So what we have here is a contemporary account by a young and sensitive volunteer, who did his duty and miraculously survived.

Few soldiers of my generation have had to endure anything like the ordeal of those who fought in the Dardanelles or Flanders. One by one, almost all of young Aitken's comrades and friends were overtaken by death: Clarke, Robertson, Paisley, and the rest. Coming from Otago, nearly all were of Scottish stock. Of the few who survived one was Hargest, who lived to fight again with great distinction as a Brigadier in the Second World War; to be captured; to escape; to write another classic, *Farewell Campo 12*; and then to be killed in 1945. Professor Aitken has more reason than most fighting men to be aware of what he calls 'the gossamer thinness of the partition between life and death'.

His book abounds in such phrases. All soldiers know how a platoon, a company, or a battalion may come nearly to annihilation in a bad battle, and then be resurrected. Here is how Aitken puts it: 'A platoon resembles a lizard with tail severed, a crab that has lost a claw, a trisected starfish; given time, it will grow the missing part and function as before, though not indefinitely often.'

As an *obbligato* to this book, there is the undercurrent of Professor Aitken's violin. (It is curious how many mathematicians have a passion for music, and Aitken is one of them.) He acquired a fiddle, and although occasionally parted from it he was able to smuggle it into the trenches both of Gallipoli and the Somme; and after he was wounded and evacuated, a friend of his contrived to see that it eventually caught up with him. Only three weeks before I write these words, I saw the very instrument in its very case, with the details of its war-time Odyssey recorded thereon in Aitken's hand. It is now a treasured possession of Otago Boys' High School—a school which has produced many outstanding New Zealanders.

On this fiddle Aitken played many times, to cheer his comrades or himself in dug-out or bivouac. Once in Gallipoli his E-string had gone, but: 'A resourceful Aucklander unraveled the strands of a short length of the 6-ply field telephone wire, and these substitutes served until I bought proper strings in Cairo next April.'

Later on, in France, possession of the fiddle brings him one of those unexpected war-time friendships which are both ephemeral and precious. He had just been commissioned, and his Colonel sent him out of the line to Abbeville to procure the due clothing and equipment of an officer. He went straight to the music shop of M. Octave Picquet, 'seventy years old, tall, dignified, and urbane, who did not in the least mind being disturbed for custom after hours by a twenty-one-year-old New Zealander', to buy some strings and a bow. They exchanged letters after the war.

Professor Aitken's memory is legendary. At the High School I met a master who had been a boy there when, for a short time after the First World War, Aitken was teaching mathematics. Apparently his facility for remembering without effort strings of figures and formulae left his pupils agape. For instance, a single reading of the names and initials of a new class of thirty-five boys enabled him never to consult the list again. He tells in this book of one similar feat of memory, when he was able to recite the nominal roll, complete with regimental numbers, of every man in his platoon; and modestly disclaims a gloss which has grown upon the tale over the years.

The precision of a brilliant mathematician's memory emerges often in this book, and is of interest as such. But of far more interest is his memory of sights and sounds and smells, and above all of people. I have never met Professor Aitken; but I know the background from which he springs, the background against which he is now living, and something of the sort of experience of which he writes.

There are no heroics in *Gallipoli to the Somme*, and the writing is restrained; but I believe that many others besides myself may rate it, with *Undertones of War*, as an epic of devotion and sacrifice.

Bernard Fergusson
GOVERNMENT HOUSE, WELLINGTON
29 APRIL 1963

Author's Note

The first draft of this account was written from memory, aided by a few maps, in Dunedin, New Zealand, between April and September 1917. It was bald and unchaptered. Crude as it was, it had the advantage in 1920 of being seen and certified by two friends mentioned frequently in its pages, Cuthbert Parr and Frank Tucker.

In 1930, having come to live in Edinburgh, I disinterred the typescript, took some pains over its revision, and put it into chaptered form. It is this version, in many parts unaltered, that has served as basis for the final revision I now present. I believe it to be a faithful presentation of my own small part in the war of 1914–18, and of my feelings at the time.

A. C. A.
EDINBURGH, 1962

1 Egypt to Lemnos

M Y ACTIVE SERVICE IN THE WAR OF 1914–18 BEGAN OFFICIALLY ON
14th August 1915. This was the date on which our draft, the 6th
Infantry Reinforcements of the N.Z.E.F., finished its four months
of training at Trentham, near Wellington, made the usual march of
ceremony and farewell through the capital, and embarked for Egypt
on the troopships S.S. *Willochra* and *Tofua*. But the first six weeks,
the long voyage broken only by a day of shore leave at Albany, Western
Australia, and a day without leave standing a mile or two off Aden,
as well as the six days in the sand at Zeitoun on the north-eastern
outskirts of Cairo, seem in retrospect mere prelude. I could recover
them with little trouble, and they were interesting to me then, but now
that authors have visited every part of the world and described every
sensation of travel, nothing is left for an unskilled pen.[1]

We had come to Zeitoun on 19th September by the usual route,
from Suez north to Ismailia, west to Zagazig, south-west to Cairo.
At Zeitoun we lived in long, wooden huts, *tectis bipatentibus* as in Virgil,
two walls with a roof across, open at both ends and floorless, planted
on the sand.[2] The hottest months, July and August, were past, but the

September equinox still had heat enough to put parades between 9 a.m. and 5 p.m. out of the question; or rather, to come to terms at once with the twenty-four-hour clock of the Mediterranean zone, between 09.00 and 17.00. There was exercise in the desert in the cool of early morning, 05.30 to 07.30; by 09.00 we were under cover in the huts except for limited leave to visit Zeitoun village, perhaps to watch, under an awning, some conjurer or contortionist; cautioned also, for our own safety, not to look too curiously into any eyes behind a yashmak,[3] lest a jealous dagger should come our way in a back street.

From 17.00 to 19.00 there was a route march, usually to Heliopolis and back, then general leave until the last suburban train from Cairo, arriving at Zeitoun after 23.00. I have nothing to say of certain demoralizing, and in some cases permanently ruinous, effects of the night-life of Cairo. For completeness and full understanding something should be said of this, but not by me, incompetent to deal with an aspect of life in barracks more than adequately described by others.[4]

Cairo at night held no attraction for me. I preferred to practise on the violin in the almost empty hut, the few who might otherwise have been attentive listeners being engaged on other things. Like almost all the occupants of the hut, these few were fated to death or injury: Singleton, who now was writing his interminable letters by candlelight, destined to lose both legs in a railway accident next year at Ismailia;[5] Paisley and Robertson farther up, now engaged in reading the Bible together (as they always did at this hour), to die in France—Robertson at Armentières in 1916, Paisley at Passchendaele on that bad day for New Zealand, 12th October 1917.[6] But now they were kneeling in the sand before turning back their blankets; and later there will be the train whistle, the influx in the dark, and more than a rumour of disorderly adventure—and yet, tomorrow, at drill in the early morning, all of this washed away as the tide washes detritus from a beach. So the six days passed. One afternoon I visited the Pyramids and Sphinx with my good friend Frank Tucker of the Wellingtons, but, again, I have nothing to describe; from Kinglake onwards, everything has been said about the Pyramids.[7] They should be seen, however, like Melrose Abbey, by moonlight.[8]

We left Zeitoun for Alexandria at noon on 26th September, marching in unbearable heat two or three miles towards the centre of Cairo. The village of Ezbet-el-Zeitoun was in a drowse; only the great ravens above the camp gates watched us departing. We spread ourselves with relief in the airy wide-gauge carriages. My temperature—from a touch of the sun or sand colic—was rising.[9] For this reason, though I was unaware of it, all impressions were unnaturally heightened. Mechanically I absorbed them; the stately Nile barges, gracefully deliberate, their tall masts like bent bows; the sudden clatterings through crowded junctions, Benha, Tantah, the equally sudden returns to Biblical scenes, here a kneeling peasant turning an irrigating rill down a furrow, there an ox driven round and round the primitive Archimedean water-screw; at last, but by this time through a film, a glaze of rising nausea, Lake Mareotis on the left, with curious fishing craft moored in its rushy edge, and mud huts on the right, eyes peering through the window-slits.[10] At the quay I staggered up the gangway, paraded sick, and was summarily sent below to lie under a blanket and digest that military cure-all, a 'Number Nine' pill.[11]

The *Osmanieh* appeared to be a cargo steamer of the Levant, perhaps captured and pressed into transport service, for which, with her limited deck space and lack of cabins, she was entirely unsuited. She was later torpedoed in the Mediterranean. Company quarters were away down in the forehold, on a grimy iron floor reached from the hatch by a long ladder. In the dim light of two portholes high above, one could just make out heaps of onion skins, remnants of a previous cargo, swept into corners. The crew of Levantines, seldom seen in the day-time, prowled abroad on that first night and stole socks and shirts that we had washed and put to dry on steam-pipes. As for rations, there was a sudden decline from the relative luxury of the *Willochra* east of Suez; the hot stew, the New Zealand butter and cheese, the bread, were at one stroke exchanged for the regular military fare of the Mediterranean zone, the hard biscuits and the small tins of Fray Bentos bully beef.

All day on the 27th I lay below, much recovered but unfit for drill, with nothing to do but order my impressions of the previous six weeks. The violin lay in its case beside me; not originally mine, but won in a raffle on board ship, some days after we had left Albany in Western Australia, by my cabin-mate and old schoolfellow R. J. Maunsell, and handed by him to me. Mediocre in tone and cheap, it was wonderful to have in such a place. Sooner or later I would have to part with it; it was excess luggage, contrary to regulations, and could not be expected to survive the strict kit inspections that would precede our disembarking on Gallipoli. I was determined in spite of this to smuggle it along as far as I could, and had begun to print a hopeful list of names on the baize lining of the case. I added one now, so that the list showed: *Indian Ocean, Aden, Suez, Cairo (Zeitoun), Alexandria.* The violin was by this time almost a platoon mascot, while the piece most in demand, Dvořák's *Humoresque* in Wilhelmj's arrangement in G major, was becoming what in later years would be called the 'signature tune'.[12]

On the 28th, recovered though still shaky, I sat above with the platoon about the deck-housing on the port side, looking west. Mr. Johnston, the platoon commander, whose orders had clearly been to use his inventive discretion and keep us occupied, was refurbishing from memory old lectures heard more than once in Trentham. Our course was north with a touch of west; we must have passed during the night between Rhodes and Karpathos and were now in the southern Aegean. I listened with half my mind; we were skirting the eastern fringe of the Cyclades, small, beautiful islands, some too small to be inhabited, rising from the north-western horizon, gliding abeam and vanishing in the south-west. In the late morning a much larger one, dark and mountainous and steep along its eastern coast, came opposite to within fifteen miles. I realized, not then, but in retrospect, that this must be Naxos, the Naxos of Theseus and Ariadne, largest of the Cyclades; this eastern side seemed too precipitous for harbour or beach, which must be round to the west. I began to think of several of those ancient legends. But it was useless; mythology had lost its meaning, the names had no conviction. Gallipoli and Anzac were everything; we were bound for there, perhaps to be actually there within another night and day; meanwhile we were sitting on this deck, listening as before to those trite themes of musketry, of judging distance, of locating objects by a clock-and-finger method, or of carrying out imagined attacks by short skirmishing rushes, as understood and last practised in the Boer War. So the magnificent island faded southward with the rest, a protecting destroyer came from the north at high speed and circled us three times, the last of the Cyclades thinned away, and in the afternoon we were in the blank waters of the northern Aegean.

All this time, and in Egypt, Gallipoli had been uppermost in our minds, yet hardly ever mentioned. Not from fear, but because it was pointless to speculate concerning a place none of us had seen, being without exception volunteer recruits none of whom had yet been in action. No one doubted that Gallipoli was our immediate destination, though rumours, which among soldiers will seize at any fortuitous possibility, did sometimes suggest Salonika. In those days Gallipoli was hidden under a cloud of official silence. Sir John Maxwell, commander of the Egyptian garrison,[13] briefly reviewing us one morning in the sand at Zeitoun, had barely mentioned it. We knew of the Landing on 25th April, which had taken place soon after our entry as recruits into Trentham, and we also knew vaguely of some of the later operations; but not of the August advance, which was too recent to be definite, and which had been moving towards its collapse when we embarked for Egypt.[14] It was true that at Suez, about to disembark, we had met some wounded and invalided men, brought on board the *Willochra* to be taken home; but inert in stretchers or lying back exhausted in deck-chairs, they were so evidently reluctant to revive painful experiences that we had left them alone. None the less, a few words had passed, an outline had emerged, and on the main points my own mental picture was exact enough; a narrow, ridgy, barren peninsula, the tail-end of Europe, probably a magnified edition of my own Otago Peninsula, sun-baked and unhealthy of late; Cape Helles on the south tip, Anzac on the west side, Suvla Bay farther up; Anzac itself, our own sector, a semicircle with centre at the beach and of radius no more than two miles, dominated by the range Sari Bair (highest point Hill 971, Koja Chemen Tepe) and its southern spur Chunuk Bair, still uncaptured. Of how far the August advance from Suvla and Anzac had failed we had no idea. Therein lay the cloud of silence.

On the morning of the 29th, much recovered, I was on deck early. Due north was Lemnos, with the great harbour of Mudros already visible, opening on the south coast and almost dividing the island into halves. We passed east of the two sentinel islets that guard the fairway, and were soon merged in an enormous fleet of vessels of every kind, close-packed for miles along both converging shores; cruisers, monitors, transports, hospital ships, trawlers, paddle-steamers, surfaced submarines, tugs, pinnaces, motor-launches, down to cockle-boats and local Aegean fishing craft moored idle against the pier. We were carefully piloted and fitted into an interstice in the pattern, close to the quay of Mudros East. Opposite us, on the other side, the towering masts, four funnels, and great hull of the Cunarder, S.S. *Aquitania*, rose Brobdingnagian, dwarfing the Lilliputian tongue of Mudros West protruding behind it.[15] For the usual and expected several hours we waited on deck with packs up, watching the ceaseless water-beetle skimming of pinnaces and motor-launches up and down the long harbour. At 17.30 a paddle-steamer, the *Water Witch*, ferried us over and landed us on the tip of Mudros West. It was almost dark when Mr. L. S. Jennings (a well-known university lawn-tennis player, killed at Flers, 15 September 1916), senior platoon commander and acting O.C., led the four platoons along the ridge.[16]

It was fully dark when we descended the farther neck of the three-mile long Peninsula, guessing at an unseen inlet on the right and striking north-west across salt marsh. The western hills were no longer visible. A cold north wind blew down the divide; for the first time on my active service I felt depression and the sense of exile in the wrong hemisphere. About 20.30 we made out a few muffled lights on a slope ahead, our apparent destination. They were marquees, candle-lit. We formed up and dismissed to quarters in them.

I felt then, as everyone else must have, an obscure disquiet. Last Post had not yet sounded, it could not be as late as 21.00; yet the marquees were almost silent, voices were subdued, men could be seen through the flaps already under their blankets. There was not a trace of the animation usual in a camp until Last Post. Only one man had had the curiosity to walk out a short distance and see us arrive; yet our arrival had been no surprise, for dixies of tea stood waiting for us. No one had asked for news of New Zealand or Egypt. There was a mystery somewhere, perhaps even a disaster; whatever it was I was content to leave it unsolved until daylight. My section was already installed in a marquee, with little room left. I wound myself in my blanket and slept half inside, half outside, my feet among the guy-ropes.

In daylight the explanation was drastically simple. The casual proceedings of the night before had been that long anticipated event, the 'joining up with the Main Body'; but this camp of a few marquees held all that was left of that Main Body or, more precisely, of the New Zealand Infantry Brigade and its successive reinforcements up to the 5th.[17] After almost five months on Gallipoli without relief, from the Landing of 25th April until the dying spasms of the August advance, never out of range of bullet or shell, tormented by flies, weakened by dysentery, these survivors had been taken off for a rest, less than a fortnight before our arrival, to the Lemnian hill-side near the village of Sarpi. The remainder, the large majority, had been killed or wounded, had died of sickness, or been invalided. Half a mile farther west, under the foot-hills, was an even smaller camp with a few horse lines. This similarly held all that remained of the New Zealand Mounted Brigade. The sixteen companies in the four infantry battalions—Auckland, Wellington, Canterbury, and Otago—had each been reduced in almost the same proportion. For example, the 10th North Otago Company had numbered before our arrival eighteen men, with no officers, no senior N.C.O.s, in fact only two lance-corporals, J. Daly and R. Day.[18] Augmented by our platoon, the 20th of the draft, it still stood at less than one-third full strength. In the whole Otago Battalion only one officer was left, Major White, of the New Zealand Territorials, an almost grandfatherly figure, seldom seen outside his tent at the top of the slope. Such was our realization of the state of affairs on the morning of 30th September 1915.

These men, who had gone to bed so early the night before, were seen by daylight to be listless, weak, emaciated by dysentery, prematurely aged. They had suffered also in nerves. The pastoral silence of the ancient island was felt to be deceptive and sinister; it was unnatural to walk abroad at large without the fear of sudden death. They were suffering, one might say, from an induced agoraphobia; it was this, quite as much as bodily and nervous exhaustion, that kept them within the marquees. They resembled in some respects the survivors of an earthquake, except that those have the compulsive urge to sit outside, not inside. I noted the startling transformation of old friends. There was Paine, known at school only a few years before, last seen among the 5th Reinforcements, as they marched out of Trentham on 12th June to the music of regimental bands; now hardly recognizable, his hollow face matching in colour his sun-faded tunic and forage cap; yet he was among the least debilitated, being in fact the one who had had the curiosity to walk out two hundred yards and see us arrive. In brief, this camp at Sarpi had been, in all but name, a hospital camp. It was significant that the prime cause, Gallipoli, was under a taboo and barely mentioned.

There were a few men who had kept physique and nerves intact; two in particular, well known to me from school or student days, Sergeants E. G. Pilling and E. M. Ryburn. Ewen George Pilling, fellow prefect and sixth-former less than three years before, was at this time in the 4th Otago Company. He had been in every action since the Landing of 25th April. That evening in his marquee some others and myself listened to an account, as free from bitterness as it was from false heroics, of such part as he himself had seen of the events of the previous five months. There would be no point in detailing it; it simply gave an individual view of what anyone is free to read in the dispatches of Sir Ian Hamilton, supplemented by the official history of Brigadier-General Aspinall-Oglander; or for that matter in John Masefield's

Gallipoli, though this last, excellent as it is, sounds, to the ear of those who actually served on the Peninsula, rather consciously literary here and there. (For example, the quotations from *The Song of Roland,* prefixed to certain chapters, seem to be out of key with Gallipoli and to break the continuity.)[19] And so I will merely note that Pilling, in those hours of 9th August 1915 before Mustapha Kemal's counter-attack by way of the uncaptured ridges and saddles to the north virtually ended the campaign,[20] had led one of those small groups that reached the top of Chunuk Bair and for a time, in full sight of the Hellespont, had held it. They were relieved (as is well known to history) by the Wiltshires, but relievers and relieved were overwhelmed and pushed back down the slope at dawn on the 10th.

Active service permanently removes any taste for the conventional poetry of war. Tennyson's 'The Charge of the Light Brigade' is so much painted cardboard, and Chesterton's 'The Battle of Lepanto' merely a cause of wonder that a grown man could write it.[21] But the classics suffer too, and, with me at least, much classical allusion, simply because Troy and Tenedos are too near Cape Helles, and Imbros and Samothrace too near Suvla and Anzac; so that in future if ever I should read of Leander swimming the Hellespont, or the vain-glorious Byron imitating him, my thoughts would soon wander to George Pilling and his group lying on the eastern top of Chunuk Bair and looking down on those very Narrows.[22] This marquee gave me my last meeting with him and my last vivid memory of him. He was, I suppose, twenty-one years old, a year older than myself. It was inevitable, in such a war, that a man of his quality should rise to a commission but should die leading a platoon to attack; as, indeed, he did, at Messines Ridge on 7th June 1917, to the lasting grief of all who knew him. But now he was about to leave Lemnos for Egypt and thence for New Zealand, to enter on an officers' training course; and I never saw him again.

All N.C.O.s of an absorbed draft automatically 'revert to the ranks'. I therefore unpicked my two chevrons. Frank Jones, our former platoon sergeant, likewise unpicked his three, but at his suggestion we made an unofficial arrangement with Daly and Day to relieve them meanwhile of all orderly and guard duties. In this way, taking sick parade each morning up the slope to the medical tent, a short furlong away,[23] I had the opportunity of judging with my own eyes the physical effects of debilitation; a halt was always necessary at half-way for the sake of one or other of the bad cases, and this with no suspicion of malingering. At night on guard during the late watches, at the two-hourly change of sentries, I could judge equally the nervous after-effects, by moans heard within the marquees, muffled shouts, upstartings and alarms, nightmare hallucinations wholly forgotten, so far as could be observed, in the daylight of waking.

2 Lemnos: Sarpi, Kastro

THIS HILL-SIDE NEAR SARPI WAS TO BE OUR HOME FOR THE NEXT FIVE and a half weeks, the quietest weeks of my active service.[1] Routine was very light, as it had to be, out of consideration for the older men—for so it was natural to regard them, though they were no older than ourselves.

Afternoons were usually free, and there was leave to visit the Lemnian villages in the neighbourhood: Sarpi, over the ridge behind us; Nea Koutalis on the shore of the inlet; Pesperagos on the flats by the salt marsh; Portianos, a small town two or three miles to the south on the way to the Gulf of Kondia; and Agriones (or Angariones) on the western hill-side. Our water-supply was a well, shared with some Australians, outside the high wall of the monastery of Athos, doubtless a daughter-house named after the holy mountain of Greece, Mount Athos, with its many monasteries on the easternmost of the three peninsulas of Chalcidice in Macedonia—I have read that for more than a thousand years its rule has been so strict as to exclude even female animals from all precincts and environs.[2] This lesser Athos of Lemnos must likewise have housed an enclosed and ascetic order;

at any rate no monks were ever seen outside its walls. Once and once only, alone on a four-hour night picket,[3] I heard them intoning at 21.00, far within, a chant in the Phrygian or some other ancient mode, too indistinct for me to memorize or to write down on the stave. Pitch was given from time to time by a bare fifth or octave sounded on some instrument like a viola; the feeling was Byzantine, and something very like it is to be found in the second of Gustav Holst's *Four Songs for Voice and Violin*, not then composed.[4] All these islands of the northern Aegean have that atmosphere that betokens and fosters, as in Iona or Lindisfarne, dedicated retreat from the world; it is evident also in the prevalence of Hagios or Ayios among the place-names.[5]

To New Zealand eyes the treeless Lemnian landscapes seemed peculiarly bare. Fuel for the field kitchens was of wood, stumps, and misshapen roots brought by flatboat from some other island and unloaded by us on the shore near Nea Koutalis. Men of the Main Body, describing the April days before the Landing, spoke of wild thyme and a carpet of flowers. There was no trace of these now. The prevailing wind was north, Boreas or Aquilo as of old—and still called Vorias—blowing down the central cleavage of the harbour and held to his course by the western ridge.[6] There was the sense of vanished races and distinct periods of occupation—Pelasgic, Greek, early Christian, Venetian, Turkish, and our modern age, though this last has left Lemnos hardly touched.[7] The villages are unassuming and harmonize with their setting; the houses of clean whitewashed stone catch the sunlight; the narrow streets serpentine up and down with little plan; the line of communal windmills stands apart in silhouette on the nearest windy ridge. The village life, austerely simple, is permeated throughout and integrated with religion; the priest of the Orthodox Church, in black habit and tall cylindrical hat rimmed at the top, is constantly seen on his visiting rounds among the houses.

These islanders made no advances of friendship or intimacy; in particular there was not the slightest opportunity for licence. We noted their Puritan demeanour, frugality, and scrupulous honesty. The usual Eastern haggling and chaffering was entirely absent. I found the quiet villages, where nothing happened to mark any day from any other, very congenial. Others of the Platoon might sample the *koniak* of the inn at Portianos, its walls decorated with stiff garish paintings of their battles of liberation—Kavalla and Navarino;[8] I was content to walk the hill-side by Agriones, to watch the matrons sitting at house-doors in the sun, gossiping and treadling their spinning- wheels.

Lemnian is a dialect marked by strong gutturals and fricatives which must come from the centuries of Turkish occupation. The first Turkish occupation was in 1478; in later centuries Venetians and Turks held the island alternately. The names of parts of the body, as one might expect, are Greek; thus ear is *ota*, finger or toe is *dhachtila*, and so on. Other words show the Italian influence; the sun is *soli*, the moon *luni*, a house *dhoma*; a window, however, is *paratheria*, not *fenestra*. I gleaned these few linguistic facts while on picket once in Agriones, beguiling the time by exchanging vocabularies with a dark-eyed and highly intelligent small boy of eight. It was nearing sunset; the unfenced white-washed houses, bluish in the morning light, were now cream in the level rays, hens picked peacefully about, the other children were in two rows, approaching and receding in a singing game exactly like 'Nuts in May'.[9] On an old O.A.S. envelope[10] I jotted the tune, question, and answer:

These guileless diatonic phrases are clearly Italian, and cannot be of date much earlier than 1800.

I dwell on such slight recollections, which have little intrinsic interest, as if reluctant to pack up and leave for Gallipoli, which indeed I have temporarily forgotten. But to write of Lemnos is to wish, in spite of the lack of archaeological remains, to revisit it, and to visit also its island neighbours so musically named: Skyros (where Rupert Brooke lies),[11] Eustratios, Imbros, and Samothrace. However, to end this pastoral interlude I will recall a day in late October, a day of leave and of wandering with a student friend, J. ('Cicero')* Johnston, through the western hills and south along the coastline.[12] By this time, with the exhilarating island air, the restful surroundings no longer sinister, the mitigated routine, and the improved rations, the veterans of Anzac were recovering health, spirits, and weight, until by the beginning of November they were almost their normal selves, though still subdued.

Kastro, a seaport on the western coast and almost at the south-west corner, is the chief town of Lemnos. It is only a small port built on a pair of harbours, netting fish for itself and carrying on a small trade with neighbouring islands. The site is of extreme antiquity, mentioned in Pliny and Plutarch. There is also a citadel on a promontory, often in the past besieged by Turks and defended by Venetians, even, in 1770, besieged by Russians, and summing up in itself most of the belligerent or defensive history of the island. I knew then only the classical associations of Lemnos with Hephaestus, and almost nothing of its later history, nor that so unlikely a person as Sir Edward Elgar had visited Kastro† by donkey from Mudros ten years earlier.[13] 'Cicero' had studied the map and proposed a visit; we contrived leave on the same day.[14] The plan was his, to set out very early, to strike westward through the rolling hills until we sighted the Aegean, then south by the coastal road; perhaps thirty or more kilometres, say twenty miles, for the double journey.

Starting well before Reveille, by sunrise we were high in the uplands above Agriones. Even at this early hour, not yet 06.00, a Lemnian ploughman was afield, guiding his ox and wooden plough of the *Georgics*.[15] He observed us but made no sign. The camp fell out of sight behind us, a range of small hills stretched away to the west; we had shot back 2,000 years in the past, or earlier still. Through ignorance we missed a chance in not climbing the highest hill, a mere 1,000 feet; for certainly on that clear morning, even at fifty miles of distance

---

* So called because he was redoubtable in university debates.
† He spells it 'Kistro'.

and with the ranges of northern Lemnos intervening, dome-shaped Samothrace, rising to 5,250 feet, must have been visible. We missed it now, keeping to the valleys, but on Gallipoli we were to see it often. We had forgotten the war altogether, swinging along and singing improvised words, choosing a tune—and none could be better for *Morgenstimmung*—the Hunting Chorus from *Der Freischütz*, which for the rest of my life would be associated with that morning in the Lemnian hills.[16] Here, suddenly, was our halfway house, a tiny hamlet called Therma, or Thermae, built around the medicinal hot springs that give the place its name. It is barely acknowledged on military maps, but I have found it since on a map of that old cartographer, Abraham Ortelius.[17] Thermae! How pleasant to imagine that this might have been the spot where Ausonian Mulciber

Dropt from the Zenith like a falling Star
On Lemnos, th'Aegean Ile;

though a rival for this distinction, if names mean anything, might be the village that still bears the name Hephaistia on the north-eastern coast of the island![18] We bathed together in the warm sulphur-impregnated water of a small stone cubicle, breakfasted on omelettes served by the first and only affable Lemnian we ever met, the host who presided over these waters, and were ready for the last seven kilometres, winding down through valleys and olive orchards, passing by ancient wells, striking the road, and reaching Kastro about 10.00. I read later, not knowing it then, that Kastro in ancient times bore a different name, Myrina,[19] with the reputation of a strange Pelasgian worship; and that Pliny the Elder had set the Macedonian Mount Athos in high relief by stating that its shadow at the summer solstice fell on a statue in the agora of Myrina. (This seems to mean no more than that from Myrina, at midsummer, the sun might be observed to set directly behind Mount Athos, forty miles off.) To our uninformed eyes Kastro appeared what in fact it was then, no more than a somnolent little seaport, in a phase of depression caused by the war, its few fishing boats moored idly at anchor in the crescent harbour. 'Cicero', at heart an economist, sociologist, educationist, soon found the local school and spent its lunch-hour in converse with the dominie—in what language I forgot to ask. Meanwhile I wandered at large in search of— well, anything, a bookshop at least; but there was nothing, no sign of book-lore beyond an untidy heap of paper-backed serials in a window near the school. The general title was translatable, *The Adventures of Nat Pinkerton, Detective*! 'Cicero', reappearing, bought a copy, which he later posted to the University of Otago; but it is unlikely that the work, in spite of its philological interest, ever reached those learned shelves.

The *kastron* or citadel, which gives the port its modern name, is perhaps the only thing in Lemnos that a peace-time tourist might consider worth visiting. It is built on the crown of an abruptly rising promontory that divides the coastline symmetrically into two bays, one to the north, the other to the south. From the landward side a steep incline leads up to it by hundreds of steps cut in solid rock; here and there on either side, caught in crevices, are old round cannon-balls that no one has ever troubled to remove. At the top a high bolt-studded door opens into a stone-flagged cutting, and from here, very much as at Edinburgh Castle, one emerges on a fort and barracks, a well-shaft, and a brass cannon, resembling Mons Meg,[20] resting on a pile of rusted cannon-balls. The cliff-edge is embrasured and crenellated; leaning through, one looks down on a shore platform 200 feet below. But on this calm day of late autumn, the western Aegean all around, we could believe neither in those old wars attested by this Mons Meg, nor in the present one raging only forty miles across the water to the east. There must have been sea-haze in the north-west, for Mount Athos (6,350 feet in some atlases, 6,670 in others) was invisible; but in clear air and in a sea of light and lovely blue with no trace of wine-darkness,[21] the green crown of an island rose up some twenty miles to the south. All islands and mountains in this region bear sanctified names, but it may be that this one, farther from the mainland than any other, out at the very centre of the northern Aegean, is the Iona or Lindisfarne of these parts. No two maps seem to agree upon the spelling of its name; it is Hagios

Eustratios, or Hagios Stratios, or Ayios Evstratios, or Eustratios simply, or Agio Strati, Ai Strati, or even the Turkish Bozbaba.[22] On a map of very ancient times it is Chryse.[23] But names tell very little. If ever—few things are more unlikely—I should set foot again in ancient Myrina, I would instruct myself beforehand as to who or what St. Eustratios was, and what part Lemnos, Eustratios, and Samothrace played when the learning of antiquity fled westward from the Turks after 1453.[24] I might also learn the history of a temple-like ruin, in what appeared to be cream-coloured marble, beyond the extreme northern angle of the barracks. Descending, we sat for a time on the sandy southern beach, watching the fishermen of Kastro drag-net a haul of fish. Then, judging direction by the stars, we ignored the coastal road and walked back by night through the hills, dropping down on the camp at Sarpi exactly as the cavalry trumpet for Lights Out was sounding from the Mounted lines. This day, uneventful as all beautiful days are, has kept an abiding freshness, fixed in memory as it is by euphonious and evocative names—Agriones, Thermae, Kastro, Eustratios—places never to be revisited, never to be thought of again without affection.

With the first frosts of November the last flies, the summer torment of Gallipoli, disappeared. The weather changed suddenly, giving a foretaste of the great blizzard at Suvla and Anzac a month later.[25] Late one night a violent gale, with thunder, blew flat every marquee in the Brigade. Continuous lightning showed men holding poles vertically, driving in pegs, straining at guy-ropes and wrestling with flapping canvas. All to no purpose; renewed gusts blew everything flat again. At length we gave up and lay among the sodden tangle till daylight.

Next came the usual and infallible signs of impending departure for some front of war—the issue of new equipment, the kit inspections, the surprise 'mobilization parades', and yet one more of many instalments of anti-typhoid inoculation.

Expectation was confirmed by a review on the salt marsh in the presence of Lieutenant-General Sir Alexander Godley himself.[26] Briefly and without flourish Sir Alexander delivered the usual exhortations; the struggle to come, the constant need for discipline, and so on; but he let fall one sentence that lingered, in my mind at least. 'Make no mistake about it, men,' he said, 'this war is going to last another three years.' He went on to give sufficient but discouraging reasons for his estimate, making, I think, oblique allusion to the Western Front (where the disastrous failure at Loos had recently taken place),[27] and certainly mentioning German pressure on the Russians. I feel sure that no one else, in those early years of the First World War, made so exact a prediction of the time of its end; for he addressed us, as nearly as I can fix the date, on 7th November 1915, just three years and four days before the Armistice of 11th November 1918.

On 9th November, at 11.00, we finally left Sarpi and marched away to embark for Gallipoli, though with battalions still at only one-third of their fighting strength. I had not so far been dispossessed of the violin; I had hidden it away during kit inspections. Now, inconspicuously transferred from hand to hand among members of my section in one of the rear platoons, it was carried to the point of embarkation.

3 Lemnos to Gallipoli

THE BATTALION BAND SAW US OFF ACROSS THE SALT MARSH AS FAR AS the isthmus; then it wheeled right, and right again, and was seen to be marching past us back to Sarpi. For the moment I thought it odd that ability to play a brass instrument should exempt a man from coming on with us to Gallipoli; but the Army was the Army and had inured us to shrug off any anomaly like that. We took the slope and within an hour were above Mudros West. The giant *Aquitania* had gone, the great harbour looked all the more spacious from being denuded of more than half its former shipping; but down there was the faithful *Osmanieh*, standing close in to take us on board.[1]

We moved out of Mudros in the late afternoon, steaming east at moderate speed. Night fell, dark and moonless, but starry. About two hours from midnight, with propellers stopped, engines silent, and the *Osmanieh* slowing to a standstill, we made out the black mass and ridgy back of the Gallipoli Peninsula, pin-pointed with tiny lights, as from a camp of gold-miners on a slope, visible to us but not to the Turks. The water, unseen below, must have been in a flat calm, for desultory rifle-shots and the rat-a-tat of machine-guns sounded across it with extraordinary distinctness. Fifteen miles to the south a warship was firing at periodic intervals; to the north a line of green lights with a red cross in the middle undulated above its shimmering reflection, a hospital ship at anchor, south of Suvla. In low tones old hands identified the contours; 'Quinn's Post just about there', 'Chunuk Bair up there', 'Hill 971 away to the left'.[2]

New-comers took it all in, silent and subdued. A swish of water below and here was a lighter against the side to take us off; we went down hand over hand (except for me, managing somehow to clasp the fiddle-case in my left hand) and were tightly packed, ring within ring, on the exposed deck. The lighter made for shore. Very soon we were crossing an unpleasant zone, about a furlong wide, where the overshot Turkish bullets plipped and plonked into the water all about. A man directly above me at the rail cried out suddenly, wounded, but controlled himself; no one could move, we could only hope he was not severely injured. Now the last plonks sounded astern; we were clear.

A pier, the North Pier of Anzac, loomed above. The lighter, heavily freighted, was low in the water, men were leaning down, evident Londoners by their quick ironical banter, hauling us up by the arms and shoving us on our way. A London corporal shone a darkened lantern across my legs and saw the fiddle-case. ''Arry,' he called, 'look at this!' The other corporal turned and shone his lantern. 'Gorblimy!' he said to me, 'you surely 'aven't forgot the 'am san'wiches?' He gave me a shove and I stumbled after the rest. We turned north along the beach and side-stepped through a hedge into a narrow trench. On the right the rising mass of the Peninsula was felt rather than seen; cold blew through the openings of important valleys, known later as Sazli Beit Dere and Chailak Dere. A 'dere' on Gallipoli is a steep water-course, deeply eroded, bone-dry in summer, probably flooded in winter. The tributary gullies that feed it are even steeper and still more suggestive of landslides, while the endless windings and abrupt variations of height in this sector make the contours on the map look like the vermiculations in a diagram of the human brain,[3] and an aerial view must show something similar. The greatest height above sea-level, 971 feet or 296 metres, occurs two miles inland at the hill Koja Chemen Tepe (otherwise 'Hill 971') on the Sari Bair range. Chunuk Bair (750 feet) is a southern spur of the range.

Beyond Chailak Dere we turned inland behind a foot-hill called Bauchop's Hill and spread out our waterproof sheets on a crumbling slope of loose earth.[4] Here we had a few hours of broken sleep.

Whether we had come up the wrong valley, or were merely waiting under cover until quarters could be vacated or found for us, we remained fastened to this crumbling slope all next day, learning the distinctive sounds of bullets and of long-sailing shells whining overhead to our batteries hidden in scrub near the beach. That night we slept again on the sliding earth, but were wakened two or three hours before dawn to go back down the valley and along and up the Chailak Dere. As we made more and more height above sea-level the gradient increased. More than once I felt like throwing the violin away down the stream-bed, but members of the section took turns with me in carrying it up the slope. At the head of the Dere we turned left, as day was breaking, into a very steep and narrow gully resembling a disused quarry. This was to be 'Otago Gully' until the evacuation. On the lee slope we dug shallow slots among the roots of the ilex bushes, a holly-scrub with acorns, and made our quarters in these.

It is a strange phase of life to remember, lying in all weathers out of doors, a fiddle-case beside me, in a kind of premature grave among the prickly ilex. On this outlandish slope under Chunuk Bair, day and night were interchanged; we kept the hours of the cat, the owl, or the bat. Any odd watch of the night would find us up in the front line improving the trenches there, or far down the Dere deepening the sap at some dangerously exposed corner, or even at the beach to carry up stores. My first such night was impressive. We were digging with pick and shovel in a clump of rhododendrons, or possibly oleanders, leaves cut by casual bullets falling all the time among us. We had perhaps three feet of safety and hoped to deepen it to five or six by daybreak. This was not a wood like those nightmarish travesties of the name on the Western Front, High Wood, Delville Wood, Mametz, Polygon,

Sanctuary, Bourlon, and the rest. It was no more than a small thicket
of oleander, but different—alien, Asiatic, and sinister. I never forgot this
first night among the falling leaves and under the bullets. From these
fatigue duties we would return to our Gully before dawn, only to be
roused again on the stroke of 06.00 by the rasping bark of an Indian
mountain battery, camouflaged on the flank of Table Top opposite and
opening the day by loosing off over the Turkish crests.

Finding it impossible as yet to acquire the habit of sleeping by day,
I explored the higher slopes of our Gully, working leftward through
the ilex until I came out on a goat-track with a few dug-outs beside
it. On the lowest of these lived an Australian stretcher-bearer, a hard-
bitten old hand but friendly and helpful. Hearing that next morning
we were to make the further climb of a quarter-mile to the trenches,
I took the violin and left it in his care. We were to occupy terraces
just behind our front line, which itself was just below the final ridge
of Chunuk Bair. The gradient at the steepest part of this ascent could
not have been much less than 1 in 1; I never did harder work than
climbing that short distance in fighting kit. At last, panting, we stood
clear on these artificial terraces, 600 feet above sea-level; between two
worlds—Chunuk, felt but not seen (had we seen it, it would have seen
us) beyond the crest above, and behind us and to the west, thirty miles
of the Aegean. My spirits rose as I turned to the magnificent view,
but were as quickly damped by an ordinary incident of trench warfare.
From the trench mouth, just at hand, a stretcher-party was emerging,
carrying a man of the Wellington Battalion, shot through the head and
dying, a friend of my own good friend, Frank Tucker.[5] A glance was
enough to show that he would be dead in a few minutes. My feeling of
reverent awe never recurred so strongly when such sights had become
familiar. The bearers passed down the slope; the next morning would
show another wooden cross in the small cemetery at the head of the
Dere. I date this initiation of mine as 12th November 1915.

These high terraces, and what could be seen from them, are my
most vivid memory of the Anzac front. They took the place of the
more usual support line, which would have been impossible on a slope

so steep and convex. The seaward view was wonderful;[6] Suvla Bay some miles to the north-west, Cape Suvla beyond, the Gulf of Saros, or Xeros, beyond again. Inland from Suvla, and apparently though not actually connected with Suvla Bay, was the Salt Lake, a shining oval sheet, dry in summer. From a rocky headland, Nibrunesi Point, on this side of Suvla, four miles of beach came in a scimitar curve with lessening sweep until it met a stranded hulk and then ran behind our scrub-covered foot-hills. Out to sea on our left, fifteen miles away, was the eastern corner, Cape Kephalu, of the mountainous island of Imbros, where Sir Ian Hamilton had his headquarters. To the north-west and forty miles away, rose Samothrace, behind the horizon and some of it below—the watch-tower of Poseidon in the *Iliad,* and exactly as Kinglake, standing eighty years before on the conjectural site of the Greek camp before Troy, had described it, 'aloft in a far-away heaven!'[7] And no wonder, for from north to south it is only seven miles across, yet rises to an exact 1,600 metres, 5,250 feet. Samothrace drew me always, our weather-mark, sometimes invisible in cloud, or dimly seen through haze, or dark mauve against the sunset. The sea between Imbros and Samothrace was at all times specked with destroyers, monitors, trawlers. The hospital ship that we had seen on the first night stood at anchor off the beach. Inland and opposite it were the small white cones of hospital tents. Eastward from the long beach the ground rose gradually to the plain, or almost plain, of Anafarta, a bare expanse dotted with sparse trees, and beyond to the Chocolate Hill and some savagely scoured hills outlined like the letter W and, indeed, called by us the W-Hills. They were the hills Tekke Tepe which should have been captured first of all in the August advance from Suvla but never were, a failure that doomed the whole campaign.[8] These features of our familiar panorama rise before me now as I remember them. For me the whole menace was centred less in Chunuk Bair and Sari Bair towering close above than in those barbarous W-Hills away to the north-east. I would scan this view with my back pressed into the terrace-wall, for though most of the shells were high whining ones on their way to our concealed batteries far down, others were shrapnel skimming the saddle and bursting immediately above.

Half of the Company had gone into the front line. The rest of us, until our turn should come, were on fatigue duties by day, such as carrying up biscuits and ammunition from the stores at the beach, or on the nightly digging parties that have been described. On the fourth day a few prospective lance-corporals such as myself were sent to the line to learn the ground and the trench routine. This was at the Apex, the highest and farthest inland part of our front at Anzac, on the curve of a hill facing Chunuk Bair but separated from Chunuk by a narrow and deep ravine. These front-line trenches were seven feet deep, chipped with the pick from a soft sandstone, with fire-step trimmed level,9 ammunition, bombs, and flares neatly labelled and stored in oblong recesses cut in the side-walls of each bay. A short furlong above us were the Turkish trenches, behind strongly stapled and rusty wire entanglements, curving farther away under the skyline of Chunuk Bair but dominating us at all points. Below them a triangular field was conspicuous, amorphous from the front but clear-cut in green from a side view; this was the 'Cornfield' of the notorious 'Farm', where the August advance had run to its end in atrocious hand-to-hand fighting.

Next morning the two halves of the Company changed places. I found myself an acting lance-corporal, in charge of a 'group' of four on a fire-step in a bay, looking directly across at the Cornfield. Fifteen yards in rear was a parallel trench, linked to ours by communication saps. This held the sleeping-quarters, coffin-like recesses cut in the wall—dug-outs in the true sense. Hours of duty were eight on and eight off, beginning at midnight and thus taking two days to complete the cycle. The routine was to keep fixed positions and fixed dug-outs, and at change-over simply to file round clockwise. In this way each man had a double share of blankets, his own and those of his opposite number on duty in the line; and on that exposed ridge, in the bitter cold between midnight and dawn, they were indispensable. We slept in our uniforms, rifle at hand-reach, and, until the December weather made it unavoidable, did not remove boots or socks, and often slept

in full equipment in case of surprise. I need not describe vermin;
Gallipoli had its several kinds, and even colours. In such conditions
we spent a cold but uneventful week, with a small number of casualties,
being relieved about 20th November by the Ruahine Company of the
Wellington Battalion.

I set down these particulars once and for all, not to be referred
to again, dull as they must seem to anyone except a New Zealand
infantryman who had manned those terraces. But the greater part
of modern war, when of the static type, consists precisely of such
monotony, such discomfort, such casual death. And so let it be
stripped of glamour and seen for what it is. On this very morning of
the relief I had occasion to observe in my own case by how slender a
margin one may escape such a death. My group had filed out, I had
myself remained for five minutes to hand over to the incoming group
leader and to point out some peculiar features; how, for example, in a
particular pair of adjacent bays one might lean breast-high on the
parapet and yet be safe from bullets. As I stepped from the trench
mouth I heard the crash of shrapnel just behind me, metallic and curiously muffled. An enfilading shell had fallen low, had ricocheted from
both walls, and burst right inside the dug-out where C. S. M. Brodie
of the Wellingtons, a popular N.C.O. and Ship's S.M. on board the
Willochra, had been drawing up a parade-state of the change-over.[10]
He had, of course, been killed instantly. A sequence of blind accident—
so it is usually described. But if so, then my own escape was equally
accidental, since if death falls in this fortuitous way, so does escape from
death. Thus it was useless to philosophize, as equally it was useless to
be fatalistic, like others of the platoon who spoke of bullets 'marked
with his number', or a shell 'with his name written on it'.

The Battalion was down in the Gully again, enjoying what was officially called a 'rest in reserve'. This rest consisted in going up to the
line by night, as before, to dig in four-hour shifts, or by day to the beach
to carry back the tins of bully-beef and biscuits, the '3-by-2' or '4-by-2'
wooden beams, the bags of rice, or the sheets of corrugated iron, past
the mouth of the Chailak Dere and the dangerous corners. Temporary

and unpaid lance-corporal as I was now, though not officially, regarded, I was sent beachward on many such parties. I learned what it was to see rice leaking from a bullet-hole in the bag of the man in front, or to lower a heavy beam of wood, wait for the critical moment, and double across the thirty yards of exposed valley. In such time as could be spared from these fatigue duties we terraced the crumbling side of Otago Gully and excavated small cavelike dug-outs or 'bivvies', instinctively burrowing for shelter against the Hellespontic winter.

In this state we were caught unready by the famous November blizzard, which must have hastened the date of the Evacuation by proving that it was impossible to live on Gallipoli during the winter months. It fell on the night of 26th November. By another concurrence of casual events the Staff, unknown to us, had planned a false alarm for that very date, to the very hour indeed, by way of testing how quickly, in sudden emergency, we could man certain reserve trenches high up on Rhododendron Spur. The alarm was raised, we threw on packs and seized rifles and cricket-ball bombs. The wind rose to a gale, lightning flashed over Chunuk Bair, thunder reverberating like gun-fire was at first actually mistaken for gun-fire. Climbing the oozy goat-tracks we reached and manned the trenches, only to learn that the manoeuvre had been experimental and that the night, in a military sense, was 'quiet'. A staff officer, Major Hastings, who had the same wide-set eyes as Lord Kitchener, passed along and made notes; we slithered down to the Gully and dispersed to bivvies. It was midnight, the temperature still falling, the rain turning to sleet and then snow, but in our high-walled Gully we escaped the full force of the north-easterly gale roaring above. I slept half in and half outside my unfinished dug-out, waking early to find myself covered with snow but fairly warm. The ground was iron-hard but mostly free from ice, since the first deluge had drained off the steep slopes and had run to the foot of the deres. We suffered a few casualties from frost-bite, but escaped lightly. The British regiments on the Suvla flats, and especially the 29th Division, living in slots in the ground that filled and froze, were said to have suffered 6,500 casualties from frost-bite, exposure, or even drowning.[11] For several days the coast had been pounded by heavy seas. No part of it was in any sense a harbour; Anzac Cove itself was not properly a cove, only an indentation in the coastline. Piers were smashed, lighters could not stand in to load food and water; even water at Anzac had always to be brought by sea from Egypt and carried by donkeys driven by Sikhs and Punjabis to the tanks at the heads of deres. For a week the daily ration was two hard biscuits, Huntley and Palmer's No. 5. On 30th November a thaw set in and the sea calmed down.

In the first week of December we received increased winter rations— bread baked on Lemnos, cheese, oatmeal, a small allowance of dried cabbage. Why recall such things? Only because to taste, at Anzac, a stew compounded of bully-beef and dried cabbage was to outdo any epicure by recovering sensations which civilization has forgotten, those sensations experienced by primitive man when first he cooked meat on a fire.

We moved up to the Apex for what was to be our last spell there. No one, of course, knew this, or for a single moment expected it. There had been, just three weeks before, an event of the highest significance, Lord Kitchener's visit and famous brief survey of Helles, Anzac, and Suvla, so casually made as to strike not a spark of rumour. No one dreamed that those wide-set eyes, more familiar in those years, especially on the poster 'Your King and Country need You', than those of Kaiser Wilhelm II himself, had already written off the campaign. Most of us visualized a winter of stationary warfare followed by an advance, presumably not at Anzac, in the early spring of 1916.

My group this time occupied the left one of those two curious bays that had parapets immune from enemy fire. We could lean over and observe, obliquely to our left, the green Cornfield and the Farm where the August advance had run to a standstill four months before. With that triangle in front as a constant reminder, and the whole wide landscape spread about like a map, from Anzac away to Suvla and thence east to the W-Hills, it was impossible not to speculate on the August advance and the causes of its failure. Not the plan, certainly, which at Anzac had justified itself by the quick initial captures of Russell's Top, Table Top, Chunuk Bair, and Hill Q, and which with slight alteration of circumstance should have succeeded and might have gone down in the books as a classic model in such operations. The cause of failure—we guessed even then, and some of us found it later in the relevant chapters, and especially the incredible footnotes, of Brigadier-General Aspinall-Oglander's official history—must have been that the forces landed at Suvla under General Stopford had unaccountably been allowed to waste time digging in, even bathing in the Bay, instead of driving inland at all costs to capture that crucial saddle, Tekke Tepe.[12] If those W-Hills had been gained, Mustapha Kemal's counter-attack from north to south down the ridges could not have been carried out.[13] But the whole campaign, on the Anzac sector at least, had been thrown off centre at the start because an unforeseen current had beached the landing troops a mile too far to the north, at Ari Burnu, with the labyrinth of deres and gullies of Sari Bair in front, instead of at Gaba Tepe, from which the drive to Maidos and the Narrows would have been shorter and more practicable. Yet again, we had not been equipped with up-to-date and efficient weapons. Consider, as one item only, the grenades, if they could be so called; the 'jam-tin' bomb, made by the individual soldier himself; the 'cricket-ball bomb', set off by striking the head on a match-striker sewn to the left lapel of the tunic, and therefore useless in wet weather. Perfunctory is too kind a word for the quality of invention that produced this. Somewhere down the Rhododendron Spur the Australians had improvised a bomb-throwing catapult, but very erratic and feared by us, I fancy, more than by the Turks. There was, in fact, the suspicion, not felt so strongly then as when, transported to France a few months later, we had a basis of comparison, that the Gallipoli campaign had been treated as a side-show, a secondary and diversionary affair, neglected and starved, or only intermittently remembered, in favour of the Western Front; in brief, that the attention given to a campaign might be assumed to vary inversely as the distance from the central directive.

What prompted a few, not all, of these thoughts, and not so strongly or precisely as yet, was that here from these two immune parapets the disintegrating remains of 10th August were before our eyes the whole time.[14] Obliquely across the ravines, half-left, on a steep slope in the inaccessible no-man's-land below the Cornfield, one could count with field-glasses, or even without them, seventy bodies at least, British, Indians, New Zealanders, Turks, lying there in every attitude of death, some face downwards, some face upwards, a few kneeling with their heads in their hands, and one, startlingly conspicuous among them all, sitting lifelike in an aiming position. It is conventional, even instinctive, to gloss over such scenes with abstractions, lest they should grate too harshly on the soft susceptibilities of civilian life. We take refuge in vagueness, or in noble phrases like the 'sombre aftermath of victory', or in traditional emollients, *dulce et decorum est,* or *sed miles, sed pro patria,* or something found in such a non-combatant poet as Tennyson.[15]

From that time on, and lastingly, such usages would rouse in me an impatient protest. Let these things be called by their proper names, and war will be extirpated the sooner. However, this is to range too far ahead in my experience, anticipating the reactions of Gommecourt, Serre, or Ovillers at the Somme next year, or of Passchendaele in 1917. Not yet clear of 1915, on this ridge under Chunuk Bair, we were continuously in danger, with every faculty turned outwards for self-preservation and little sympathy to spare for those forlorn dead, little more than a rueful interest, leading us to verify that every single corpse had been stripped by the Turks of its boots.

During these final weeks a report went about that the Turks were bringing up 10-inch howitzers to drop shells at a steep angle into our trenches and gullies. This sounded plausible.[16] We were set to work constructing deep dug-outs, large square vaults described as H.E. Shelters (but promptly named 'funk-holes'),[17] with tunnel entrances descending by fifteen steps a foot high and a foot across, perhaps resembling on a smaller scale those elaborate underground galleries occupied by the Germans at Thiepval and other parts of the Western Front. We spent each night digging at these, officers even, such as Mr. Gillman, warming themselves occasionally with a turn at the pick.

Meanwhile with equal energy the Turks were digging by daylight high up the opposite slope. Watching from my safe parapet the shovel-fuls of earth thrown up against the skyline, I saw my first Turk, tall, in grey-black and carrying a black cloak, clamber out of the support trench and stand up to full height on the parados.[18] Conditioned by now to reflex automatism, in one action I slid the rifle-sight to '450', aimed, and fired. Not one but two shots echoed over the ravine; the man in the bay on my right had fired simultaneously. The Turk plunged into the trench in a swirl of dust, the cloak trailing behind. An ordinary incident of trench warfare, this, and during the rest of the day I was too much occupied to think about it. At night, in the dug-out after the change-over, it returned upon me. It seemed that the two shots could raise nine possibilities, in three of which at any rate I might have killed or had a part in killing a fellow human being.[19] This, of course, was what I was there for, but it seemed no light matter, and kept me awake for some time. I could come to no conclusion except that indi-vidual guilt in an act of this kind is not absolved by collective duty nor lessened when pooled in collective responsibility. I further found that I bore the Turk no trace of enmity—nor for that matter did any of us; he was to us 'Johnny Turk' or 'Joe Burke', almost a fellow sufferer. We were not indoctrinated against him, as we had been against the Germans, by propaganda, the cartoons of Louis Raemakers, and tales of atrocity.[20] But I saw, still further, that this Turk, at the moment of shooting, had not even been a person; he might have been big game. It was a single step to the thought that certain 'colonial' campaigns, not infrequent in our annals, might have been conducted in almost this game-hunting spirit. Here I balked; to become analytical might lead to doubt of the cause for which we were fighting; for this had been called, in those early years, the 'war to end war'. I was far from such doubt then, and would have repudiated pacifism.

These last days on Gallipoli ebbed quietly away, with the usual random but steady drain of casualties, the Sikh or Punjabi, perhaps his donkey too, killed by machine-gun bringing water up the Dere before dawn—this was a constant drain; and friends also, Sergeant Fred Bartlett and Corporal Will Rowan, well known at Trentham, killed in the early morning of 8th December, both already buried, when I learned it, in the small cemetery at the Dere-head. I mention these two because in a way quite out of character each was said to have independently expressed a premonition a day or two before. It must have been imagination, but sometimes, when a man had died in this way, I seemed on looking back to have felt in him a preoccupation, a resigned retreat into himself.

The Company was down in the Gully for the last time. Almost at once I was detached for a remote duty, to take three men, M. Allan, T. Wilson (killed at Armentières, 28 May 1916), and H. E. Walter, to Rhododendron Spur, to be at the disposal of the Auckland Battalion for a week. I saw afterwards, but not then, that our assignment had to do with the Evacuation. We were to dig in the reserve trenches, occupied on the night of the alarm and the blizzard, a square cave of a size to hold 80,000 rounds of ammunition, all to be cleaned and oiled, and some boxes of grenades. This store must have been for use in a rearguard action, in case the Turks should learn of the Evacuation while it was in progress. We rationed with a section of Aucklanders living in roomy dug-outs close by the trench called Grafton Road, but we bivouacked out in the open in coffin-slots among the rhododendrons or oleanders. I brought up the violin, which for weeks had lain in the empty dug-out of the Australian stretcher-bearer, he himself being by now ill or wounded. Each night we had a muted concert in the largest dug-out. My E-string had gone, but a resourceful Aucklander unraveled the strands of a short length of the six-ply field telephone wire, and these substitutes served until I bought proper strings in Cairo next April. There was no room for the sweep of the bow-arm, while the *Humoresque*, or anything like it, was out of key with Gallipoli; but Christmas was near, and carols with muted *obbligati* were softly intoned. In its time *The First Nowell* will have been sung in strange places; this dug-out under Chunuk Bair must have been one of the strangest.

After the last of these subdued concerts I stooped under the water-proof door-sheet and stood for a minute waiting for the diffused light to show me the way to my slot-bed. The contrast was extreme; inside, the warmth and comradeship of men far from home but remembering it and forgetting the war for a brief hour; outside, the ink-black valley, the hill just visible in the frosty starlight, the desultory rifle-shots or bursts of machine-gun fire sounding as always along the line. From far to the south, away down towards Cape Helles, came the periodic boom of a great gun from the sea; the shell could be heard, like the noise of a distant train high in the air, crossing over the Peninsula to the forts in Asia. I began my walk, but stopped at half-way, conscious of danger, as of a rattlesnake. A string of hisses, rapid and even as semiquavers, sounded just in front of my knee, accompanied by soft thuds somewhere to the right; machine-gun bullets at the end of a very long trajectory. A forward swing of the arm, and the violin-case would have been perforated. I stood still; the hisses ceased for a few seconds, returned, ceased, returned. I jumped high over the spot and dashed for my earth-bed, roughly grounding the violin. For a while I lay awake, shaken by this escape from the arrow that flieth by night,[21] and by the gossamer thinness of the partition between life and death; but I slept none the less soundly.

4 Gallipoli to Lemnos

I T WAS THE END OF THE SECOND WEEK OF DECEMBER, AND THE AIR WAS ALIVE
with rumours. Men returning from night fatigue at the beach had
seen numbers of Australians sitting about the shore with full pack up,
and reported unusual activity about the pier. The Regimental Band
was said to have come from Lemnos and had been heard practising
in some hidden valley near the sea. Only one man, the Aucklander
who had improvised my E-strings, suggested that Gallipoli was to be
evacuated; no one believed him. The general belief was that either we
were going to Lemnos for another spell of rest or, more probably, that
Australians and New Zealanders were to make a third landing, not at
Suvla but at the narrow Bulair waist farther north,[1] and were to reorganize and rehearse this on Imbros. No doubt these rumours were
deliberately fostered in order to keep secret the real plan of evacuation. By the afternoon of 13th December we had finished timbering
the cave and cleaning the communication trench, when a runner
coming up the goat-track handed me a message: 'Report 17.00 Otago
Gully with party and equipment'. We cleared up and reported on
time. The violin had to be left; I scribbled a hasty note to Chadwick,

batman to Major W. W. Alderman, asking him to look after it if he could. The Apex had been taken over by the Auckland and Wellington Battalions. In Otago Gully everyone was sitting in full equipment, waiting for darkness.

We filed down the long sap to the foot of the Chailak Dere and turned left parallel to the beach.[2] Less than a hundred yards before this last turn a Main Body man, Page, who had been with the Battalion since the Landing, was killed by a bullet.[3] Two or three of his friends remained to give him quick burial and follow on. Farther along the beach halts became more and more frequent, until at last a hold-up of several minutes occurred at every twenty yards. The embarkation away ahead must be in difficulties. This might put us in serious danger, but it was weighing little on the spirits of a small group behind me, detailed to carry the jars of rum. I was annoyed by their ribald merriment; but the night would have been incomplete without some such Shakespearian foil, some Ancient Pistol, or the Falstaffian captain who was giving these fellows countenance, in return for surreptitious pannikins of rum.[4] An hour before dawn it was clear that at this rate of progress we should never reach the pier on time. The order 'about turn' came along, we hurried back and off the exposed foreshore, past the opening of the Chailak Dere and up Bauchop's Gully, where, exactly as five weeks before and on the identical slope of crumbling earth, we lay torpid all day. At nightfall we had again packed and were ready to move.

This second attempt ran without a hitch. We filed down without casualties, and along the beach by Fisherman's Hut to the pier. A company of Ghurkas was being slowly put on board a lighter, every man with frost-bitten feet swathed in white bandages. Taken on board a neighbouring lighter, we crossed for the last time the zone of plipping and plonking bullets (I think a few men sustained slight flesh wounds) and were transferred shortly before midnight to a transport, the *Reindeer*. After pannikins of cocoa in the cook's galley, we slept here and there in any odd corner of the deck. The sea was choppy, the wind was icy, the balaclava helmets gave scant protection. I lay aft, my blanket spread among the folds of a tarpaulin covering some lumps of coal. Frank Jones lay beside me, and beyond him K. C. Finlayson (8/918), a Main Body man. We shall hear of him again; both lost their lives in the first battle of the Somme.

The fact of the Evacuation was now realized and confirmed. At the first light of dawn Finlayson reached over Jones, who remained fast asleep throughout, and lightly touched me; but I was already awake. Cape Helles was receding in the north-east, on its right the fainter coast of Asia Minor curled away east and south; between the two continents the Dardanelles, like the mouth of a wide river, streamed grey-white. Steeped in the *Aeneid* as I was in those years, I was at that moment deaf to every classical echo. Later, in harbour at Mudros, I realized that we had been looking astern directly towards the site of Troy, and that by a partial turn of my head to the right I could have taken in Tenedos as well, might, indeed, have been able to quote of myself in after-years

Est in conspectu Tenedos, notissima fama
Insula . . .[5]

and the rest of that famous description, which remains today just as true of the island that the Turks call Bozcaada. But Troy and Tenedos did not exist; I had eyes only for Cape Helles and Achi Baba.[6] Without a word, and Jones sleeping peacefully the while, Finlayson and I lifted our heads every few minutes until the promontory, as the light strengthened, slid under the sea. We then lay back to sleep among the coal. It was high day when we awoke, about 11.00, at anchor in the almost land-locked calm of Mudros East.

The wrench of this leave-taking, though not acute then, being just dull bewilderment, though driven under for many months by the incessant mobility, change, or routine of active service, returned on me at length, and lastingly. I have never since then been able to pass a map, small or large, of the Aegean region. First in the north-west it is three-pronged Chalcidice that catches the eye, the trident of wonderfully named peninsulas—Kassandra, Sithonia, and Athos (three fingers pointing south-east from Macedonia to Lemnos), and Eustratios and the northern Sporades. For a moment the eye may linger on the mouth of the Struma, the Strymon of Orpheus and the Virgilian cranes,[7] but it flits quickly over 'Imroz' to 'Gelibolu', the uncaptured city of the Hellespont once known to us as Gallipoli.[8] On the west coast of the peninsula Gaba Tepe and Ari Burnu are as before; the name Anzac naturally does not appear. Last of all the eye moves north-west again to Samothrace, no longer Semadrek but Samothraki. Like Lemnos, since the Treaty of Lausanne in 1923 it is now not Turkish but Greek once more; but for the rest of my life I cannot imagine it as belonging to any country that ever was.

5 Lemnos to Egypt

THE GREAT HARBOUR WAS ALMOST EMPTY. WE DISEMBARKED IN THE late afternoon at Mudros East, marched three miles inland, and pitched tents in the foot-hills. No one put into words the fear present in all minds. What if the Turks, when the numbers left at Anzac were reduced, should suspect, or discover, that an evacuation was in progress? My own mental picture was of a cinema film run backwards, the Landing reversed into a rearguard action.[1] Keeping this thought at bay we pitched additional lines of tents ready for the three battalions still to come off. At intervals of two days they appeared, Canterbury, Wellington, Auckland, finally the whole Brigade except a small rear-guard of honour, under Major Alderman, composed of the survivors of those who had landed at Ari Burnu eight months before.[2] On 20th December this rearguard marched into camp. No cheers, speeches, or demonstrations greeted any of these arrivals; only, as was fitting, the quiet individual welcomings of friends and the matter-of-fact settling into the tents provided.

The Evacuation of Gallipoli is doubtless by now a classic in military history.[3] It seemed pure fantasy that in a week of stealthy withdrawal there had been but a handful of casualties. This was a result of the absolute secrecy that had been preserved, the anticipation of all contingencies, the punctilious execution of all plans. I recalled the puzzling order, given out early in December, to lie low and keep complete silence for forty-eight hours. At the end of half that time a strong reconnoitring Turkish patrol, sent over to Walker's Ridge, was captured entire by the Australian Light Horse. This would deter the Turks from crossing over if a similar silence should again occur, as it was bound to occur in the final stages of the Evacuation. Frank Tucker, arriving with the Wellingtons and coming to seek me out, described how in the last days, when the number left at Anzac had been reduced to less than half, small parties carrying towels as if for bathing parade had gone down open saps and come back up covered ones, circling on their steps like a stage army. The Regimental Band had, indeed, come from Lemnos and had played in a secluded gully. Rifles, cleverly mounted with triggers wired to tins into which water dripped until trigger-pull was attained, had kept firing random shots along the front for hours after the last man had left. The last party of all had rigged up barbed-wire obstacles behind them here and there as they came down the long communication trenches. Some other details bordered on the fanciful, but I later found most of the above authenticated in Masefield's *Gallipoli* and in Brigadier-General Aspinall-Oglander's official history. Thus for us at Anzac the Gallipoli campaign ended, as not long afterwards, in the first weeks of 1916, it ended altogether by the withdrawal of the British forces from Cape Helles, to become henceforth an epic, a legend, or the subject of endless post-mortem revaluation and recrimination.

The Brigade remained only three days more on Lemnos. I hardly walked abroad; I might have done so had I known that names like Palaiokastro and Hephaistia lay over the hills to the east. I had been regretting the violin as lost, left to the Turks. However, Chadwick, Major Alderman's batman, now came looking for my tent, the violin-case in his hand. The Major (later Colonel in the A.I.F.) had been kind.[4] 'Shove it in with my stuff,' he had said, 'some fellows get attached to these things'; and thus it had been among the last personal belongings to come away from Anzac. With a due sense of this I printed *Anzac, Apex, Mudros East* on the baize.

We rested quietly for these days, reading a mass of delayed mail sent on from Egypt—none had reached us since we left Lemnos for Gallipoli in November—and multitudes of back numbers of the *Auckland Weekly News,* whose social and personal columns seemed meaningless in the surroundings. Routine was nominal, being little more than short route marches among these eastern foot-hills. We remained in Lemnos just long enough to hear, on the last night, extraordinary rumours of a general insurrection in Egypt. These originated in the revolt of the Senussi in the Western Desert, quelled on Christmas Day in the brief action at Mersa Matruh.[5]

We left Lemnos on 23rd December, packing up before daylight and passing the great military cemetery of Mudros East, one of those that later came under the War Graves Commission. After the usual and expected hours of waiting about we were transferred by lighter to the *Huntsgreene,* formerly the *Derfflinger,* a German transport captured and renamed. Here, in one of the lowest of the several troop-decks, in ill-lit quarters that were at once eating, sleeping, and living rooms, we spent a Christmas fully in keeping with the anticlimax of the Gallipoli campaign.

6 Egypt: Ismailia

WE HAD PASSED BETWEEN THE CYCLADES AND THE SOUTHERN Sporades, so that Salonika was out of the running as a possible destination.[1] Rumour ranged quickly in the opposite direction and suggested Alexandretta.[2] However, the tall lighthouse of Ras-el-Tin and the famous breakwater proved it to be Alexandria after all. We remained on board only long enough to hear the reading of a general order concerning the suppression of the Senussi revolt, then disembarked. The train, for once, was drawn up at the platform. We were hustled into the carriages and sent off with all speed; doubtless because in our motley, frayed, and faded uniforms we were no sight to enhance British prestige after such a set-back as the Evacuation.

The timeless world of the great Delta had lost much of its fascination. At nightfall an eastward turn off the main line put Cairo out of the question; Zagazig and Tel-el-Kebir suggested Suez. Rumour shot ahead to Aden, Mesopotamia, even, in a flight of wish-fulfilment, garrison duty in India, when the train slowed down nearing Ismailia.[3] We detrained a little south of the town, marched two miles, and bivouacked at midnight under the open sky, tentless on the sand, halfway between Ismailia and the small village of Nefisha.

It would be tedious to describe in detail the next three months of reorganization and training, beginning again, as if we were once more recruits entering Trentham, at squad drill without arms and ending with divisional manoeuvres; for it was here that the New Zealand Infantry Division was created.[4] I will summarize quickly and pass to 5th April 1916.

This, to all appearance, temporary bivouac, in the area between the high embanked Ismailia-Nefisha railway curve and the Sweetwater Canal, was the first surface-scratching towards the foundation of a great permanent camp, the famous Moaskar Camp. It began with rough shelters of brushwood, planks, native matting, anything that might serve as a wind-break against driving sand and as a canopy against the heavy dews before dawn. Here the Maori Contingent gave a lead in resourceful ingenuity, and we were content to copy them. Daily routine included only a few hours of drill, but evening leave, which could be to nowhere except Ismailia, was restricted to an almost negligible percentage, the Brigade being thus virtually 'confined to barracks'. This leads me to glide quickly over a piece of insubordination on New Year's Eve, when resentful troops broke camp in large numbers, streaming along the sandy road to Ismailia. The clink received a fair quota from this escapade. It seemed to me, reflecting on the matter (and being now a corporal again, I had remained in camp), that the reason for the very restricted leave was simply this, that pending an issue of new uniforms we were not presentable.

Still without tents in our improvised shelters, we endured two days of high winds and sandstorms; sand in the eyes, down the neck, in the stew, sand even percolating as fine dust inside close-lidded mess-tins. Tents arrived by rail, the whole area was rectangulated and subdivided, Australians came and settled south of us towards Nefisha; quickly the great oval of bare desert was transformed into the regular rows of white canvas cones. The tents arrived just in time;

the sandstorms were followed by a week of tropical rain. About 9th January 1916 the 7th Reinforcements arrived from Zeitoun.

This was a confrontation. Until that day I had not realized how uncouth we must have appeared—though still more uncouth, unshaven, and bearded on Gallipoli, where water, non-existent in our sector, had to be brought by sea, as has been described, and rigorously economized. Our uniforms and equipment were heterogeneous. Some men wore caps, some slouch hats, some pith-helmets; some had long trousers, some shorts, some riding breeches; some had puttees, some none; some had long Lee-Enfield rifles, some short. All clothing was frayed, torn, sun-faded. Parade-ground drill had degenerated, men sloped and ordered arms by the principle of least action in a single circular movement, avoided saluting, kept step but little else. Judge then how by contrast—and everything is relative— the 7ths looked like young Apollos, physically fit, sun-browned, spick and span, executing their movements before us with all that click and swank of simultaneity so dear to the military eye and ear. They looked with critical sadness on our rough state, they were disappointed at having missed Gallipoli—as though it had been the Hesperides![5] Some even lamented that they had probably missed the war.

Next came the New Zealand Rifle Brigade from Mersa Matruh, first the 2nd Battalion, nicknamed the 'Square Dinks' (a 'square dinkum bloke' being idiomatic Australian for a genuine fellow)[6] from the distinctive black patch on the upper sleeve; later the 'Diamond Dinks', who wore a diamond patch and had been in action with British and Sikhs in the defeat of the Senussi on Christmas Day. The alternative name of the Rifle Brigade, the E.L.O. (Earl of Liverpool's Own), had been quietly allowed to lapse. These battalions were as fit and fine-looking as the 7ths. The camp, greatly enlarged, spread inland to the other side of the Ismailia-Nefisha railway embankment and far out into the desert on that side. The 8th Reinforcements and the 3rd and 4th Battalions of the Rifle Brigade arrived, and now the New Zealand Infantry Division of three brigades was created, the original Infantry Brigade of Gallipoli being the 1st Brigade, the 2nd Brigade being formed from reinforcements later than the 7th, from returned wounded, and from dismounted cavalry, and the former E.L.O. being the 3rd or Rifle Brigade. The original Mounted Brigade, which later went to Palestine and served with Field-Marshal Allenby, was quartered at Serapeum, farther down the Suez Canal. Many of its reinforcements were transferred as infantry to the 2nd Brigade and some to the Pioneer Battalion, to which also all the Maoris were transferred. The last and most spectacular stage in the grand reorganization was the arrival of the 2nd Maori Contingent.[7]

It was a Saturday afternoon, the second Saturday in February, if I remember rightly. We *pakehas* treated the railway embankment as a grand stand, lining it in tiers, soon after the midday meal, to have the best view of the symbolic tribal ceremony about to be enacted on the arena below. The Contingent was expected to detrain at Ismailia about 14.00; marching by the long strip of sand parallel to the embankment it should reach Moaskar about 14.30. The veteran Maoris of the 1st Contingent, much reduced in numbers by Gallipoli, squatted on the sand in a circle, bare to the waist as in the days of *pa* and *taua* and wearing, specially woven for the occasion, skirts of reed.[8] A line of scouts, each kneeling on one knee at the alert, stretched at fifty-yard intervals some way towards Ismailia. The farthest out was Himia, the oldest and most respected, reputedly the son of a chieftain of noble and remote genealogy, but more immediately the banker of a highly profitable 'crown-and-anchor' board.[9] He poised a spear, which at the appropriate moment he would launch in the path of the oncoming strangers; they, it was to be presumed, would walk over it without picking it up, in token of peace and friendship. All this was visible and well understood from the embankment.

The ceremony proceeded exactly according to anticipation; the distant train whistle, the clouds of rising sand as the column approached, the hurled spear, and the backward bound and intent gaze of all the scouts. I breathed with relief to see the officer at the head tread the weapon into the sand, whereupon the squatting circle sprang to its feet in a rhythmic dance of welcome, the new Contingent forming close column meanwhile and sitting down to watch.*[10]

The dance ended with the dancers in a semicircle and a Maori orator declaiming in the midst. This was great oratory, of a kind known in ancient Greece, and partly in our own day to Latin races but not to Teutonic. The emotional meaning, the elegy for the dead and the exhortation of the living, came through with no need of translation. A Maori chaplain responded,[11] more *hakas* were danced, Brigadier General F. E. Johnston (killed at Messines, June 1917)[12] in prose after poetry briefly addressed the Contingent, his words being rendered into Maori by the earlier orator, Te Rangi Hiroa, (the late) Dr. Peter Buck, physician and anthropologist,[13] to whom is chiefly due the revived pride of the Maori race, and the interest of anthropologists generally, in a legendary history and an antique culture. Last of all, the old Maoris filed along the ranks of the new and greeted and shook hands with each. Next morning veterans and new-comers were indistinguishably assimilated.

Fitted out with new clothing and equipment, we worked through the whole infantry curriculum from squad drill without arms to divisional manoeuvres. The sun rose daily higher in the sky. In khaki shorts and short-sleeved singlets with open neck, we may perhaps by the end of March have looked as the Main Body had looked on their first arrival at Lemnos, almost a year before; or as John Masefield described them, leaving in the ships for Gallipoli on 23rd April, the day of St. George, of Shakespeare, and of the death of Rupert Brooke, in all the strength and joy of life in young men about to be broken in war.[14] It never crossed our minds for a moment to ask where next we should be sent to serve.

---

* This rite was carried out as described, in the presence of Her Majesty Queen Elizabeth and the Duke of Edinburgh on their arrival in the Maori part of New Zealand during their tour of 1954.

7 Ismailia and the Suez Canal

Landscapes around Moaskar were monotonous, the tawny desert undulating to west and south indefinitely, varied only by the Suez Canal, widening out here into Lake Timsah, and by the Sweetwater Canal turning westward beyond Nefisha to Tel-el-Kebir.[1] We could trace its course by the distant masts of barges along the skyline. These barges sometimes bore sail, but more often were dragged by natives on the tow-path and camel-track, where Moslems might be seen at sunrise and sunset prostrating themselves in prayer. The tow-path carried the traffic from village markets or the booths of Ismailia; the Arab would ride ahead light-handed on a donkey, the woman, presumably his wife, would follow with a truss of straw or other heavy burden balanced on her head. Nefisha was a small squalid village where Arabs, ill-featured and often one-eyed, pestered us to buy their oranges, while no naked toddler with fly-ringed eyes was too small to whine 'Baksees, mistah!'[2] The only pleasing part was the vista of palm-groves and native gardens on the other side of the tow-path, watered by channels furrowed off from the Sweetwater Canal. To the west, inland, on the other side of the railway embankment, the desert was unbroken for miles, a brown sea of wave-shapes and hummocks of sand; yet however far out we manoeuvred, however blank this surrounding tawny ocean, Arabs would appear at the midday halt as if by magic, chaffering their oranges. 'Orang-ghees big-one, very-good-very-sweet-very-clean, two-for-half!' After the usual beating down it would be ten for a half (piastre), that is, eight a penny.

Mirages were a daily commonplace. Cavalry on the skyline would seem to be splashing in a silver lagoon. Once, glancing back from the marching column, I saw the whole of Ismailia reflected in a lake of shimmering air.

Ismailia itself, in its northern part, is French, residential and attractive, having sprung up with the Canal itself sixty years before; a broad quai, with trees, near the margin of Lake Timsah, wide streets, fine private houses covered with flowering bougainvillea, cool public gardens studded with small sphinxes and pharaohs bearing hieroglyphics. The Place Champollion commemorates the great decipherer of the Rosetta Stone.

The southern part of the town, which we had always to cross first when on leave from camp, was utterly different. There were the native quarters, filthy narrow streets cluttered with booths and vegetable stalls. Rotting oranges lay everywhere, we jostled donkeys and trod a way through squawking fowls. On our return to camp conjurers squatting in the sand would waylay us, jabbering their 'ghilli-ghilli-ghit, ghilli-ghilli-ghit' while pulling coins from our noses or working disappearing and reappearing tricks with corks and copper tumblers. A cork is placed on the sand, a tumbler over it, a larger tumbler over that. The tumblers being removed, the cork has disappeared; the tumblers being replaced and again removed, the cork reappears in the original position. All very elementary, but diverting; and this and much more for a piastre. Contortionists we had already seen at Zeitoun; I still remembered the sick sensation of watching a young girl, trained since babyhood, arching her legs behind her back until the knees came down over the shoulders, a model for Doré's illustration of Arachne in Dante's *Purgatorio*.[3]

In late February we moved to Ferry Post, north of Ismailia and on the eastern side of the Suez Canal, where it debouches into Lake Timsah. This fortnight, spent in guarding the lines of communication to the trenches on the Arabian side, was the happiest interlude of our active service. Fatigue duties included a new kind, the ferrying of transport across the Canal and back, in barges winched by underwater chains. We turned these winches in four-hour shifts, though natives not only willingly but with alacrity worked their passage. Our freights were varied; platoons of infantry, mounted men, camels, refractory mules pulling limbers—hardest of all, these, either to get on or get off—staff-cars, war correspondents in green uniform, and finally the Prince of Wales himself on a tour of inspection of the outer lines; young, only lately come of age, popular, known by all to be chafing at the ban of royal succession that prevented him from serving actively in France with his own Regiment.

Lake Timsah, with bathing parades in its warm water, is the background to the memory of those days at Ferry Post, but is indissociable from another background, of sound, the rattle of chains and derricks and the engine-throb of vessels coaling in the lake, the throaty monotone of the native coal-carriers, and the high chromatic wail of their foreman gesticulating above; all fusing into something harsh, exotic, utterly eastern, as characteristic as the famous *Ei-ouk-nem* of the timber haulers of the Volga;[4] 'Aya-lis-sa, aya-lis-sa, hi-li hi-li, aya-lis-sa'; or sometimes 'sa-li-a-na' for 'aya-lis-sa'. With diffidence and aware of anomalies, I venture a rough paraphrase:

At night, on forty-eight-hour spells of duty, we guarded lonely bastions on the Canal bank, sweeping at sunset a belt of sand along the water's edge and scanning it periodically for footprints. The nights were of such pellucid clearness and starry brilliancy that the Pleiades could be counted as ten stars rather than seven, and detail appeared in familiar constellations such as is never seen in temperate zones. There, for example, the Bull, in the Zodiac, is no more than the hint of a head, with the bright red star Aldebaran for eye, and the Pleiades and Hyades near by; but in these Egyptian skies other faint stars appeared, so that one began to imagine horns and shoulders as well. In the deep night there was no sound except, rarely, the soft wash from ships passing down with only one light at the masthead. Once a startling call came out of the dark from the forgotten civilian world, 'Hullo there, New Zealand!' On strict guard, we lay low and made no answer.

With regret we returned to Moaskar for the final day-long divisional manoeuvres, sham attacks made far out towards Tel-el-Kebir, or on the other side of the Canal towards Serapeum, and a night-long one that turned us into somnambulists. Its purpose still remains obscure. We marched with battalions abreast, and each in column of companies, many miles inland. From time to time Brigadier-General Johnston could be seen in the lead on horseback, outlined against the stars. At midnight the whole formation, preserving all relative orientations, wheeled deliberately through a complete right angle, from west to north, marched for some hours in the new direction, and was halted at daybreak, gazing blankly into a nullah.[5] Neither in manoeuvres nor in real service did we ever do anything remotely resembling it.

Now came the usual signs of impending departure, the kit inspections—and still the violin escaped being impounded—the uniform provision of short, 'high velocity' rifles, revaccination, the rehearsal for a review, the granting of a percentage of leave to Cairo. I was by now once more a corporal. Of my section of a dozen men, whom I could name as if reading from the old roll-book, but do not need to, men of English, Scottish, Irish, and New Zealand birth, all were eventually wounded once or more, and seven, perhaps eight, were killed. With these men I spent the best and happiest days of my active service.

My leave to Cairo fell on my 21st birthday, 1st April 1916. I went in by night train, 155 kilometres, with H. Parsonson of my section, but was abroad alone at six in the morning, taking the cool air in the Ezbekieh Gardens. I visited the Jardin Zoologique, briefly surveyed the Citadel, and spent much of the afternoon writing letters home from the Y.M.C.A. at Ezbekieh. The purchase of some violin strings and a rubber chin-rest completed a day curiously unreal, spent as it was in the unconcerned civilian world.

The review passed off well. On the next day, in an address to the 1st Brigade, Sir Alexander Godley divulged that we were going to France. We knew very little about the Western Front. Ypres was already a portent, and I think I had heard that Neuve Chapelle, the Aubers Ridge, and Loos had been disastrous affairs;[6] but I knew no details. At any rate France must surely be preferable to Gallipoli, which had seemed like a marooning on another planet. As it happened I was carrying in my pack one or two small anthologies of French poetry of the nineteenth century, Lamartine, de Vigny, Hugo, Leconte de Lisle, and so on, sent to me from New Zealand, together with a book of travel by one R. E. Prothero, called *The Pleasant Land of France*.[7] I was destined never to read the book, but I looked forward to seeing for myself that pleasant land.

8 Egypt to France: Hazebrouck

LATE AT NIGHT ON 8TH APRIL WE FINALLY LEFT MOASKAR, ENTRAINING at Ismailia and travelling the forty miles to Port Said standing up in open trucks; not at all unpleasant, indeed almost exhilarating in the cool starlit night. We were tramping at two in the morning through back streets, shuttered up and totally deserted, and after lying for an hour with packs up in a compound near the quay, marched to the gangway of the troopship. From pure habit I had been expecting the *Osmanieh*, and was quite bewildered by corridors glowing in these early hours with electric light, uniformed and attentive stewards standing there, cabins with white sheets and pillows, in a word by all the luxuries of peace-time travel, obliterated from memory by Gallipoli and the Levant. This was the Cunard liner, S.S. *Franconia*, later, like the *Osmanieh*, torpedoed in the Mediterranean.

The voyage, lasting a week, more than fulfilled the expectations raised. Day after day of cloudless blue and halcyon sea, shadowed only by the thought of enemy submarines; drill almost nominal, apart from the serious routine of lifebelt and lifeboat practice. No land was sighted, not even a remote cape of Sicily, before we entered the Gulf of Lions; and so all the more paradisal, to eyes that had forgotten the colour of grass, was the green of certain low hills rising behind Toulon. It was 13th April. We had stood to before dawn in lifebelts, roused by an alarm and the rumour, never verified, that a troopship following close behind had been torpedoed.[1] We passed the islands in the fairway west of Marseille, and soon were drawn up on the quay.

Briefly marching across the port we entrained for a long journey. A few dingy back streets had brought the war closer to hand, more believable than ever before, transferred as it were from a foreign campaign, such as Gallipoli had been, to home country; for these people were visibly besieged on their own soil, and though it was not mine, I felt a sympathy with them and the truth of a saying I had somewhere read, *chacun a deux pays, le sien et puis la France.*[2] At first, no men were seen, only women and girls, at the heavy work of loading and unloading railway trucks on sidings; and when at last some Frenchmen appeared, they were past middle age, reservists on home guard, superintending batches of German prisoners. In their baggy uniforms, shouldering their rifles with bayonet vertically skywards, they looked unsoldierly enough. On our long journey to the Belgian frontier we were to see them at every bridge, railway point, or level crossing. The train moved out at 1 p.m.; we have left the region of Mediterranean time.

For fifty-seven hours, at an almost uniform twenty kilometres per hour, we went from south to north of France, from the Gulf of Lions to the Straits of Dover and then south-east from Calais to Hazebrouck near the Belgian frontier; quite comfortable, except for crowding, in our 2nd-class carriages, rather rueful to pass or be passed by other trains in which the defenders of their native soil were boxed up in closed trucks labelled *hommes 40: chevaux 15*; or sometimes *hommes 40: chevaux 15 en long,* 12 *en large*.[3] Our own compartment had a large wall-map and a railway guide, so that at all times I knew to within a few kilometres where we were. The route was, of course, the usual one, Marseille to Paris by Lyon and Dijon, then to Calais by Amiens and Abbeville, and then, as has been said, south-east to Hazebrouck.

All that first afternoon, from the fleeting glimpse of the sea near the mouth of the Rhône to twilight somewhere near Vienne, I was riveted to the window by the beauty, in this early spring, of southern France between Languedoc and Provence. The book of R. E. Prothero lay in my pack, still unopened; I was content to leave it so, and to gaze on the reality rather than read descriptions. Arles, Tarascon, Avignon, of which it were sacrilege to write; Orange, where we stretched our legs on the platform and drank strange-tasting tea, sweetened, but certainly not with sugar; and where the young and charmingly and most courteously inquisitive *dame de la Croix Rouge*[4] was puzzled by an anomaly, that (to translate) 'you call yourselves New Zealanders and yet you seem to be white'.[5] Then to the train again, and more trundling, and Vienne and darkness, at which we lay down to sleep in a huddle of limbs on the seats and floors of the compartment.

In the early morning the name Macon passing by in an evaporating mist showed that we had left the Rhône for the Saône; greyer skies and more chastened greens marked a sober and more northern region, Chalon-sur-Saône, Beaune, Dijon, and those others, Joigny, Sens, Montéreau, leading northward to Paris; but by now, tired of the map, the twenty kilometres per hour, and the interminable journey, I joined the rest on the floor. On the early morning of the third day a blear-eyed inspection showed us to be beyond Paris, not yet at Amiens but clank-clanking away at the same snail's pace somewhere in rear of Roye, in landscapes winter-bitten, dreary, bleak, and northern. Branch-railways of military purpose, a multitude of French troop trains, thickets of barbed wire everywhere, and a general pervasive miasma showed that at this point we could not be far behind the front line. Held at Amiens by signals, we moved on and reached Abbeville at the mouth of the Somme; then in the afternoon, again clank-clanking past Étaples, Paris-Plage, Camiers, Dannes, Boulogne, and Wimille-Wimereux, so slowly that we had time to perceive at leisure the scarcity of men—none to be seen except soldiers on leave, sitting in pairs on seaward-facing seats in utter blankness and *cafard*[6]—and the large proportion of comely young women wearing deep mourning. Here for the first time Verdun began to shape for me, as Ypres did later, in great black letters.[7]

We were now swinging towards Calais. As with signals against us we slowed down, rumour had its brightest and briefest moment, but the vision of chalk cliffs was dashed by the sudden change of direction, south-east, until with Audruicq and St. Omer crawling by we came to believe that we had merely left the Ismailian desert for the Belgian firing-line. At last, in darkness, at 9.30 p.m. on the third day, 15th April, we detrained a little way from Hazebrouck and marched from the muddy siding on to the cobble-stones of the village of Morbecque. At intervals the muffled tread of footsteps under the shuttered windows was punctuated by faint but ominous reverberations—cannon in the distance. The shutters above us parted once in a narrow chink of light, and a woman's face looked down; but the arrival of troops by night was too ordinary an event here to excite interest.

A map of large scale shows a hamlet called Le Grand Hasard, half-way between Morbecque and Hazebrouck,[8] the usual estaminet and cluster of houses at a cross-road, so typical of Flanders. This was our destination, a deserted camp, tents of disintegrating canvas pitched on marshy and ill-drained ground chequered by paths of duck-boards, those flat wooden grids, unknown on Gallipoli, like short footbridges placed end to end, familiar paving of hundreds, perhaps thousands, of miles of sodden trench in France at the time. The most casual glance at the site suggested a breeding ground of fever.

Thus with sky, climate, and soil all changed in ten days, we trained for a month in this region between Morbecque and Hazebrouck (ancient villages, shown on those old maps of Abraham Ortelius),[9] learning many new things and unlearning a few old ones. For example, the Victor McLaglen system of bayonet-fighting, graceful as fencing, compli-cated, spectacular, but as useless in this war as pike or quarterstaff; it had to go.[10] In its place we were taught the recent and business-like British system (of which we shall hear more as the battle of the Somme draws near), as simple as it was brutally efficient. It consisted in benumbing an enemy with the foulest blows of foot or rifle-butt, and then killing him economically with the bayonet, the whole to be carried out in a brisk forward motion. To describe it accurately in detail is to indict civilization.

In a similar way we were to forget altogether our primitive cricket-ball bomb of Gallipoli and to learn to admire the savage beauty of the new one, the lemon-shaped Mills bomb, Mark 1, No. 5, with its grooves deep-cut in lines of latitude and longitude, so that it should 'form a shrapnel on detonation'.

Gas and gas masks were a further addition to kit and repertoire. Selected officers and men were sent to army schools of instruction in these recent additions to infantry training; to gas schools, grenade schools, schools of camp sanitation, bayonet-fighting, and so on. Graduating after a brief course, usually of a week, these experts either became instructors in divisional schools or returned to give direct practical teaching in their own units. And all this time the route marches about Morbecque were demonstrating the difference between Egyptian sand and Flemish cobbles.

The air was warmer each day, trees were leafing, ditches by the roadside were lively and loud with young frogs. In a field near Morbecque we paraded to hear a British officer lecture on gas, how to recognize it in time, how to adjust the helmet, how to exhale by the valve. With helmets duly adjusted we entered and filed along some thirty yards of trench, stated to be full of chlorine. It may have been chlorine—there was, indeed, some pale sulphur-coloured gas there, and some sort of hissing from a pressure cylinder; yet my buttons came out untarnished, and some said that a frog had been carried through without ill effects. All this is, of course, very trivial.

Hazebrouck was not an attractive town, though I should like to see it again in conditions of peace. It contained at that time many refugees from French and Belgian towns in German hands. Some were lace-makers. One might watch, in a certain corner window, the graceful finger-juggling of three Belgian ladies, evidently sisters, the tiny bobbins flying up, crossing and re-crossing in an intriguing figure. Dialect was interesting. Adults here seemed bilingual, speaking guttural Flemish in private among themselves, but using French to their children, whose school-taught speech was easy to understand. An undersized boy of fifteen vividly described to me the overrunning of La Bassée by the Germans in 1914 and the flight of the inhabitants, himself among them.[11]

9 Hazebrouck to Estaires

THE CAMP AT LE GRAND HASARD, VISIBLY UNHEALTHY FROM THE VERY first, was now certified by the M.O.[1] to be actually so. We moved out of it and began a small peregrination around the neighbourhood. First to a farm near La Belle Hôtesse, a little north of Steenbecque, another of those hamlets of a dozen houses grouped about an *estaminet*. Platoon quarters were in a straw barn with a high thatched roof and two principal compartments, separated by a passage with breast-high walls on either side. We were specially favoured in this, other platoons being housed in pigsties or in stables opening on manure-pits in the quadrangular courtyards of French farms.

There were the usual small humours and trivial incidents of billeting, such as must have happened to every regiment quartered on such farms.[2] For example, the straw-stack-and-compensation act. This is of the simplest; to place, as it is certain Madame did, a small stack of straw close to the barn door, to be inevitably raided by men who were short of bedding; then would follow a complaint to the O.C. about the theft of *la paille*, with compensation much in excess of the actual value. This little act was played before us that first evening by Madame and a collusive neighbour; *'La paille, la paille!'* alternately over the half-walls. Their indignation sounded forced, but nothing could be done except send them up the road to Captain Buddle.

We seemed entirely taken up with trivialities like these. Rations were poor, the vibrations of our arrival seemed late in reaching the quartermastering department, men had received no pay since Moaskar and could not supplement their scanty bread with French rolls. All these petty grievances fused into a parade of protest conducted by the privates themselves, at a time before morning parade, in fact at 8.50 a.m. on 25th April, the first anniversary of the Landing at Gallipoli. N.C.O.s watched with interest through a chink in the wall of the barn. The parade was quite orderly, without arms, the spokesman being our Ancient Pistol, Private K—,[3] the original nominative and living embodiment of the verb 'to wangle', sporting two unauthentic rows of campaign ribbons, some of the campaigns being simultaneous in widely separated parts of the world. Captain Buddle, riding down to 9 o'clock drill, seemed to listen sympathetically to K—, and the ordinary work of the anniversary went ahead without further hitch. A popular officer, Captain P. Mackenzie, drew on his own credit in London and advanced several francs to each man.

Such was the flat prose of life in billets, and I merely note it; drill, and straw, and shortages, and evening leave in the *estaminets*; with such exceptions as Frank Tucker might make in finding a church organ in Steenbecque, on which to play from memory his favourite preludes and fugues of Bach or Mendelssohn, hiring a small boy, the son of a munition worker at Thiennes nearby, to blow for him. (It was in this family circle that I heard French and Flemish alternately spoken.) But now an alarm parade, at the end of April, broke up our rustic idyll. N.C.O.s rushed to *estaminets*, dragged men out, and hurried them back to camp and into equipment, hustled them along the road to the rendezvous three or four miles off. We arrived half an hour late, were reprimanded by a staff officer, and sent back to our barns and stables. This must have decided the authorities against keeping platoons so widely separated; and so we returned to Le Grand Hasard, now renovated and drained and fresh with new duck-boards and white tents. No sooner were we settled in than we received marching orders. From the slight ridge at La Belle Hôtesse I had often at night-time seen the flashes of guns on the skyline. In this direction we set out early in May for the town of Estaires on the Lys.[4]

Before starting I put my pack and all that I carried on the quarter-master's scales. I record (and in 1961 *heu quantum mutatus ab illo!*)[5] the statistics for my own future interest: web equipment, 120 rounds of ammunition, valise with clothing and greatcoat inside, waterproof sheet and blanket, rifle and bayonet, steel shrapnel helmet, two gas helmets, filled water-bottle, entrenching tool and handle, haversack with rations; contraband additions, nominally not allowed but so far connived at: some books and the violin and case. Total weight, 74 lb., statutory weight, 62 lb.[6]

This march was one of the most trying we ever did, not from its length—for it was only thirteen and a half miles[7]—but from the Flemish cobbles, all the harder and more angular because our feet were still soft from the desert. We went by the Forêt de Nieppe, emerging via the Berquins, Vieux and Neuf, on to the Strazeele-Estaires road, which was one continuous stream of motor-lorries. Australians, preceding us in France by a fortnight, were billeted in all the intervening villages. In this march of four and a half hours no one fell out; but feet were badly blistered, and we were glad to settle down in billets in a disused flour-mill not far from the church of Estaires, on several floors over-looking at the back the River Lys, a dull-coloured stream polluted with effluents and sewage, and commanding a view in the direction of Neuve Chapelle.

Of Estaires I can say little. I was 'under open arrest' for most of the time that we were there—which was rather a shock for a conscientious N.C.O. The matter is hardly worth recording. On arrival I had been made corporal of the guard, but had leave from the sergeant to lay out my equipment on an upper floor. The sergeant himself was ill-advised enough to stroll fifty yards up the street in quest of local beauty and elegance; in the interval a prisoner escaped and was recaptured.

The sergeant and myself returned simultaneously to find ourselves under open arrest. There is nothing in all this; it simply meant that until I should go before Orderly Room, and be acquitted, I was confined to the flour-mill with one of my own rank, Corporal McInnes, an old schoolfellow, shadowing me in the most intimate details of my personal life; such was the way of the Army. Thus, while the rest were at drill or route-marching, we rested our feet, and he provided audience for much violin practice, including Bach's *Chaconne*.[8] Time hanging heavy on our hands, we explored the whole mill, and found, scribbled on loose sheets, in local dialect and with many faults of grammar, a crude ballad—one might render it *The Belle of Estaires*—a small drama in rhyme founded on the coming of the English soldiery, and by no means prudish. If I recall, as I seem to do, that one refrain was something like

Mainte jeune demoiselle
Portera un bébé,[9]

I need say no more by way of description. I lost these sheets; linguistically they might have had some interest, for, as the several place-names already mentioned indicate, this region where French and Flemish meet is the Teutonic strand against which the farthest waves of the Latin tongue, in early centuries, lapped to a bilingual standstill.

At Orderly Room, I should add, Sergeant B——[10] found a characteristically ingenious excuse for his brief absence from guard, but was laughed out of court and reprimanded.

These petty incidents are postponing our approach to the front line. But not for long; that very afternoon brought it into clearer focus. A German aeroplane was seen, surrounded by woolly puffs of smoke; shells fell over by Laventie, one or two heavy ones bursting near the railway at La Gorgue, only a mile away across the Lys. Our long spell away from the guns was nearing its end.

10 Estaires to Armentières

WE WERE NOW JUDGED PROFICIENT IN THE BRITISH SYSTEM OF bayonet-fighting and ready to move up to the line. Next afternoon we left Estaires, crossed the Lys, and marched by Sailly and Erquinghem to Armentières, which we reached at dusk.[1] As night closed down, the rattle of machine-guns from the line became more distinct, the great curve of the salient itself being marked by a wide semicircle of rising flares or Very lights, bluish-white parabolas.[2] Here is something impossible to describe. Danger cannot really be brought home to the man in safety; only from actual experience can one know the special awe these sinister arches of light inspire in one viewing them for the first time when moving up to the front by night. As we entered the dead streets we met an English regiment leaving, the two columns passing each other in the darkness without a word spoken; nothing but the muffled tread of feet marching in opposite directions, mysterious and impressive. A Yorkshire guide showed us to our billets, my section being quartered in the 'Quatrième Classe'[3] of a French school, with holes in the roof of the shelter-sheds and craters in the playground, and in the classroom a large shell-hole in the floor in front of the teacher's desk. The guide remained with us overnight, telling us till a late hour, and in a dialect at first unintelligible, interesting details about the previous summer and winter in the trenches. He also worked off on us many of the stock japes of his regiment, which, understanding only a word here and there, we received in blank puzzlement; then he would chuckle or roar laughing at our simplicity—and I imagined him telling his mates afterwards what greenhorns had come into the line! In glimmerings of comprehension we made out that the Armentières salient had been a quiet or 'cushy' spot for the previous six months, neither side being much inclined to harass the other; I also understood him to say that in the autumn he had gone brambling in no-man's-land—but this may have been one of the stock japes; at any rate he said that patrols had met in no-man's-land and had passed without mutual molestation, and that during whole weeks hardly a shot had been fired; in short, a 'cushy spot' indeed, a 'rest sector'. It did not remain so much longer.

We changed our billets next evening for the Hospice Mahieu, an almost deserted charitable institution which still sheltered a few old men and several devoted Sœurs de Charité, one being Irish and thus able to interpret. The stone floor of a long room or ward in this building was to be our home, when not in the line, during the remainder of our stay in the Armentières salient; oblong and high-ceilinged, it resonated well and was excellent for violin practice. The Hospice was in the square of Notre Dame, the only church in the town at that time which had not suffered from shellfire; the rue Sadi Carnot led to a second square with a clock pointing perma-nently to 11.30. This square was always referred to in orders as 'Half-past-eleven Square', and no one troubled to ascertain its real name. The western part of the town, near Erquinghem and Nieppe, was still in some degree inhabited, but the eastern part was almost deserted and badly smashed by shells; the extreme eastern suburb of Houplines had suffered most of all and was still suffering daily, and the station of Armentières itself, though already reduced to ruins, was still regularly shelled.

While in the Hospice we had to send fatigue parties up to the line at nights to improve the trenches. At the edge of the town we took to the duck-boards, which were on ground-level until we came to the inevitable gap in the hedge and sidestepped down into the trenches; but here they were long zigzagging communication saps. They were, indeed, very unlike the trenches at the Apex on Gallipoli; the yielding nature of the low-lying ground had called for much sand-bagging, the sides also were not perpendicular but sloping outwards; so that, used to the narrow vertical cuttings of Gallipoli, we could not at first feel any security in these long grooves of V-shaped cross-section. From their appearance, too, nothing of consequence had been done to them for months, even in the way of patching up parts where the sides had been breached and bullets were apt to drop low. During our stay in Armentières, from this May until August, we duck-boarded trenches and saps along their whole length, strengthened them with new sand-bags, repaired breaches, and put wire-netting on duck-boards to give us a better footing, with the frequent exasperation of seeing a good piece of work blown away by high explosive.

Before we went into the line proper I was corporal of a forty-eight-hour 'gas guard', at a level crossing on the disused rusty railway leading to Lens and Carvin. It was south-east of the town, in the crossing-keeper's cottage, ruined and deserted; in rear, a pressure cylinder and large motor-horn, the sentry's duty being to transmit any alarm in the front posts.[4] This, the least strenuous of guards, left ample leisure for playing cards and admiring the countryside: the northern spring for the first time; the birds—we had heard and seen none on Gallipoli, and in Egypt only the great ravens on the gates of the Zeitoun camp; wonderfully, at daybreak on the first day, from a clump of trees near the line, the cuckoo of the northern hemisphere, never heard by most of us before except in cuckoo-clocks; the trees and the plants green and ready to flower, a very delicate shimmering light green, lovelier, though transitory, than our darker New Zealand evergreen. This clear morning, but for the ruined houses in rear and the broken roof above, might have been a spring morning in peace-time; the idyll was sharply shattered when batteries began to blaze away from copses all around, and enemy batteries in systematic search of them sent salvoes of shells screaming overhead and crashing into the outskirts of the town and the Asile des Aliénés[5] close by. Aeroplanes soared high above amid puffs of anti-aircraft shrapnel, dropping red flares as rangers to their batteries; we flattened ourselves against the wall under the narrow eaves as the small, hot, jagged fragments came down with a humming whirr. A few hundred yards in rear, behind a row of cottages at a cross-road called Shrapnel Corner, an old Frenchman was placidly ploughing in a field. Suspicion, of course, fastened on him. Why so immune there? He must be signalling to the enemy, and by some code. It was even fancifully surmised that he might be sending messages by ploughing with horses of different colour from day to day!—and so, *pauvre vieux*,[6] he was carefully watched. At night the crackle of machine-guns from the line was curiously muffled and echoed back from the cuckoo's clump of trees, an effect that varied extraordinarily with atmospheric conditions.

In a day or two we entered the trenches of the Western Front line (for the first time), a little to the right of the Armentières-Lille railway. It will be easier for purposes of future description to use the numbering and nomenclature then current on the Western Front. The front was divided into stretches of length from 200 to 300 yards, numbered from right to left; the part taken over by our Company was described as 'trenches 71 and 72', the support line parallel to this and about a furlong in rear being 'S 71 and S 72', the third or subsidiary line, parallel to this and several hundred yards in rear again, being 'SS 71 and SS 72'. The rusty and grass-covered railroad crossed the trench-line at the 'Railway Salient', '73 and 74'. To the right, at '69', the opposing line of trenches converged to within a distance of seventy yards, this part being named, from its appearance on the map, the 'Mushroom'.[7] In the wide semicircle of the whole salient the long communication saps ran out from the town as centre, like the radial threads of a spider-web, to intersect subsidiary, support, and front lines; to a mathematician it was merely a diagram in polar co-ordinates,[8] with Armentières as origin.

When we left the Hospice after the middle of May the system for each Company of the Battalion was to have been four days in the front and support line, four days in the subsidiary line, changing about, and then eight days in billets. This was not adhered to for long; as the date 1st July approached, the worst day in the whole history of the British Army,[9] we spent longer and longer intervals in the trenches, being in fact in them for forty days continuously in June, July, and early August.

The 10th Company went first of all into SS 71 and SS 72 for four moderately quiet days of rest and sleep in the dug-outs, but four nights of working parties mending the front and support lines in various places, most of them away from our own immediate sector.

It is a severe test of conviction to stand upright on the parapet of a support trench on a moonless night, taking on trust the assurance that if you remain still when the Very light opens out its beams you will probably pass unobserved; at first I found the test too severe, and would generally jump down. But the piece of trench on which we were engaged this first night was peculiar. Because it lay in some dip in the ground and was perhaps masked by the front line itself, the machine-gun bullets cleared its parapet by some seven feet; at least we were assured so, and had reason, standing on top and patting down the thrown-up sand-bags, to believe it. There were brick walls behind, the single remaining ones of houses often breached but rarely blown right down, since the shells on penetrating would pass an appreciable distance beyond before exploding; and while we patted with the flat of the spade, a traversing stream of machine-gun bullets a foot or two above us would chip the walls afresh, with whiplike cracks and a line of sparks. This enemy machine-gunner, with his fine judgement of eleva-tion, went by the nickname of 'Parapet Joe'; in the front line he had the height of the parapet to an inch and was able to cut the bags along an arc of 200 or 300 yards; sometimes he would make his spray of bullets switch suddenly back, to catch any unwary head.

Another precarious job was the 'pushing party'. This consisted in bringing forward supplies from dumps in the subsidiary line or in the outskirts of the town, across country on a truck pushed by several men over rails exposed in places to machine-gun fire. From such tasks we would return in the early hours of the morning, unless we had been wounded, to our dug-outs in the subsidiary line. Lying on my back for the first time under my low roof of corrugated iron I perceived, fixed in the beams, a book in a red binding. I drew it out, and found it to be, of all things, Carlyle's *Sartor Resartus!*—left here, no doubt, by some metaphysically minded Scots private or corporal, whose fate might be doubtful.[10] In the remote days of peace I had opened the work, flinched at its appearance, and shut it again. Well, here it was. The patcher repatched! I myself needed some repatching. I made efforts to read, but Teufelsdröckh and the Carlylean philosophy of clothes obstinately refused to be fitted into the surroundings, and so I returned him to his crevice.

The violin was my companion in this dug-out; I slept with it by my side. However, since to play it in the open was inviting trouble and to play it in the confined space of the dug-out was impossible, I left it next time at the Hospice under the special care of a Sister.

11 *Armentières Salient:*
The Front Line

A T THE END OF THE FOUR DAYS[1] WE WENT UP TO THE LINE IN 71, where a double dug-out accommodated Mr. Gillman, Sergeants Jones and Day, and myself—I should add that I was still a corporal. In a letter to my sister I had described, item by item, my surroundings in the dug-out just quitted; the details will serve well enough for a typical picture:

> ... three-quarters of an inch of candle dimly lights up a space too cramped for one man to turn round in comfortably, much less to provide sleeping and living quarters for three; there is a sixth of a pound of butter in a tin at the left of the candle. Resting on a sandbag is half a tin of jam, and on a ledge with a sloping board above it on which, if you started up in the night, you would strike your head, lies bedding; three waterproof sheets and three great-coats, no blankets. The remainder of the limited air-space is filled with three sets of equipment, bandoliers with ammunition, six gas helmets, three shrapnel helmets, three mess-tins, several puttees, three rifles, a violin case, some cheese in a piece of paper and

some crumbly bread in a sack. The roofing iron is sufficient to keep out the sun, but lets in the rain.[2]

Three of these four days were fairly quiet. In the day-time a few sentries kept a look-out from the bays while the rest slept; in the night-time everyone had to be on the fire-step under full equipment until Stand-to in the chilly dawn.[3] Trenches here were very tumble-down, and enfilading machine-gun fire dropping at long range actually came from behind—so extreme was the curvature of the salient—and had wounded two officers of the Company which we relieved, the 4th Company, at their dug-out entrance; snipers were active and had already killed a tall officer of the same Company, Mr. Hall, popular in the 6th Reinforcements, in the front line.[4] Stale, foul-smelling water from the winter rains stagnated in the floor of the trenches under the rotting duck-boards, and there was a pump for removing this over the parados to the muddy unsightly terrain, full of stinking pools in shell-holes large or small, that lay between the front and the support line. Our dug-outs were on the edge of this morass, low shelters topped with old sand-bags or corrugated iron. Large, well-conditioned rats infested the line at nights, scampering along parapets or gnawing at haversacks in the dug-outs, supplementing their vampire meal. But the line was quiet, quiet in no ironic Remarquian sense;[5] there was no shelling here, nothing but the echo-awakening crackle of Parapet Joe and the hiss of rising flare-lights, soaring to their parabolic apex and shedding a bluish or greenish light over no-man's-land. Our own flares seemed inferior to those of the enemy; we fired them up rarely and almost apologetically; indeed, we generally left the illumination of no-man's-land to the Germans, who had excellent flares, sometimes with parachutes attached, below which they might swing gracefully for what seemed a full minute.

On the morning of the third day, 28th May if my reckoning is right,[6] shrapnel came over early, killing Tom Wilson, one of the men who had been with me in those last days on Rhododendron Ridge, mortally wounding Tom Meikle of the 7th Reinforcements on the same fire-step, and sparing Tom McCone, who had been sitting between the other two. McCone had had curious escapes; in the last, at Mudros East in Lemnos, he had been shot through the cheek by a bullet exploding in an incinerator which he was tending.

On the evening of the fourth day our side began the period of 'activity' with a bombardment, the first drum-roll—relatively *pianissimo*, but it was hard to realize that—of the long crescendo that was to lead up to 1st July. Word was passed along that at 5 p.m. Australian artillery in rear would 'strafe' the Mushroom, and that we had best be prepared for a retaliation on us. Shells soon skimmed our parapets and sent the German sand-bags flying; but no sooner was this observed through periscopes than the retaliation came—shrapnel, high explosive, and large trench-mortar bombs. Frank Jones, Dick Day, and I were standing under the corrugated iron roof, trying to look unconcerned, Dick Day, a Main Body man, even making some show of cracking jokes; but jokes rang hollow as a succession of shells and bombs neared the dug-out; noises like an express train passing at high speed through a station, a thud as the missile, whatever it was, buried itself in the earth just over the parapet, then the shock of the explosion, a sulphurous and phosphorous smell, and a spitting out of dust and rust. The last concussion, mercifully the last, knocked us on to our knees, a thick smoke enveloping the dug-out; it was later found that this particular 4·1 or 5·9, or perhaps *Minenwerfer* bomb,[7] had made a great crater just outside the parapet, banking up and blocking a sunken ditch which was used at night as a sally-port for stealing out to no-man's-land. After an hour the main retaliation ceased; but 'pineapple' bombs[8] kept dropping till nightfall into the muddy pool behind the dug-out; in the soft ooze very few of them exploded, while those that did explode merely threw up mud-geysers, bespattering the dug-outs with black slime.

As we waited for relief by an Auckland Company an increasing drizzle set in after dark. The orders were passed over, we filed back in gloom and rain, ten yards and a half-turn to the left, and so on alternately and interminably. Duck-boards were greasy and in places still unrepaired; Sergeant Carruthers (killed Passchendaele, 12th October 1917) went through, spraining an ankle. At the outskirts of the town it was discovered that a 'listening post' of six men out in no-man's-land had been forgotten in the relief. As the nearest N.C.O. I was ordered to return to the line, see them relieved by six Aucklanders, and bring them back to the Hospice. Relievers and relieved grumbled equally, the former at being stirred out, the latter at being left in wet, cold, and danger until midnight. We came back along the sunken ditch, over the loose earth of the new crater and under the hanging waterproof sheet of the sally-port, reaching the Hospice between one and two in the morning. Henceforth no listening posts were omitted in the reliefs.

Eight days were spent in billets on the fatigue parties and guards that have been described. With the coming of June the crescendo advanced suddenly and in no slight *sforzando*.[9] I was on guard in rear of the Hospice, on the night of 2nd June, when a great and continuous drumming of gunfire began beyond the northern skyline, where Ypres lay sixteen miles away. YPRES! The name startles me still as I write it now—the letters seem to magnify themselves into the Cloth Hall and the ruins.[10] As it turned out, I was never to be there; but once, later that same June, passing in a bus on a summer afternoon along the Bailleul highway and bound for a grenade school, I saw, on a signpost at the right, YPRES, with a direction-finger, *Der Wegweiser* of Schubert if ever there was one;[11] and for the moment I was dazed and shaken, as though I had read the words, *per me si va nella città dolente!*[12] On this night one could hear above the *ostinato*[13] rumble the occasional cough of giant 'crumps', as we called them, with their feeling of wholesale death arriving at speed. If it was like this from sixteen miles away, what must it be from near at hand? And which side had begun it? For a fortnight the heavy crumping continued. A test alarm was held, we fell in quickly in the quadrangle, and the Sisters of Charity, thinking that the Germans had broken through, were in tears and had to be reassured by Captain Buddle, this being the first disclosure that the alarm was false. It was not until we were in SS 76 that we learned from newspapers, brought from town by fatigue parties, the details of the attack of 2nd June, the concentrated bombardment on the Canadians, the leisurely crossing of German infantry with full packs up—they had imagined that nothing could survive—the loss of a Canadian Major-General and a Brigadier-General and the last resistance of a handful of Canadians.[14] All these, if we had realized it, were omens for ourselves.

The route to SS 76 and SS 77, the subsidiary trenches which we now occupied, was more varied than that to 71 and 72. We went by way of Half-past-eleven Square through the suburbs by the 'X' route to a lane in the outskirts, descended into the zigzag saps through a hole in a fence by a shattered house rumoured to contain a grand piano, and passed under the wall of a ruined distillery and through some dismantled buildings called Buterne Farm,[15] where Platoon 12 remained, the other three platoons continuing farther along the side of a low-lying stream bordered by willows, and turning at right angles into the subsidiary lines, for there were two here, parallel and about a hundred yards apart. The path by the stream had a sylvan name, Willow Walk; in the mornings after a night of machine-gun fire it was less sylvan to note fresh bullet-holes in the willow-trunks and some in the handrail of the footbridge. Battalion H.Q. in the subsidiary line to the left of Willow Walk consisted of a line of cosy little dug-outs excavated from a bank in front of which a group of trees leaned together in such a way as to conceal the abrupt ten-foot drop of the ground into a hollow. A hundred yards up the sap leading to support and front lines was the dump, from which the railway line of the 'pushing party' ran to Houplines. A stream of the most dubious appearance, with every indication of rats, flowed in a ditch past the subsidiary line, but was used for tea and stew, the days of fastidiousness being a remote civilian memory. We spent eight days in this part, not taking our turn in the front and support lines, since the officer commanding there had decided to spend the whole period in the line, intending next time to spend eight days in the subsidiary line. He could not know that the 'raids' would dislocate his programme.

12 Armentières: The Crescendo

D URING OUR STAY IN SS 76 AND SS 77 I WAS PROMOTED TO LANCE-sergeant and transferred to Platoon 11, which now had Frank Jones as sergeant. Once more, as in Trentham, Lemnos, Gallipoli, and Egypt, to my great satisfaction and, I dare say, to his, we were working together. We shared a dug-out. The raids had begun and bombardments were of nightly occurrence. At any hour of the night, as we lay facing rearwards under the low inward-sloping roofs of corrugated iron, the dim outlines of the town, barely discernible against the dark skyline, would be silhouetted in the white light of flashes, followed in a few seconds by the scream of shells overhead and the rumble of guns. Retaliation would begin at once, and the darkness would leap in the other direction with the distant white flashes of guns and the nearer red ones of bursting shells. In concussive effect the 'minnies', that is, mines thrown by *Minenwerfer*, were the worst, huge canisters with a thin metal case and a great weight of high explosive, which burst with a terrific rending report to make holes ten feet deep and fifteen feet or more across. At other times a gas alarm or gas alert made us stand to; for whenever there was an east wind, as indicated by numerous wind-vanes all along the line, a gas alert was ordered, sentries had to listen for the possible hiss of gas escaping from pressure cylinders, and all ranks wore gas helmets pinned on tunic fronts, ready to be slipped over heads on the first alarm. Sometimes this would come from a flank, and night would then be hideous with the sustained doleful hoots of horns, the tappings and clangings of the suspended shell-cases that served as gongs, and the tolling of church bells in the town.

During this increasing surge of activity there was little sleep to be had at night; perhaps a few hours between Stand-down after break of day and nine o'clock or so in the morning, when the guns began again. It was quiet also in the evening until Stand-to at dusk, when machine-guns opened out once more. Enemy artillery battered Armentières severely. In the day-time great shells soared overhead into the town, and what might be at one moment a large brick building would vanish at the next in a spinning cloud of carrot-coloured dust, which in turn would clear away to disclose nothing but the skeleton framework. I recall a Sunday morning when there was a thin blue haze over the landscape and the faint far-off chime of church bells. A German battery was sending single shots, twos, and fours into the outer buildings of Houplines; having no urgent task for an hour or two I counted them mechanically— 178.

My turn now came for the pushing party with Corporal O'Brien, who was fatally wounded in the front line three weeks later. The trolleys had to be pushed from the dump in the subsidiary line to the edge of Houplines, there to be piled with food, timber, barbed wire and 'concertina' wire, corkscrew iron pickets to string the wire on, sand-bags, sheets of corrugated iron, and petrol tins filled with chlorinated water. Two trips had to be made on this night, each from the dump to Houplines and back; the trucks gave out such a creaking and rattling as the Germans could not but hear, or so it seemed. Cover was good for most of the way except at an open stretch where machine-gun bullets struck fire from the rails; here—and I was forcibly reminded of Chailak Dere on Gallipoli—we had to wait for the opportune moment before pushing past with all speed.

After about a month in the line I saw my first German, a prisoner, a young fair-haired Saxon captured in a scuffle between night patrols. As we came off Stand-down I was ordered, with scant time for a meal and none for a shave, to report at Battalion H.Q., to take this prisoner back to Brigade and Divisional H.Q. to be interrogated, and then to Army Corps H.Q. in its château at Lamotte-aux-Bois, eleven miles from the nearest part of the line. The escort proved to be two men of my own section, Keith and Norman. The prisoner flinched at the sight of fixed bayonets—no doubt New Zealanders had the reputation, among the Germans, of being cannibals—but he flinched more in Half-past-eleven Square, where knots of angry Frenchwomen let him know, rather close to his ear, what they thought of him and what they would have done to him had we not been present. And so he was interrogated twice over—at Brigade and Divisional H.Q. His Company? Some Leipzig Company. How long in the line? Did he notice any effect from our snipers? (Here he and the interpreter seemed at cross purposes before *Scharfschützen*[1] was hazarded.) And so forth. This done, I was ordered to send Keith back to the line and proceed by staff car with Norman and the prisoner to Army Corps H.Q.; and this was the real interest of the morning. The wooded region of the Forêt de Nieppe is beautiful, and the château was well appointed; there was much evidence of paper-work at desks and tables and alcoves, and it happened to be the hour of morning coffee. I felt the professional gap, inevitable and natural, between the Staff and ourselves; the social distance, too, for I was a trench-stained N.C.O., unshaven that morning. (Divisional Orders next day included a brief sentence or two about the necessity of daily shaving in the front line and its effect on morale.) Some memoirs over-emphasize the jealousy existing between the Staff and the combatant troops. There was certainly a tincture of this; it could not be otherwise, where one department of the Army lived in civilian comfort and the other in perpetual squalid discomfort and peril. But in fact we in the line hardly ever thought of the Staff, or, if at all, only when things which they were presumed to have planned went wrong; when things went right it was simply an uncovenanted boon. Something more on this will be said when we move into the first battle of the Somme.

It was now past the middle of June. No hint came to our ears of all those regiments moving forward from back areas in the south for the day that would alter the whole feeling of the war, the 1st July, postponed as it was from the original 25th June. After it, nothing would ever be the same. Meanwhile, with us, the crescendo was still only gradual.

13 Terdeghem:
A Grenade School

I<small>T WAS AT A SLIGHTLY LATER DATE THAT I BEGAN TO TAKE NOTICE OF THE</small> communiqués which tersely described, or in most cases avoided describing, the doings of each night on the Western Front. In particular I noted a limited selection of euphemistic adjectives, such as 'sharp', 'brisk'; e.g. 'the enemy was ejected after brisk fighting'; 'there was sharp retaliation', and the like.

It required some experience of the raids of July to learn to construe correctly these communiqués; but 'briskness' could certainly include some deadly grenade-throwing. For my own further education in this I was now ordered to report with pack up at Brigade H.Q., in readiness to proceed to the 2nd Army Grenade School at Terdeghem, a small village some twenty miles away, between Steenvoorde and Cassel.[1] There were some Australians waiting, but only one other New Zealander, Gunn, a sergeant of the Rifle Brigade (killed at the Somme, 15th September 1916), who came forward and made friends at once.[2] A bus took us by Erquinghem, Bac St. Maur, Croix du Bac, and Steenwerck, our railhead, to the highway at Bailleul. It was along this highway that I saw the signpost pointing to YPRES and seeming for a moment to darken the air. But on this lovely afternoon of midsummer, with Flanders at its best, one could almost forget the war. The fields border on the roadside with no hedge or fence between, cultivated to the last foot, the only demarcation between field and field being the line where different colours meet. Hops luxuriated on their frames of slanting poles; thin blue smoke from cottages wavered in a gossamer haze. Escape from the line, brief as it was, produced a lightness of heart not to be described, nor ever quite recaptured. The little villages, each with its church in a clump of trees, the highway, shaded, as in Dutch or Flemish paintings, by a long avenue of poplars, these to New Zealand eyes held a peace, a mellowness, the ripeness of an old civilization. Amid such scenes we passed through Météren, Flêtre, Caestre, Sylvestre-Cappel, villages each on a rise, turned right at the last of these, and reached Terdeghem about 4 p.m., finding ourselves among English, Scots, Canadians, and Australians. Some of the Canadians could speak at first hand of the affair of 2nd to 15th June;[3] their account differed in certain respects from that of the newspapers. I formed friendships with one or two of them, those war-time friendships of a few days, clouded by never meeting again and never knowing, a few months later, whether the friend was living, mutilated, or dead.

If I had had a map of the district I should have known that the small historic town of Cassel, crowning a hill 515 feet high and descending a little way down its sides, would have given an unsurpassed panoramic view of the old front line from the dunes at Nieuport in the north to the slag pyramids of Lens and Loos in the south, and even farther. It was only three miles from Terdeghem. As it was, I took no leave from camp at all, but like a student preparing for examination, revised my lecture notes and made careful scale-drawings of the bombs, or rather *grenades*, that we were studying. (They were *grenades*, but the thrower, since he could not be called a *grenadier*, was a bomber.[4] Such distinctions were dear to the British Army.) Into five days was packed a fairly intensive course, theoretical and practical. Theory, expounded in lectures, concerned itself with the nature and principle of grenades, not only our own but those of the Germans—and I remember how complicated were the German rifle-grenades of types 1913 and 1914; with their articulation, how to assemble and disassemble their component parts, and so on. Practical tests included bowling at marks in the open and from trenches for accuracy and distance; and here, to my pleasure, the sergeant-instructor was an old Otago schoolfellow, H. C. Alloo, one of that celebrated family of ambidextrous bowlers and batsmen in inter-provincial cricket, and now at Terdeghem a bomber of deadly length and accuracy, dropping his Mills Mark 1, No. 5, to within less than a yard at forty yards. There was instruction also in methods of grenade attack and defence; and specimens, mounted in constructive detail in trenches in the park, of characteristic enemy death-traps against which it was well to be forewarned. The most impressive of these was a concealed gate of barbed wire horizontally suspended, which by the pulling of a wire would fall to a vertical position and make a cul-de-sac, to be promptly raked by a concealed machine-gun. We were invited to regard this ingenious portcullis as outside the bounds of reasonable fairness; a one-sided idea, since modern war consists so largely in the grossest deceptions ensuring the foulest opportunities.

Mr. Lewis, the officer who lectured in so quiet and donnish a voice on these refinements of attack or defence, as if it were analytical dynamics, let slip an obscure allusion by which I concluded that some part, perhaps a very considerable part, of the Army or armies might be out of the line at that very moment rehearsing for a great offensive. I did not think of this again until later in June when one of my own men, James Burnett of the 7th Cameronians, lent to us from Cape Helles, his ear to the ground in a dug-out in SS 70, told me of a continuous rumble of artillery many miles to the south. We were thus prepared for the opening of the first battle of the Somme.

At Terdeghem there was a kind of conspiracy of silence, the very antithesis of rumour, concerning some incident of not long before. Skirting round the topic—though it was too vague to be called even that—I imagined, rightly or wrongly, that there had been an accident in the lecturing room, where it might be that a bomb, perhaps defective, had exploded in the course of demonstration. If it were so, and if it had been a Mills, it was not difficult to reconstruct the scene. And on the Thursday of this week I saw for myself, in a minute-long act of suspense, how easily such an accident might occur; indeed, I am sure that some others and myself owed our lives to our Irish instructor, Sergeant Flanagan. The squad of six, a little drowsy in the heat of the summer solstice, was seated round a trestle table on the lawn, dissecting grenades in turn and demonstrating their action; to do this with safety it was, of course, necessary to unscrew the base-cap and remove the detonator. It was the turn of an Australian, Corporal G—, who at that moment was in the act of pulling out the pin that checked the spring-lever but without having previously removed the detonator. The bomb was the familiar Mills, five seconds from pin-release to explosion. I had noted the trunk of a substantial tree, and was wondering whether I could be behind it in five seconds, when with great presence of mind Sergeant Flanagan, keeping the corporal's action suspended by some smooth deliberate talking and correction, and looking him in the eye, quietly put his own hand across and closed it gently but firmly on the corporal's, all the while talking about the lesson, drew away the bomb, lever down, and re-inserted the pin. On another occasion Sergeant C—, also an Australian, bowling a live bomb over a parapet at a target, swung his arm, after letting the pin go, no fewer than three times for better aim. We flung ourselves on the trench-floor as the bomb, bursting before reaching ground, shrapnelled back over the parapet. On that Friday night there was a lifelike, or deathlike, sham attack, officers versus N.C.O.s, a confused affair of smoke bombs, Very lights, and weakly charged grenades, discussed in all its aspects at the final lecture on the following morning, and pronounced very successful.

Our own return route in the afternoon was by Nieppe and the Pont de Nieppe, where a new phenomenon, high up in the cumulus clouds, caught the eye, a fountain of liquid streaming down, vaporizing, bursting into more fountains, falling in this way until it poured on the ground, then catching fire and leaving long trails of smoke.

Instinctively we reached for helmets, fearing that it might be some new poison gas; next, that it might be an incendiary bomb for setting fire to the ripening crops by the road to Nieppe; but finally learning that it was an invention of our own, a petrol-shower incendiary bomb to be used by our aeroplanes against enemy observation balloons.

The Company, not long out of the trenches, was in the Hospice. The violin was in such good condition that I could almost believe one or other of the Sisters had been keeping it in tune. The activity preceding that *dies infanda*,[5] 1st July 1916, was at its height. The town had suffered considerably from retaliatory bombardments; the church of Notre Dame had been neatly decapitated, its spire hanging downwards—like the more famous Virgin of Notre Dame de Brebières at Albert,[6] seen later on our way to the Somme—but the base still held somehow in the masonry. The interior had been badly damaged by some scores of shells.

14 Armentières:
The Raids Begin

D URING THE LAST DAYS OF JUNE WE RETURNED TO THE SUBSIDIARY
line, SS 69 and SS 70, in rear of the Mushroom, immediately
to the right of the sector which we had first occupied in May. It was
this time the 'V' route that took us to the edge of the town near the
Asile des Aliénés at a point where three disused and grass-grown
railways diverged, the middle one to Lille; we skirted the right-hand
one, which ran south-east, until we reached the gas-alarm post already
described, then turned left through the inevitable hedge-gap into
the saps and, filing past a brickyard with a very tall chimney, came
to the rear of a line of houses along a road. The last house in the
row was pierced; the sap passed under its roof. From this point we
walked in a doubtful immunity above ground for a little, shielded by
the line of houses on the other side of the road, until at the end of
the hamlet we came to Square Farm, a large walled-in court, and so
finally dropped in to Lothian Avenue, which ran past a cemetery to
the line.[1] I believe that not only New Zealanders but Scots who served
there, if ever they came upon this description, would recognize every

feature of it. German machine-guns had spared the cemetery, though stray bullets had unavoidably damaged the glasswork. I remember that once, when the subsidiary line here was being heavily shelled, I had two or three minutes of moral struggle. Should I stick it out in the open, where I happened to be at the time, or should I take cover in the cemetery? The instinct of self-preservation prevailed; I lay among the green mounds, ashamed afterwards of having thus taken advantage of the dead.

It was now nearing the end of June, and high midsummer. Lush grass and green stalks trailing golden flowers, doubtless mere weeds but unknown to me and beautiful to the eye, covered the gashes in the earth and spangled the dead ground between the lines. The woods on the slope of Pérenchies,[2] behind the German line, were in their densest foliage; crimson poppies bloomed among the wire of no-man's-land. Lieutenant Hargest (later, in the Second World War, Brigadier Hargest), Mr. Rae, Frank Jones, and I explored the ground between our part and the support line to know it by heart in case we should ever be summoned to go overland and repel a raid. Long grass had so overgrown the barbed wire that the critically important gaps were hard to locate. It was almost unnatural to be thus walking at large above ground, to discover a ruined cottage with a garden with currant bushes and apple and plum trees, unpruned and untended since the flight of the owner in 1914, and the flower-beds choked with weeds.

Raids and counter-raids by night and bombardments by day abruptly marked the beginning of July. Within a fortnight each Battalion of the Brigade had suffered in its turn severe losses from artillery and *Minenwerfer* fire directed on its sector. This began one midday with enfilading fire on the support line from a German battery far to the right and—such was the curvature of the salient—virtually behind us. The trench-line was breached in several places and many of the Wellington Battalion were killed and wounded.

We were called up from the subsidiary line to repair the damage. Some connected the bombardment of this support line with the desertion to the enemy of Private— of the Wellingtons, who had been on sentry-duty in the Mushroom the night before.[3] It is unlikely that he was responsible, but for the desertion at least he had some provocation; he was of German birth, and it was said that his parents in New Zealand had been subjected to abuse and ostracism, of which he had lately learned in letters. In barest justice it is difficult to see what more those parents could have done than send their son—for this was before the days of conscription—to fight on our side and possibly be killed by men of his own race; but there is no arguing with xenophobes.

The battle of the Somme had now begun, but as yet we knew very little about it, for we were beginning the longest of all our spells in the trenches, and the few official communiqués read out by the platoon commander referred to places, Fricourt, La Boisselle, Hem, Curlu, and so on, with names quite unfamiliar.[4] Sometimes a newspaper was brought from Armentières, but there the news was equally meager— indeed, the British newspapers of that fortnight almost provide the classic example of evasion and downright misdirection.[5] There was also the mysterious affair of 30th June at Richebourg St. Vaast, only ten or twelve miles south of us.[6] Enough noise had been heard from that direction to warrant the belief that two or three divisions were attempting to break through to Lens or Carvin; yet this had been merely described as a 'strong raiding party penetrating the enemy's third line', and nothing further had been heard of it. No news, of an attack, was mostly bad news—one felt that, even if it were intended only as a diversion on the eve of the great attack farther south, a costly set-back had been played down. From a scrap of conversation overheard between officers I judged that losses on an unprecedented scale were being incurred at the Somme, but I did not learn until later that the casualties sustained on 1st July, most of them within two or three hours of the launching, were equal to those of the whole fortnight at Loos, were twice as many as those of the whole Boer War, and numbered over 7,000 in officers alone.

It was about this time that the word 'attrition' acquired a vogue, though only in 1917 did it have a general use and an accompanying theory. There can be little doubt that both the word and the theory were the by-product, the cover, and an attempt towards the palliation of the enormous losses sustained in these great 'pushes', which for the gain of ten miles of advance might mean the loss of 200,000 men. Much of this was not attrition at all, but the arbitrary throwing away of lives. And the trouble about attrition was that it was reciprocal; each side wore down the other, subject became object and object subject. If on the large scale it had begun for the French at Verdun on 21st February 1916, it began for the British on 1st July.

In these early days of July, however, the Somme was for us a distant, indefinite, and ominous reverberation. Burnett, my Scot from the Cameronians, whose ear was that of Highland Jessie at the relief of Lucknow, reported to me each day on its variation.[7]

Late at night on 6th July a heavy bombardment began to fall on front-line 75 and 76, to our left, a tremendous 'crumping' of shells alternating with the rending crashes of *Minenwerfer*, the red flames shooting up almost continuously. This was the exterminating pattern of several such bombardments. It was falling on the Aucklanders.[8] Our own retaliation was weak, some of the supporting artillery having been moved to the right to assist an Australian raid. After two hours it seemed impossible that anyone could have survived.

In the morning every available man was summoned up to repair the damage. We found S 75 and S 76 almost obliterated. Stretcher-bearers were still at work bringing back from the line the dead bodies or as much of broken flesh as could be found and put in sand-bags for burial; for men had been blown to pieces or entombed. Front-line 75 and 76 had suffered less, though damaged far worse than any trenches had been before that day. Many men had been killed by concussion alone; I saw in a low dug-out four signallers, all dead without a mark on them; they had remained at their telephone post and had been blasted out of life together. A glance through a periscope at the point of junction of 75 and 76, where the line had suffered most, showed at once why the front line had escaped the extreme damage of the support line. Some fifty yards out there had formerly been a disused

parallel trench which curved in to join 76 at the place we were about
to repair, now entirely blotted out by a honeycomb of great shell and
Minenwerfer craters. Clearly the Germans had supposed this to be
our real front line and had treated it accordingly. Had it been as they
supposed, it is doubtful if any in the line could have survived; as it was,
the Auckland Company had suffered 110 casualties, a large number
being fatal. Compared with what was happening away in the south this
was, of course, a mere trench incident, and I can recall no mention
of it in the communiqués. If it were mentioned it would have been in
some such noncommittal terms as the following: 'After a strong artillery
preparation the enemy attacked our line east of Armentières, but was
beaten off after some fighting.'

There had, indeed, been raiders, but their mistake regarding our
front sufficiently explained why they had not entered our real line.
Other causes were the self-sacrifice of an Auckland machine-gunner
in an advanced post covering the front. Survivors said that through the
explosions they could hear continually the rat-a-tat of this machine-
gun; it was also known that the advanced post of bombers had resisted
to the last. All of these men were now reported as missing. There was
a strong rumour that one of the raiders was still in hiding, somewhere
between the front and the support lines.[9]

The bombardment had knocked down the trench walls of 75 and 76
and had piled up in their place a bank of tumbled earth and sand-bags.
To cut a new passage-way through this was the work not of days but
of weeks. We made a beginning, but were then ordered to return to
SS 70 for our belongings and to relieve the Aucklanders, who doubled
down the sap, or what remained of it, with unconcealed alacrity. Thus
from now on most of our afternoons were spent in rebuilding the line,
putting the trenches once more into defensive order, and making new
dug-outs in rear of them, for almost all the old ones had been blown
to pieces by *Minenwerfer*, against which there is no protection. At the
right of our sector, the join of 75 and 76, a gap was left, a sally-port for
advanced grenade posts and wiring parties to use at night, for there was
extensive cover outside in the honeycomb of enormous overlapping

craters. And now all this ground has been described for what was to happen there a week later.

The barbed-wire entanglements in front had for the most part been buried or blown away entirely. Wiring parties therefore went out each night to put up a new set, working by the standard method in which a dozen men, each carrying out his special part—for example, one man in the middle stringing out a roll of 'concertina' wire between the two parallel hedges of barbed wire—were presumed to be able, on flat ground, to make an obstacle thirty yards by ten in some twenty minutes. I write from a professional recollection, since at a slightly later date, in 77, I was permanent 'wiring sergeant' of a picked party, including Keith, Norman, L. W. Smith, and other experts in bush-clearing and fencing on farms and back-blocks in New Zealand. 'That out wiring sensation' was the subject of one of those quasi-humorous drawings of Captain Bruce Bairnsfather,[10] which in 1916 were rapidly waning in popularity, since humour of that kind is strongly relative, depending on which end of the stick one is pulling; and the war was producing, besides its other attritions, an attrition of the sense of humour. What might raise a laugh in 1915 would hardly raise a smile in 1916; what it might raise in 1917 or 1918 I did not remain to learn.[11]

Two nights later, 9th July, the 1st Canterbury Battalion had its turn, and an even worse ordeal.[12] First notice of this came to us in 76 by the sudden descent on our sector of a 'pinning down' barrage. Evening Stand-to was almost over, the long twilight was shading into dark about nine o'clock, when our whole length of trench quivered under the sudden explosion of 'whizz-bangs',[13] shrapnel on extreme enfilade. All through the afternoon the Germans had been ranging with trench-mortars on a part of the disused trench in front and now, amid the shrapnel, one could hear dozens of great bombs bursting there. Fortunately for us they evidently still supposed it to be our real front line. I met Mr. Rae on his rounds at a point where shrapnel was specially bad; he considered the possibility of sheltering in an old dug-out near by, but I remembered the Auckland signallers. We moved off in opposite directions. Crossing again on our rounds we met at the same point to find the dug-out blown to pieces by a dropping shell and stinking of phosphorus. High explosive now joined the shrapnel; among the several casualties in the bays was Corporal O'Brien of the pushing party, mortally wounded.

This barrage on us was a mere diversion. It lifted a little, and now it could be seen that a mile to the right, at 69 or 70, a bombardment of shell and *Minenwerfer*, exactly like that which had overwhelmed the Auckland Company, must be falling on the Canterbury men. The fuse-lights of the *Minenwerfer* bombs were traceable as parabolas rising quickly from a point about a thousand yards in rear of the German lines, curving slowly at the apex and rushing steeply down. Then, after four or five seconds, the rending crash. This bombardment, like the other of three days before, lasted for exactly two hours and ceased suddenly. Word came that raiders were in the Mushroom, but later the bombardment was resumed for a few minutes and it appeared that they had returned to their trenches. The Canterbury Company had suffered, I believe, 135 casualties,[14] a 'box barrage'[15] down communication trenches cutting off all escape. This time the incident was regarded as important enough to be mentioned in a communiqué which read: 'Raiders eastward of Armentières were ejected after half an hour of fighting.'[16]

It now began to be possible to construe the communiqués, somewhat as follows: (i) 'ejected'; it could hardly be said of any raid by either side that 'the enemy were ejected', since artillery or mortars did the smashing up, raiders came over and had a look at it, perhaps captured a prisoner or two, and then went back at the time decided upon: (ii) 'sharp' or 'brisk'; this could mean that at least one company had lost 50 or more per cent of its effective: (iii) 'fighting'; this meant that hardly anyone on one side saw anyone on the other, the heavy casualties being due exclusively to shrapnel, bombs, and high explosive, with machine-guns added if it was a case of crossing no-man's-land. A future historian, if he leaned at all on these carefully sieved accounts, would be quite misled. On the other hand, where our own reverses were concerned, we found the German communiqués fairly accurate.[17]

Three battalions of the 1st New Zealand Brigade had now suffered severely on separate occasions, with casualties on an ascending scale. But for having moved across on the 7th to relieve the Aucklanders, we might ourselves have taken the brunt of this bombardment of the Mushroom. There was also something disquieting in the pattern: 75 and 76, then 69 and 70; one might half expect 73 and 74, or 71 and 72, and about 12th July. One might also expect about 150 casualties, for the box-barrage problem seemed insoluble. It proved to be more, but this time the raid was from our side, and the 4th Otago Company was exterminated in a different way from the others.

15 Armentières:
The Raid of the 4th Otagos

I T MUST HAVE BEEN A LITTLE EARLIER THAN THIS DATE THAT DIVISIONAL Orders included a short paragraph of posthumous commendation of Private William J. Clarke, 8/1432, 10th North Otago Company. He was the first of my old section to die. I first heard of the circumstances from Dick Burt, another of my old section, who had to control himself for a moment or two before telling me any more than that 'Clarkie is dead'. It happened in the following way: Burt, Clarke, and three or four others had been given the task of unscrewing Mills bombs, examining for defectives, cleaning, and reassembling, and this in a covered passage in a building, blind at one end and lacking windows. I never learned who was responsible for such an irresponsible choice of place for such a task; Sergeant Flanagan of Terdeghem would not have allowed it for one moment. A defective bomb, it would seem—there were occasionally such, 'shorting' across a badly cut fuse-tube—began to go off in Clarke's hands. He called 'Run, chaps!' and had just time to lie on it against the inner wall. Burt and the others escaped with their lives, though two were wounded by the fragments that Clarke's body had failed to intercept. It must be left at that, for the divine words that meet the case are known to everyone.[1] There was brief talk, among those who knew Clarke, of a possible posthumous V.C., such as later in 1918 was awarded when an English subaltern had similarly thrown himself on a bomb in a front-line trench. Clarke himself was a quiet man who never in any circumstances thought of reward, only of duty; and for me it is enough, in pride, however undeserving, that he once belonged to my section, to be permitted to describe his last act with precision and to associate it with his name.

While the bombardments of early July had been falling on the outer salient the whole of the 4th Otago Company had been in Armentières, training for a raid of ambitious scope, as may be judged by the number, not much less than 200, of those preparing to go over the top. In retrospect it appeared ill-considered to have trained so many men in the town. Rumour may have been wrong in believing that Armentières harboured spies, or that the occasional pigeons seen flying eastward over no-man's-land carried messages to the enemy. But apart from that, those who had to do the raiding could never see the point of the large raid, in which by the nature of things we were almost bound to suffer losses quite disproportionate to the damage inflicted on the enemy, to the number of prisoners taken, and to the amount and quality of the information presumed to be gained. These losses were not due to inefficiency. The men trained for a raid, like those trained for the attacks at the Somme, did not fail to carry out their orders; indeed, had they been allowed a small margin for independent judgement, more would have survived. Were raids for pure destruction? Then the artillery and mortars could safely be left to do that. Were they for the purpose of identifying the regiments opposite? Then the most efficacious were the silent raids, in which a small party crept across no-man's-land without advertisement and surprised and captured a few prisoners; as the Maoris—very restive in their pioneer capacity—demonstrated a fortnight later in a raid up towards Plugstreet.[2] But these were vain afterthoughts, prompted by the complete disaster of the Otago raid.

The night before the raid, the 12th July, was heavy and still, with the brooding feeling, in my mind at least, that a *Minenwerfer* bombardment might suddenly start on the right. At dusk a flute was heard playing in the German trenches; unfamiliar airs, German folk-songs, with the same affecting turns and cadences as occur in Schubert's *Morgengruß* from the song-cycle *Die schöne Müllerin*.[3] This was melting while it lasted; but with true German gallows-humour the unseen flautist, knowing that we must be listening, modulated into a travesty of the Dead March in *Saul*, bizarre and truly macabre.[4] To me it seemed to say, 'For you tomorrow night, *Kameraden!*' Such musical and other demonstrations from the trenches opposite were not new; there had been a morning in early June when a tremendous tin-canning and beating of shell-gongs had begun in the north and run south down their lines to end, without doubt, at Belfort and Mulhausen on the Swiss frontier; in celebration of their 'victory' at Jutland or of the sinking of the H.M.S. *Hampshire* with Lord Kitchener on board, or both.[5] And now a single bullet seemed to fulfil some part of the flautist's omen.

Three cadets studying for commissions, formerly N.C.O.s in Guards regiments serving in many parts of the front and latterly at Vimy Ridge, had come up to our sector to do officers' night routine with our own Company officers. I had seen them not many minutes before, two over six feet and one not so tall. Just now, after Stand-down, they were with Captain Hargest, himself of medium height, in the short alley leading off the trench to Company H.Q. Four heads in a straight line; a single bullet killed both tall men, sparing the other two by inches only.

On the morning of 13th July I stood to, with the Dead March on the flute and the death of the two cadets unpleasantly in the foreground of my mind. This, the day of the Otago raid, was quiet enough except for intermittent ranging shots by our artillery on the German wire, which seemed a gratuitous piece of advertisement. The front to be raided was immediately to our right, opposite 74, close to the disused Armentières-Pérenchies-Lille railway.[6] The companies on the right and left of this sector, ours being on the left, were each to supply a 'covering party' of a platoon or so, who were to go out half-way across no-man's-land two hours before the time of the raid and were to lie in cover, facing outwards, to counter any flanking attack. This was perhaps according to the textbook; but two well-placed machine-guns would have served as well. Perhaps my prejudice owed something to the fact that I myself, borrowed from Platoon 11 and now a sergeant since 1st July, was one of the N.C.O.s in charge of the covering party; but I felt in any case that the plan showed little imagination.

During the afternoon we studied through periscopes the ground where the party had orders to lie, beyond the outermost of our own wire entanglements, to the left of a line of blasted trees, pollarded willows, running obliquely across no-man's-land, a line of trees destined to haunt my dreams in after-years. The N.C.O.s and most of the men of my old Platoon 10, with myself from Platoon 11, were to be under Mr. Johnston, platoon commander, my own platoon commander in the impossibly far-off days at Trentham. I did not enjoy being lifted out of Platoon 11 for this job; but I was glad to be under him again. Night came on, even quieter, more brooding, more sinister than the previous night of the flute-player. There was very little machine-gun fire. I was ready to have passed an oral or written examination on those trees, and where the gaps in our wire lay with respect to them; besides, this was ground fairly well known to me from wiring parties. After dark the password was given out, chosen with incredible lack of tact and feeling: *Cadet!*

About 10 p.m. we were to be out there, settled in whatever cover could be found. At 10.15 p.m. a casual bombardment, not heavy, was to fall for a while on the sector to be raided and then gradually to die down. A little before 12 midnight a heavier one was to open out, and exactly at 12 midnight the main raiding party was to begin its dash. And so at 9.45 p.m. a party from Platoon 10 went out under Corporal Fitt, an old fellow student; my orders were to go with them, to find the gap, and then to come back and lead the rest through it. We crept in silence from one great crater to another until we came to the first of the blasted trees. At its base, as I was well aware, ran a small grass-grown ditch; we crawled down this to the outermost entanglements.

Some distance to the left I found the gap, saw the party through on all fours, and came back for the others. By 10.15 p.m. we were all lying out beyond the gap except for some half-dozen whom Captain Hargest himself—almost as if he had foreseen the event and had decided to save some men at least—took out and placed in a large crater, which they occupied all night; and luckily for them, for though later under great shrapnel and machine-gun fire, they were in excellent cover and suffered no casualties.

Beyond the wire the rest of us faced half-left, our right being by the tree-boles, our left not far in front of the gap. On making a rapid tour I felt that Sergeant Bree (a Main Body man with a very early number, 8/13) on the right had his men too near the trees, which could be a good ranging mark for mortars, and that they were facing so much to the left as to be side-on to the enemy, and thus unprotected from the really dangerous quarter. As the first bombardment was due in a minute I had to return to my end, where my smaller group had occupied an uneven line of shell-holes and were deepening these with entrenching tools. I shared a crater with George Allington (soon promoted to corporal, but killed at Messines, 7th June 1917);[7] only one man, Alf Hughes of my old section, was farther to the left—I could have touched him with my rifle; to the right and behind, in a crater overlapping ours, were two other men, Dunlop and Wilkinson. We joined the two craters into a single post and put up head cover with the sand-bags we had carried out, disguising these with grass and loose earth. At 10.15 p.m. the first bombardment fell, followed by a lively retaliation which for the most part went overhead. After 11 p.m. the noise died down, the men had dug themselves in, and all was quiet except for desultory crackles of machine-gun fire and the faint hiss of the rising Very lights, showing diamonds of dew on the grass-stems close to our faces. It was now near midnight, and cold; for what seemed a long interval there was complete darkness and silence.

The sky above the town behind us was suddenly lit up by dozens of flashes. Shells whined over, there was a series of crashes along the German line to the right and a tremendous din for a few minutes, though all sense of physical time was lost. At 12 midnight my luminous wrist-watch and a hiatus in the firing told me that the main raiding party had begun its dash, but simultaneously scores of flares rose from the German trenches, spun like Catherine wheels high up in the air, and shook out spangles of red light. Evidently a preconcerted signal, for in a moment from front, right, and left came the scurry of German shrapnel, pelting down on no-man's-land, machine-guns adding their streams of bullets in a deadly cross-fire. High explosive tore up the ground about us, and trench-mortar bombs burst along the line of trees. I wondered how the main raiding party was faring, but was more immediately concerned about the right half of our covering party, which seemed to be under severe bomb and shrapnel fire. I had the impulse to go along, but it was useless and, indeed, impossible in such intense fire to leave our post and try to give help, the retaliation continuing undiminished for over two hours. Looking behind me for a moment after a quarter of an hour of it I saw, outlined in a flare-light, the figure of a man at the gap in the wire, apparently wounded, crawling through, plainly visible in the bluish-white glare. I called to him not to move, on his life, but before the flare fell to the ground he had struggled through and must have been observed. From that instant the bombs, mortar-bombs in the usual steep parabola, began to fall on us. With each bomb a Very light rose to give the observers a gauge of their shot. Once Allington passed into my hand a hot piece that had hit his shrapnel helmet and bounced into the shell-hole. I do not know how we were spared; for the ground all about was seen in daylight afterwards to be pockmarked with bomb-holes. Of the others of the party to the right only one, McLeod, was unwounded, and he got back to the trenches early, reserved merely for death next year at Passchendaele. (The original plan had presumed us all to be back in the trenches by 12.30 a.m.) The continued bracing-up against a fate that did not come had begun to tell on us by dawn, when the firing at last died down. Half-way and more across no-man's-land we could quite clearly hear conversation, some of it an angry altercation, in the German front line. While it was still dark, I looked back in the light of a flare and was startled to see a figure without helmet or tunic crawling through the gap in the wrong direction, crawling in fact towards us, careless of danger. With difficulty restraining an impulse to shoot him, I saw that he was Lance-Corporal McEvoy (killed at Messines, 7th June 1917), and that his arm was bandaged. I dragged him down into the shell-hole, where he told me in bursts that all of those on the right of our group had been wounded or killed, that most of the wounded, including himself, had got safely back to the trenches, but that one, Corporal James Harper, his special friend, lay out there very badly wounded, that another man, Robertson (the William Robertson whom I had seen nightly at prayer with his friend Paisley in the sand at Zeitoun), was either wounded or dead along there, and that Sergeant Bree, he feared, lay killed close by. This took time to piece together; for he would break off, half-demented, and would begin to crawl out of the shell-hole, but I would pull him back to hear more. It had seemed a little while earlier that we might have to lie out all day, but now the firing died down to normal, and the voices in the German trenches seemed very close. It might at last be safe for Allington, Dunlop, and Wilkinson, with Hughes on the left, to make a dash for our lines; dawn would break in a few minutes. The better to carry in Harper, should we find him alive, I shed my equipment and rifle—contrary to regulations but surely permissible for once—and gave them to Allington, ordering him and the two others to make for our trenches as fast as they could. But there was Hughes also, on my left. I reached across and stirred him; he was dead, and had been so for some hours, lying with rifle and arm at full length in an aiming position. There was a faint grey light in the sky and normal machine-gun fire, but Allington and his two got in safely. Meanwhile McEvoy and I half-walked, half-crawled, under slight fire, random and not aimed, to the line of trees, more blasted than ever. There Sergeant Bree and William Robertson were lying, the former grievous to see, even in the half-light, but Robertson without a mark on him and his face calm, even smiling. Death is said to be equal-handed for all. Yet in that minute of growing light, though I realized this, I was glad for his unmutilated body and undisfigured face, remembering how he and Andrew Paisley, his friend (killed at Passchendaele), had never failed to practise in their lives what they had never feared to avow. I could think of no single falling away, no single selfish thing, in either of them. I looked again at Bree, thinking of his young widow, for he had been married in England during his last leave in April. Two or three yards beyond this pair we found Harper lying, his thigh badly fractured, but calm and in full possession of his senses. We asked if it was very bad. He simply said, 'I think I'm done for.' 'Don't think that, Jim,' said Paddy, 'they'll fix you up all right.' 'No, Paddy, I know.' He spoke quietly, with the same high calm, far beyond his years—he was, I suppose, my own age, twenty-one, perhaps twenty-two—and he knew better than we, for he had lost too much blood to recover, and died of wounds a week later. He was of heavy build and we could not move him an inch without causing him pain; but at this moment I caught sight of a group of men, carrying a stretcher with them, coming through the gap and towards the trees. It was a volunteer party, led by Captain Hargest, always the first to think of his men, and including Sergeant-Major Howden (killed at the Somme, 27th September 1916),[8] Sergeant Carruthers (killed at Passchendaele, 12th October 1917), and Sergeant Frank Jones (died of wounds received at the Somme, 22nd September 1916). These men laid Harper on the stretcher and carried him in, I following with all the rifles, as dawn was breaking. In the trenches we learned the full story of the raid.

The covering party of the 8th Company on the far right, under Mr. Thompson, the only officer out of eight to escape death or wounds, had not suffered; they had been in large and deep shell-holes; but the main raiding party, on clearing the parapet, had been met by a storm of shrapnel and machine-gun fire. What actually happened is not clear, but it was said that Captain Jolly, O.C. 4th Company, seeing that further advance was suicidal, fired up the rocket—perhaps a green one that I fancied I had seen among the red ones—that was to have been the signal for return. Some dozen or less managed to scramble back unhurt, but nine-tenths of them at least were already hit. Captain Jolly was wounded, but refused to be taken back on a stretcher, saying that there were others much worse off than he; a little later he received a second and fatal wound. Mr. Gillman, though already wounded, went out again with bombs single-handed to silence a machine-gun which he had located in no-man's-land; he also was wounded again, this time mortally, and was brought in from the wire next night. Lieutenants Black and Millard were killed, Lieutenants Clark,[9] Johnston, and Salmon were wounded. Mr. Johnston, platoon commander of our party, himself severely wounded, had carried in Corporal Fitt, who was seriously wounded, under heavy fire. Sergeant Bain of the 4th Company (killed at the Somme, 27th September 1916) had carried in several men under fire. Private S—,[10] a more or less permanent inmate of the clink (not for moral faults but from a congenital recalcitrance to discipline), had asked to be given some remission of punishment by taking part in the raid. He was wounded, but went back over the parapet at least a dozen times, bringing in a wounded man each time, and at dawn had to be restrained by main force—a hot-tempered and impulsive man— from going out again. His sentence was remitted; a decoration, in the circumstances, would hardly have been appropriate, but he received mention in Divisional Orders. No doubt there were many other individual acts of bravery that were never known, yet any honour that came to the Battalion seemed little compensation for the long list of killed and wounded, numbering about 180. The 4th Company might be regarded as extinguished.

Naturally there could be no mention of such a set-back in our own communiqués, aiming as they did not at truth but at gloss.[11] A German communiqué of 15th July referred to 'unsuccessful enterprises . . . by minor British detachments south-east of Armentieres'. Since two other such 'enterprises' were also mentioned, it must be assumed that two other companies somewhere in the line were likewise annihilated.

1. Aitken with his father and siblings, on his last home leave before embarkation in August 1915. *Centre for Research Collections, University of Edinburgh*

2. Title page of Aitken's 1961 manuscript.
Hocken Collections, Uare Taoka o Hakena, University of Otago: MS-0717/001

1961

Memoirs of an Anzac

A. C. Aitken

8/2524, 1st Otago Infantry
Battalion, N.Z.E.F. 1915

First draft, Dunedin, 1917.

Revised, Dunedin, 1920.

Revised and put into chapters,
Edinburgh 1930.

With some excision,
Edinburgh 1961

A. C. A.
36 Primrose Bank Road,
Edinburgh 5.

1

Foreword

These recollections of a year of
infantry service, 26 September 1915 to
28 September 1916, were written
from memory, aided by a few maps,
in 1917. I was for three months in
2nd London General Hospital, St
Mark's College, Chelsea; for part of
the time on crutches from foot
injuries, and almost incapacitated
from writing by the arm injury. I
was invalided home to New Zealand,
reaching Dunedin in March 1917.
Until 30 September I was a daily
outpatient at Dunedin Hospital.
During these six months I jotted down
in pencil, in the form of a long
discursive letter to no one in
particular, and with no regard for
literary style (which I imagined would
put a false gloss on the facts), a
tolerably full and accurate record
of my service; for I remembered
all incidents, regimental numbers

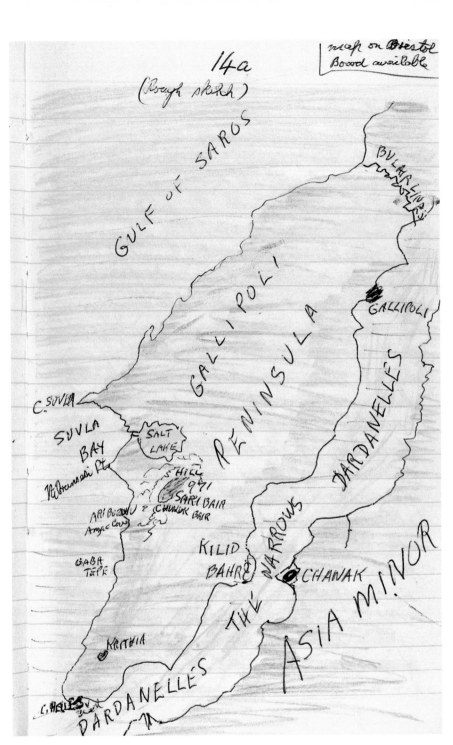

3. Aitken's hand-drawn map of Gallipoli from the 1961 manuscript.
Hocken Collections, Uare Taoka o Hakena, University of Otago: MS-0717/001

4. 'New Zealanders return to Gallipoli by picket boat
after a rest in Lemnos'. *Imperial War Museum: HU 53360*

A CROWDED. BIVY AT THE 'APEX'

Looking towards Suvla Bay of No 2 Outpost Gallipoli Nov 1915

5. 'A crowded Bivy at the Apex' *(top)* and 'Looking towards Suvla Bay'.
From the photograph album of Major J.M. Rose, 1st NZEF, 1915.
Te Papa Tongarewa Museum of New Zealand: O.040616 and O.040664

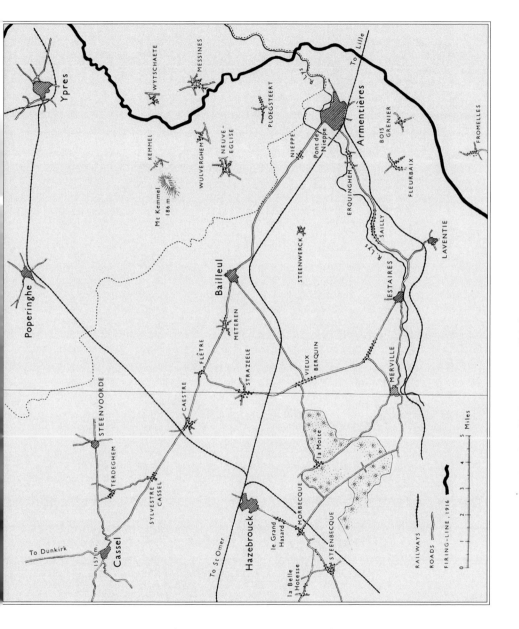

6. Hazebrouck, Armentières, and vicinity (from OUP edition).

a

b

c

7. Mathematical Shapes.

(a) Parabola: 'The
night sky is lit up by
the bombardment of
Beaumont-Hamel'.
Imperial War Museum: Q 7.

(b) Rhomboid: 'Tank go
into action at the Battle
of Flers-Courcelette, 15t
September 1916'. *Imperia
War Museum: Q 2488*

(c) Polar Coordinates:
'An aerial view of the
Cordonnerie Salient'.
*Australian War Memorial:
G1534BD*

8. Aitken's violin and case. *Photography by McRobie Studios, Dunedin*

9. Detail showing trenches near Armentières, from 'Belgium and Part of France, edition 8A Sheet 36 NW, correct for 24 September 1917'. British trenches in blue; German trenches in red. *The William Ready Division of Archives and Research Collections, McMaster University Library: 049 WW1MAP*

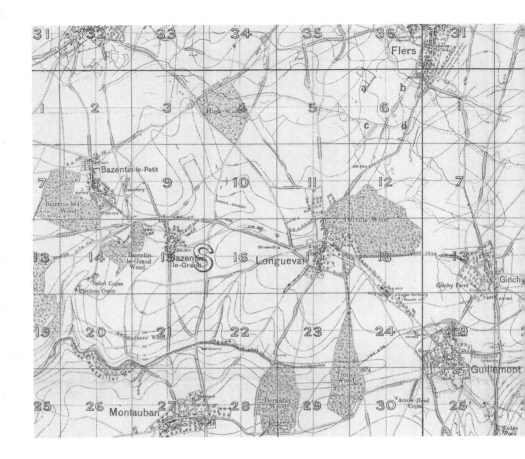

10A. Detail of the Somme battlefield, showing the sector where the
New Zealand Division was introduced in September 1916. From
'France, 57C SW edition 3B, 28 Sept 1916'. *The William Ready Division of
Archives and Research Collections, McMaster University Library: PC0397*

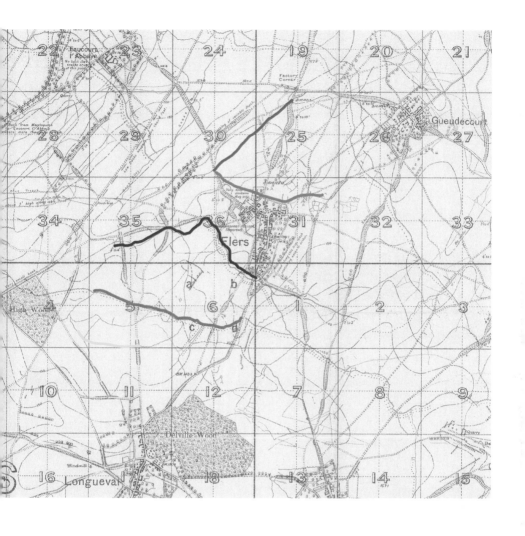

10B. Detail showing advance of New Zealand Division at the Somme,
15–27 September 1916. From 'France, 57C SW edition 3B, 28 Sept 1916'.
Yellow line: starting point; green line: first objective; brown line: second
objective; blue line: third objective; red line: final objective. *The William Ready
Division of Archives and Research Collections, McMaster University Library: PC0397*

11. 'New Zealanders making a trench by joining up shell craters, 15th September 1916'. *Imperial War Museum: Q 191*

12. The same scene a little later. 'Reinforcements crossing the old German front line during the advance towards Flers, 15 September 1916'. *Imperial War Museum: Q 188*

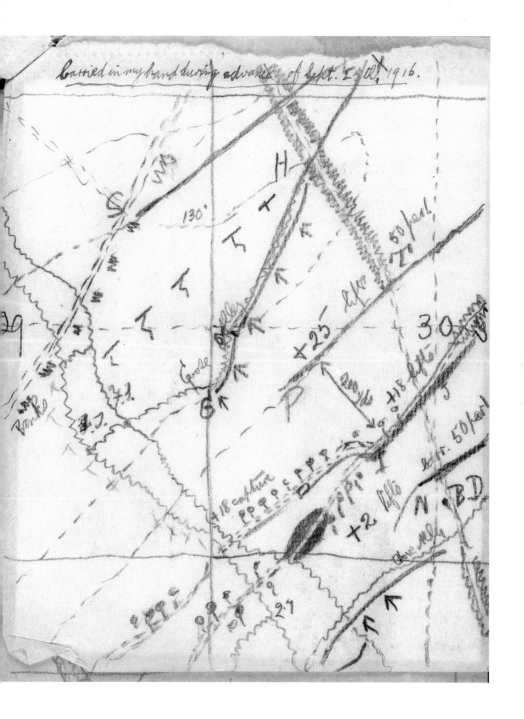

13. 'Carried in my hand during advance of Sept. 25 1916.'
Aitken's hand-drawn map. *Centre for Research Collections, University of Edinburgh*

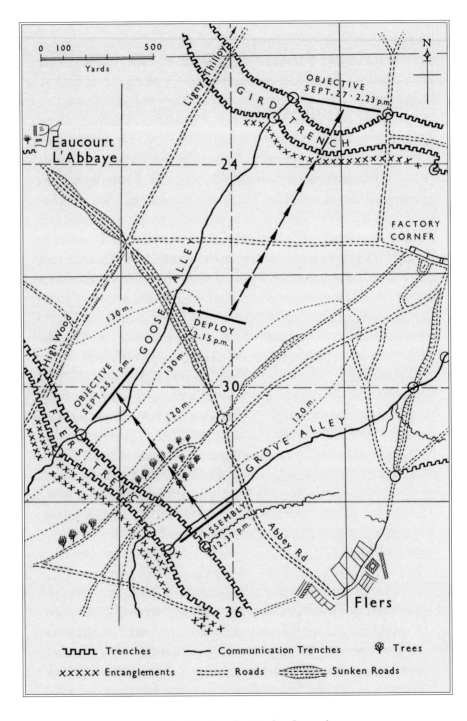

14. Map showing the attacks of 25 and
27 September 1916 (from OUP edition).

15. Second Lieutenant Alexander Aitken, London 1917.
Centre for Research Collections, University of Edinburgh

16. Professor Aitken in later life. *Centre for Research Collections, University of Edinburgh*

16 Armentières:
After the Raid

THE 4TH COMPANY, REDUCED TO A BARE HALF-PLATOON OR LESS, WAS placed in reserve at Buterne Farm until reinforcements should bring it up to something like normal strength. Our own 10th Platoon was at very low strength, lacking a platoon commander, a platoon sergeant, and several corporals. One man was still unaccounted for, Noble, a youth of eighteen or nineteen who had joined us with a very recent draft.

On the next evening, 14th July, a party went out two by two with stretchers in the general charge of Mr. Brockett to bring in the bodies. Platoon commander of Platoon 9, he had asked specially for this duty; for an order had recently come round that officers were not to go into no-man's-land on missions that N.C.O.s could competently perform. The night was the quietest yet; all the bodies were brought in, including that of Noble, who was found in the ditch by the line of trees. The party was now all inside except Mr. Brockett. Since he still failed to appear, Sergeant-Major Howden, a completely intrepid man, went out again alone into no-man's-land, exploring the line of trees until he was so close to the German trenches as to distinguish conversation in them. Returning and quartering the ground outside the gap in the wire he found, in the dark, Mr. Brockett lying dead almost in the same place and attitude as Hughes the night before. I remembered how, a fortnight earlier, he had been on a repetitive and wearing duty, taking a party of bombers night after night to the Mushroom a mile away to make a diversion with smoke-bombs while a raid was in progress elsewhere. Each night the party (it included William Robertson) had been in position, expecting quick retaliation after their bomb-throwing; each night wind and moonlight proved unfavourable at the last moment. This had gone on for a week, until the Germans, as has been seen, countered by raiding the Canterbury men at that very place.

Now that he was dead I remembered a conversation carried on between us not long before, at 2 a.m. one quiet night under the stars and the Very lights, and not as between officer and N.C.O. but as if between two undergraduates,[1] on the paradox of which we were part: that so-called Christian Europe, at a time when the beginning of the third Christian millennium might be entered upon in old age by infants now living, should be offering up its young men to the Moloch of war,[2] while pacifist non-Christians of other continents—Hindus, Chinese, Moslems—must surely be looking on, perplexed at this urge to suicide. Did Christianity, not of saintly individuals but of nations and sects and denominations, contain an impulse to aggression? This had balked us, so that we fell back on the theme, which still in 1916 had some currency, though rapidly devaluing, of the 'war to end war' and some future league of nations;[3] and on this note of vague Tennysonian aspiration we had parted and continued on our rounds.[4]

To return for a moment to the early morning of this day, 14th July. In no-man's-land I had been sustained by responsibility and self-preservation. The instant I was safe inside the lines a sudden reaction had come, taking a strange form, that of rounding on the nearest person, who happened to be Mr. Brockett, concerning the stupidity of the whole plan of the raid with its wanton expenditure of life. Yet even as I 'blasted' him I felt false, divided into two persons; this one, who was speaking, was not really sincere, was taking an advantage of a gentleman, and should have been checked by that other, who, however, was holding back. I wished to apologize; but he had moved on, looking gravely concerned, and since he was killed on that same night my apology was never made. This splitting of the personality was unpleasant, and was doubtless one of the symptoms of minor shellshock, wearing off after a fortnight. Less complicated symptoms were a jumpiness at shell-bursts, and broken sleep. It is, of course, true that to certain persons in places of safety, and even to some psychologists who have never had the experience of enduring hours of bombardment in a shell-hole or confined dug-out, or of seeing their comrades blown to pieces, shell-shock indicates a lack of moral fibre. Captain Hargest was not of this persuasion. With his usual observant solicitude he took me along to his own dug-out at Company H.Q. and ordered me to lie down on the coco-nut matting and try to snatch some sleep. This proved impossible; each time I closed my eyes I heard again, as though it were in the dug-out itself, the whistle of the falling mortar-bombs, and I saw Hughes, Robertson, Sergeant Bree, Harper, and the line of trees. But gradually, through and across these repercussions, I became aware of a conversation in low tones going on somewhere behind me, apparently between Captain Hargest and Mr. Rae, and perhaps occasionally someone else—but I am not sure of this. However that may be, something was missing; a roll-book; the roll-book of Platoon 10, my old Platoon. Urgently required, it seemed; Battalion had rung up, requesting a list of the night's casualties and a full state of the Platoon. Apparently surnames were available, but the book was nowhere to be found. This being suddenly clear, I had no difficulty, having a well-trained memory now brought by stress into a condition almost of hypermnesia, in bringing the lost roll-book before me, almost, as it were, floating; I imagined it either taken away by Mr. Johnston or perhaps in the pocket of Sergeant Bree in no-man's-land. Speaking from the matting I offered to dictate the details; full name, regimental number, and the rest; they were taken down, by whom I do not know.[5] To me the essential thing was to help Captain Hargest out of his quandary.* Captain Hargest gave further proof of his unobtrusive consideration, so unobtrusive that for a day or two I failed to put two and two together. Stuart Macdonald, Orderly Room Sergeant at Battalion H.Q., had just been recommended for a commission and his post fell vacant. I was sent back to fill this vacancy. The position, so far as it concerned me, was almost a sinecure, the work being mostly clerical and carried out by a small staff well trained in its details. Though the respite was at first welcome I soon longed for the freer society of the Platoon. These relatively commodious quarters, under the lee of the shelving bank and safe from everything except deliberate high explosive, though barely half a mile from the front line, were in an utterly different world, an unreal world that soon palled.

Dates for this week or two have become somewhat vague, but I must still have been at Battalion H.Q. on 19th July. This was the date on which the 5th Australian Division in the Fleurbaix-Fromelles region to our right launched, together with the 61st Division, its unsuccessful and very costly attack. Its losses, I have read, were 5,500, those of the 61st Division, 1,500.[6] The Germans, it seemed, had allowed them to capture certain low-lying trenches which proved, however, to be flooded. In any case it was not clear what purpose this attack was presumed to serve. It could hardly lead to a break-through, and it was not on a scale large enough to have drawn away from the Somme any appreciable percentage of the German forces or artillery. It simply added one more to the now monotonously repetitive catalogue of attacks on narrow fronts which began with apparent success, ran into unforeseen difficulty, and ended with casualties utterly disproportionate to any alleged gains. This was reflected in the respective communiqués: the British communiqué, obviously heavily censored, referred to 'some important raids on a front of two miles, in which Australian troops took part. About 140 prisoners were captured': the German communiqué spoke

---

* In later years this incident, to which I attached no importance, was much exaggerated by legend; as late as 1933 I met it again, with the Platoon expanded to a battalion!

truthfully of '481 prisoners, 10 officers, 16 machine-guns . . . sanguinary repulse'. Thus this region, south of the Armentières salient and east and south-east of Laventie, continued to be ill fated; Neuve Chapelle and Aubers in 1915, Richebourg St. Vaast only three weeks before, and now this costly set-back at Fromelles, with 7,000 casualties.

Simultaneously with this attack, and doubtless with the intention of masking it, there was an all-night demonstration round the whole of the Armentières salient. Like soundboards our dug-outs in the bank transmitted the vibrations in an extraordinary manner. Guns bombarded, Stokes mortars fired hundreds of rounds, gas was discharged in three different places, and three raiding parties, small ones this time, went over successfully and, for the first time, with few casualties. About 21st July I was recalled to the line to be Platoon Sergeant of my old Platoon 10, replacing Sergeant Bree; this without doubt had been Captain Hargest's intention from the outset. The surge of activity in the salient had now spent itself. Much to our relief, naturally; we were allowed no time to reflect that we were being groomed and reserved for the third movement of the battle of the Somme.

The junction of 76 and 77 in the extreme eastward part of the salient showed on the map a name l'Épinette, but the small hamlet at the cross-roads and the *estaminet* that must have displayed its fir-tree sign, A l'Épinette,[7] were razed to trench-level, a mere pile of shattered bricks. Here, in a cleared space among the rubble, we had our 'wire dump', a store-house of barbed wire, 'concertina' wire, and corkscrew pickets.[8] All about this part were many indications that at one time, probably after the Germans had been driven back from Armentières, the salient had extended to a still greater radius, and that there had been heavy fighting before it had been so reduced. Among the trees by Willow Walk and in the spaces between front, support, and subsidiary lines were many wooden crosses, for the most part bearing the names of officers and men of the North Staffordshire Regiment and the date January 1915—to me seeming as remote as June 1815—or simply marked 'To the memory of an unknown hero'. This must have been the sequel to the famous 'Christmas truce' of 1914, when men from both sides, recalling the day and remembering their common humanity, had spontaneously crossed no-man's-land and exchanged gifts, a procedure that, on our side at least, had scandalized G.H.Q. and brought upon itself severe disciplinary measures.

On days free of haze we could see the great wood of 'Plugstreet' (Ploegsteert) three miles to the north, the red roofs of Messines on a hill six miles to the north, and Mount Kemmel, a little over 600 feet high, farther to the west. Somewhere up there, under the earth, was our Mining and Tunnelling Company;[9] and even as early as this there was rumour of a surprise in store for the enemy, no doubt referring to the nineteen large mines sprung under the Wytschaete-Messines ridges ten months later, at 3 a.m. on 7th June 1917.

We have been long enough at Armentières; and so, feeling the attraction towards the flame, the pull of the Somme, I pass quickly over the days of early August, windless days of low ground mist for some hours following dawn, with consequent prolongation of Stand-to and postponement of breakfast; mornings on which I crawled about in no-man's-land and in the dead ground between front and support lines, salvaging dozens of Mills bombs from a brick cellar, and making myself unpopular by bringing to the dump a complete 'pineapple' bomb, many German stick-grenades resembling old-fashioned wooden potato-mashers, and two small landmines. Presuming excessively on the training in grenades at Terdeghem, I unscrewed the head and percussion cap of the aluminium-painted pineapple bomb (looking exactly like a pineapple, with the addition of a hollow tail bearing three fins) and found that the German assembler had failed to insert the detonator. I scraped out the cupful of donnerite and for a time kept this pineapple as a souvenir until, during the long marches towards the Somme, it went the way of all unnecessary ballast.

We were not yet quit of the line. Another Otago Company relieved us, and the Platoon then spent several days in a 'quadrilateral strong point' officially called S.P.X., another platoon occupying its twin, S.P.Y.[10] Ours was concealed from enemy view by a line of trees; a 'cushy' spot free from shell-fire, disturbed only once, by two light rifle-grenades fired experimentally at very great range. It was part of a deserted farm; sand-bags of new potatoes, gathered in one of its fields, were an agreeable addition to our rather dull rations. From S.P.X. we returned for the last time to SS 77 and the too-familiar firing-line 76.

During this last spell in the Épinette it was noticed that the Germans were using trench-mortars where they had previously used howitzers, clear evidence that they had moved some of their heavy artillery south to the Somme. They sprinkled us liberally with 'pineapples' and with a new type of bomb, large, barrel-shaped, and somersaulting, but as before they concentrated for the most part on the disused trench in front, a delusion which over the whole of these six weeks must have saved us at least 200 casualties.

On both sides, during this fortnight, there was a notable lack of the previous 'briskness', a sense that the military organism had been enfeebled by the continuing drain of blood in the south. And still from there, after five weeks, nothing definite, only names—Bazentin, Delville Wood, Pozières. Other names heard of earlier seemed now to be hushed up—Gommecourt, Thiepval, Beaumont Hamel—and one other, sinister even in the sound of its name, Serre.[11]

In the second week of August we were relieved from the Épinette by the 1st Auckland Battalion and came out of the line to the Hospice Mahieu, which we had not seen since the last days of June, six weeks before. Tramping in the gloom through Houplines we could see that the suburb had suffered still more from the shelling of July. The brick wall surrounding our billet in the rear of the town had been cracked by a shell, but the Hospice itself was untouched. We did not go into the line again except on the usual fatigue parties, being relieved about the middle of August by a Scottish division that had been in action at the Somme.[12] From men of these regiments—easiest of all for men from Otago like myself to understand and feel at home with— we learned in advance the full scale and ferocity of this unprecedented battle campaign, and knew what to expect. On the last night of our stay in Armentières the enemy must have known that it was occupied by double the usual number of units, for he shelled it indiscriminately, causing precipitate exits from the *estaminets* and the cinema, but actually doing very little harm. Our Ancient Pistol, Private K—, was wounded at last, and was thus incapacitated from going on to the Somme.[13] In the Hospice we took final leave of our kindest friends, the devoted Sœurs de Charité, and on request, and in token of farewell, the violin for the last time in the Hospice played the ever-popular *Humoresque*.

17 Flanders to Picardy: Citernes

N EXT MORNING WE MARCHED THE FIVE MILES TO RAILHEAD AT Steenwerck, meeting further Scottish battalions on their way to Armentières. They were, I think, the Gordon Highlanders, who had suffered severely at Delville Wood; naturally no trace of this could be seen as they swung past in the kilt to the skirling of pipes. After the usual delays we entrained and moved out westwards past Hazebrouck. Unvisited Cassel, extending a little down the southern side of its commanding hill on the right, now took my eye at last, a symbol of the opportunity that does not come a second time. The journey was unexpectedly short; we stopped, still with Cassel in view only six miles behind us, at Ebblinghem, a wayside station midway between Hazebrouck and St. Omer, detrained, and marched some five miles south and west to a small sequestered village called Wardrecques, where we were quartered in the usual barns and stables.

Wardrecques was on a plateau from which the ground fell suddenly to the south-east in the direction of the low-lying ground of the Lys Canal from Aire to Merville and the front line east of Laventie. The adjacent ridge gave a view far away across a rolling plain of the country about Neuve Chapelle and La Bassée. On clear days certain faint black dots in the sky denoted observation balloons; at night we could hear a dull rumble and see distant flashes. To the far south-east, as we had noted in those early weeks, now so remote, at La Belle Hôtesse—itself only ten miles off and near enough to be visited on bicycle by a nostalgic W.O.—two slag-heaps, conspicuous as the Pyramids in a wide expanse of plain, were the only things that broke the view.[1] The country about Wardrecques was very beautiful; but more than that, it had the undertones of history, for the quiet tree-shaded roads and wooded parkland where our route marches took us had known the camps and campaigns of English soldiers in those French wars of four and five hundred years before. I remember feeling this especially when passing an ancient chateau near Clarques or Thérouenne, the Terouenne of Canto VI of Scott's *Marmion*, 'where England's king in leaguer lay'.[2] All about us lay fields of good crops, ripe or overripe, standing uncut for lack of labour to cut them, a waste keenly felt by George Keith and George Norman, both farmers in my Platoon. A military order of those days invited us wherever possible to help the French to cut their crops, but since Wardrecques did not seem to have a single Frenchman left in it, and since routine gave us no unoccupied time or opportunity, this was never more than a benevolent wave of the hand. It was not yet certain in our minds whether we were really bound for the Somme; rumour, whose tongue had been much less insistent on the French front than in the unimaginably far-off days of the Levant, had suggested that an attack had been projected elsewhere, for example between Ypres and Armentières, an intelligent guess that anticipated Messines by ten months. Whatever our eventual destination, we ourselves were busy all day with realistic bayonet-practice.

After a week at Wardrecques we packed up, surreptitiously leaving some blankets and, regretfully in my own case, the small books of French poetry and R. E. Prothero's *The Pleasant Land of France*, still unread and never to be read, in the loft of an old barn. In the after-noon we marched in the direction of St. Omer and entrained at Arques, the Arques which 'brave Crillon' missed,[3] for a long journey, retracing in part that longest of all journeys from Marseilles in April, ages and ages ago. Slight incidents engrave themselves on the mind when great events are forgotten, and impressions of this journey stand out for me with peculiar colour; chief of all a level crossing between St. Omer and Audruicq, where a dog-cart carrying two girls was waiting for the train to pass. They had distinction, and one was beautiful; and I had the sudden vision of a lost former world, containing poetry and the music of Chopin, to which mud and dust and khaki were strangers and unknown; the incident of a moment, a spark in the night at once extinguished but never to be forgotten. So, too, I remember the train slowing down a little before Audruicq to pass a village called Ruminghem, and the kindly old people who waved to us from their gates in the evening. The light of eternity shone on them in the level western beams; mortality did not touch them, they were the fixed and we the transitory: they must be dead these many years, but to me they will always be as those undying simplicities in paintings by old Dutch masters—a woman, it may be, drawing water from a well in a court, or a girl reading a letter by a window. At Audruicq we ran parallel to a line of trucks, all smashed to pieces, apparent relics of an explosion in the great depot there; also portentous piles of duck-boards, fifteen or twenty feet high, which, by their augury of an expected winter campaign, extinguished any hopes we might have had that the war would end in 1916. Then Calais, and then, in reverse order, the sequence remembered from the April journey, Wimille-Wimereux, Boulogne, Dannes, Camiers, Étaples, and the rest, so that as night fell we guessed we were bound for the Somme at least. About 11 p.m. we reached Abbeville, detrained, spent some time in a field having a late meal, then began a long march inland under the guidance of the billeting officer, Mr. Thompson, whose degree and post-graduate study in France had doubtless gained him this thankless job.

In memory I group together three marches: the shortest but the worst, going up the slope to the terraces and trenches at the Apex on Gallipoli; the march on the cobbles from Morbecque to Estaires;

and this night march from Abbeville to the village of Citernes in Picardy, which we reached between six and seven in the morning. Mr. Thompson must have tried a short cut by farm roads and found it a long way round; by daybreak, at any rate, we were walking under low-hanging apple-trees and from thirst, or the mere desire to munch, pulling down the dangling green apples and chewing them. No one fell out, but all were thankful when we looked down on a small village among trees, with the first thin wisps of blue smoke rising from cottage chimneys hidden in the leaves. We were quartered as usual in farms and deserted steadings.

The sergeants of the Company lived together on the upper floor of a deserted house, the general quarters being on the lower floor and in the outbuildings. On the boughs of trees in an orchard at the back we hung stuffed sacks and practised bayonet-fighting, short jabs and under-swings of the rifle-butt, even during the evenings and at other times outside the regular hours of drill. Route marches, still more bayonet-exercise under the supervision of an English sergeant-major— a V.C. who, having killed, it was said, a record number of men at the Somme, was now resting on his laurels a little—and practice in attack under barrage protection occupied most of our time. The old system of advancing in skirmishing order by rushes, and ending up with a charge, a fifteen-year-old survival of the Boer War, had at last gone out of fashion, effectively abolished by German 77-mm. shrapnel and masked machine-guns. In its place, according to principles elaborated by General Horne, so it was said, from experience at the Somme and elsewhere, there was the new system of walking across to the enemy behind a timed and phased barrage of our own shrapnel.[4] We practised sham attacks of this kind every day, moving behind 'barrages' (of signallers carrying flags) to the 'objective' and 'consolidating' it when gained; accuracy in timing was the all-important point. Once an aeroplane co-operated, as if in real battle; on capturing the objective we set alight red flares that burned for a minute, placing them in imaginary shell-holes to give the pilot our line and the extent of our advance. I mention all this here because it was repeated with even greater exactness of detail in an actual and successful attack beyond Flers on 25th September.

Here also at Citernes we were visited by a renowned authority of the time on bayonet-fighting, a Scottish major who delivered his own standard lecture, 'The Spirit of the Bayonet', a blood-curdling utterance which, with its unvarying examples and anecdotes, was becoming stereotyped and in danger of defeating its own ends. (How extraordinary that I should be destined, thirty and more years later, to meet and to know this lecturer, by that time an old retired Colonel, the gentlest and most courteous of men, and actually to be of help to him in certain peaceful activities!) It is clear from their memoirs that Mr. Blunden and Mr. Sassoon shrank as I did from the first impact of this lecture;[5] but considering the matter as dispassionately as I could, I was forced to admit that bayonet-fighting was a profession in which an apologetic or half-hearted attitude was inconsistent and self-stultifying. The Major's position was severely logical; in this technique of the human abattoir an instructor must be starkly realistic or nothing at all; there neither was, nor could be, any halfway house between this *Schrecklichkeit*[6] and Christian pacifism.

Citernes, like Wardrecques, was surrounded by many acres of crops, overripe and in danger of rotting. Only one adult Frenchman was ever seen, a bearded old reaper returning, scythe over shoulder, each evening at nightfall from the fields. Villages here seemed older than any I had seen before, Citernes itself producing an extraordinary feeling of age—or was it perhaps that, like Hardy's Jude wandering in the streets of Christminster, I felt that sense of time past, this *Vergangenheit*, more than the villagers themselves?[7] In these villages and their clumps of trees, separated more widely in the undulating plain than those of flat and densely populated Flanders, I felt a remarkable difference of atmosphere, easy to perceive, difficult to analyse. The very windmills were different, those of Flanders having seemed noisy and consequential, these of Picardy—or was this again subjective illusion?—lost in reverie of the Middle Ages. The homely *estaminets* of the Flemish crossroads were here replaced by solitary crucifixes, symbolic of desires less worldly than those of food and wine. So it was all through, this sense of being more deeply embedded, more deeply embowered, in the shadow of past centuries.

On the last evening, 28th August, of my non-commissioned rank the Sergeants' Mess of the 10th Company, buying two ducks, paid a French mademoiselle several francs to roast and serve these as part of a dinner *à la française* in my honour, of four or five courses, and wonderful it seemed, and voice and violin suitably responded. By comparison the cereals of the Officers' Mess with the 4th Otagos next morning were frugal and austere.

Without our knowledge several others and myself, on leaving Armentières, had been recommended for commissions in the field; this had gone through, and we were now received by the Brigadier-General.[8] Promotion, antedated by three days, was really from 26th August; the other new subalterns were Sergeants Bain of the 4th Company, Gabites and Rallinshaw of the 8th, and R. Q. M. Pascoe.[9] For me the Brigadier-General's handshake meant wounds a month later on 27th September (though as an N.C.O. I might well have been killed), for three of the others death—Bain and Rallinshaw on this same 27th, Gabites at Polderhoek Château on 3rd December 1917. Pascoe may have survived; I never saw his name in print again.[10] Sergeant-Major Howden and Frank Jones had already been granted commissions a month earlier; Frank Jones died of wounds on 22nd September, Howden was killed in the disastrous attack on the 27th. The life of a subaltern at the Somme or Passchendaele was apt to be Hobbesian—'nasty, brutish, and short'.[11]

On 29th August the five young subalterns were congratulated by the Colonel[12] and given leave to proceed to Abbeville and invest their kit allowance of £25 (equivalent in those days to 697 francs, and with my simple tastes I had plenty of unspent pay also) in procuring an officer's clothing and equipment. Next morning after breakfast we took bicycles, except Rallinshaw, who preferred to ride a horse, and so pedalled for the main road and the mouth of the Somme. After a gentle rise we reached level ground above Hallencourt, a village which crowns the slope coming up from the river and from which the contours also fall away eastwards on the inland side to the rolling plain around Amiens. From Hallencourt we free-wheeled, in the mood of peace-time summer holiday, down the long steep hill to the bridge at Pont-Rémy, then up a gradual slope for a few miles to the pretty villages of Épagne and Épagnette, with a final smooth run down into Abbeville.

In Abbeville, clean and attractive, Ordnance Stores seemed to have nothing but boots and riding-breeches, and, naturally enough, there was no British military tailor. We returned inland empty-handed and separately. I left quite early, though first finding by inquiry the kind of address I was looking for—'Professeur de Piano—Vente et Location de Pianos, Musique et Instruments: 94 Chaussée du Bois'.[13] This proved to be M. Octave Picquet, seventy years old, tall, dignified, and urbane, who did not in the least mind being disturbed for custom after hours by a twenty-one-year-old New Zealander. I bought—such was my irrational optimism—a complete set of violin strings and, still more strangely, a bow, which M. Picquet helped me to choose while Madame smilingly supervised. Unfortunately, mounting the bicycle and trying to acknowledge their adieux, I somehow broke the bow across the bar, but went in immediately and bought another. M. Picquet could not but have been vexed, though he showed no trace of it, at this treatment of a good bow, while at the same time gratified at my readiness to pay for another. Madame, however, seeing only the incongruity of the two sides to this matter, laughed until the tears came. To this admirable and warm-hearted couple I wrote later from New Zealand, and will transcribe part of M. Picquet's reply, which gives the spirit of northern France at the time, 1918, of the tremendous drive for Calais and Boulogne:

> nous sommes heureux de vous savoir rentré en votre pays . . . de pouvoir rejouer du violon avec votre 2me archet d'Abbeville; nous nous souvenons parfaitement de l'incident . . . les Boches sont venus à une vingtaine de kilomètres de chez nous et pendant six mois nous avions toutes les nuits des bombes et des torpilles par la visite de leurs sinistres oiseaux . . .

enfin la guerre est terminée et maintenant les Boches sont chez eux . . .
espérons qu'ils n'en sortiront plus . . . Malgré nos 70 ans Madame Picquet
et moi sommes heureux de vous envoyer l'expression de nos meilleurs
sentiments.[14]

On the return journey an evening of violet light turning to grey
worked more and more on my solitary mood. *Mentem mortalia tangunt;*[15]
the ubiquity of death; curtains of mortality hanging about the world.
I crossed the Somme at Pont-Rémy, dismounting at intervals and
wheeling the bicycle and at last walking altogether. After Pont-Rémy I
saw no one except an old woman coming down from Sorel, who held up
her jug of milk to me with 'Buvez, buvez!'[16] Here I finally dismounted
and pushed the bicycle up the long hill in a solitude unbroken for
miles by any village. The aura of place was tangible along these roads,
not far from the Forest of Crécy, that held the past suspended in their
air.[17] Walking in a trance, almost a levitation, the handle-bars seeming
to draw me on with no volition of my own, no sense of fatigue nor
feeling of body at all, I had come to doubt the reality of externals and
of my own existence, almost on the top, now, of the hill at Hallencourt,
a dim dark plain rolling under me eastward, and not a sound. There is
a type of dream that oppresses with an unearthly sense of the infinity
of the past and of the elsewhere, a twilight world in which the spirit
knows that it is dreaming, even notes for remembrance—though these
dissolve in the moment of waking—strange features of the landscape,
yet feels that if there were only will-power enough it could break the
shell and escape into the light of day. In such a dream, familiar yet
unfamiliar, I was entangled, I was noting such landscapes; if I could
only shake it off I might wake in some morning of the southern hemisphere and find alive and well about me the friends imagined as lost.
At this moment, as if in answer to such an effort of will, a single white
flash winked on the horizon inland, supernatural and unnerving; after
an interval it opened and shut again like an eye. It continued to do
so, at regular intervals, and brought back the ordinary captivity of
seconds and minutes. I awoke now, but to the simple realities of place

and of 30th August 1916; those were, of course, the rearmost guns, too far away to be heard, sending death as usual. The distant eye, somewhere east of Amiens, was still opening and shutting as I pedalled down from Hallencourt to the billet, where all were asleep as I climbed quietly aloft.

Before leaving Citernes we had a Battalion concert and Battalion sports. Most battalions bound for the Somme, as if obeying a uniform instinct of *morituri te salutamus*,[18] seem to have had these. Our own concert took place in the village hall of Citernes, a large, bare, barn-like building with one side open to the air, and a stage flanked by ante-rooms devoid of 'properties'. Items were varied. Private Sheehan led off with a pianoforte solo, a brilliant *Valse de Concert* of Paderewski;[19] but this standard could not be maintained. The Colonel followed, singing 'Ching Chong Chinaman' with acceptance; then Mr. Rae with 'The Village Pump'—here one could join in the refrain.[20] Someone next recited 'Gunga Din' with Kiplingesque fervor—it sounded extraordinarily out of keeping;[21] then, in some comic turns, there was a sudden drop to level but very broad ground. The Colonel was watched to see how he was taking the mixture of *risqué* and Rabelais. He was observed to laugh, but with diplomatic rather than real heartiness, or so to me at least it seemed; but my own thoughts had wandered, to other concerts, far away now in time and distance, with the Australians in the Y.M.C.A. marquee at Sarpi in Lemnos.

The sports were held in a field of stubble by the Citernes-Oisemont road, where that apparent anachronism, a train on the Oisemont-Doullens branch line, might occasionally be seen. They were regarded as a success, but seem now to belong to an age severed from the present, or visualized from reading in a book; for more than half the men who competed died on the battlefields of the Somme, Messines, or Passchendaele.

18 Citernes to Fricourt

O<small>N RECEIVING MY COMMISSION—AND PROCURING SOME KIND OF</small> officer's tunic from our own Q.M.[1]—I was transferred from the 10th to the 4th Company and was now platoon commander of Platoon 1 of the 1st Otago Battalion, a numerical fact that put me, less than a month later, in a position of the most critical responsibility.[2] Not without a pang I left my old Company, especially the Platoon of which I had been a member so long, and the men, already thinned by casualties, that I knew so well, even to their regimental numbers and addresses in New Zealand—survivors have said that I knew the numbers of their rifles also, but this is too flattering a legend! No sooner had the Officers' Mess of the 4th received their new member than we had marching orders, and pushed on by a village, with the curious name of Mérélessart and the most pungent cesspool yet encountered, to the small town of Airaines on the Oisemont-Doullens railway.

At Airaines we had the best billets we ever had in France. After so many barns and lofts and steadings it seemed to me like taking part in some charade or masquerade for three of us to be entertained as guests in a house of taste and to be given, though for one night only, a room of one's own with bed and sheets; indeed, I slept indifferently, waking up more than once with a feeling of guilt and trespass, and testing the reality of sheets and pillow. The others were Howden and Cuthbert Parr, younger brother of the science master at my old school. In the town proper, across the railway line, were billeted the O.C., Captain Herbert (killed 27th September 1916), the second in command, J. P. Hewat (killed September 1918), and Sutherland (killed 25th September 1916). In the later stages of our eastward journey, when quarters became less and less civilized until the nadir was reached in wet shell-holes at the Somme, Parr and I made light of much discomfort with the watchword, 'Remember Airaines!' Such kindness!—it is as in a dream that I see us arriving travel-stained and hot, to be received with a tray, biscuits, and cider, by Madame and her two charming daughters, aged about eighteen and sixteen. We walked in the elegant garden; weeds and fallen leaves were getting the upper hand; only one old gardener was left. Monsieur was serving at the front, had been, I believe, at Verdun; M. Picquet of Abbeville, to whom in my letter from New Zealand of 1919 I had described the house and the kindness we had received there, wrote back in early 1920 that—so far as I could decipher the spelling of the name—this would be: 'M. Cavillon . . . blessé à la guerre et comme vous il est rentré.'3 If this was, indeed, the house, then I am glad that Madame was not bereaved, as she might well have been, in the dreadful losses, worse than our own, incurred by France. Alas, our stay was all too short; we took regretful leave next day of Madame and her daughters. We pushed on again, crossed the river at Hangest-sur-Somme, passed a village called Yzeux, where with the corner of my eye I caught a notice on a gate: 'The mayor asks that no one not enters here, as this house is lived by two old women'; then from beyond Belloy-sur-Somme looked in sunlight across the river to the many-towered château of Picquigny, seeming still to hold a sky of Agincourt. We halted at the twin villages of La Chaussée and Tirancourt, opposite Picquigny. The rest of the officers found billets in an *estaminet* and a small château at Tirancourt, overlooking the river, clear here and deep enough for a bathing parade; I found myself installed alone in La Chaussée, in an old room with a high bunk and a wardrobe full of the most ancient clothes, military and civilian, like the back premises of a fancy-dress purveyor. During the two days spent here we continued the incessant bayonet and attack practice, with aeroplane co-operation, manoeuvring on upland fields by St. Vaast, from which the eye was drawn downwards to the cathedral of Amiens some miles away, towering extraordinarily above the city and dominating the whole plain. At all times of day and night British infantry and artillery-men streamed eastwards through La Chaussée, with their perpetual question, 'Hast tha' coom from t' Somme, choom?' A fortnight later, seeing the limber-men still riding eastward but through shrapnel and high explosive, I understood the urgency of this question.

By now we were moving quickly, spending only a day or two in each village. We pushed ahead as if to Amiens, but turned aside to the left before reaching it and halted for one night at a village called Coisy. I made my bed, still remembering Airaines, on the counter of a deserted shop, Parr and Howden on the floor. Now the rumble of the guns—it was the first week of September, about the time of the capture of those heaps of rubble and charred wood, Guillemont and Ginchy—was plainly heard, insistent and inescapable.[4] On this evening of late summer an aged Frenchman, the only man who seemed to be left in the village, stood with me in an apple orchard. We listened together to a sound like distant breakers on a coast, a steady and even rolling, except where here and there a larger explosion would surge up and seem to command a momentary silence. The old man remembered, from his prime of forty-five years before, the Franco-Prussian War of 1870–1. So it had been then, and now it had come again but worse, he said. 'Ké malheur, ké malheur', he sighed in his Picard dialect, 'ké malheur que la guerre!'[5] He repeated the words again and again, wrung his hands, refused to be diverted from this theme.

On again, until the rumble was near at hand and suddenly, for five minutes, like oceanic thunder from behind the neighbouring hill, then dying to the former dull rumble as we emerged on the Amiens-Albert road and changed direction. We passed through La Houssoye, Army

Corps H.Q., and followed the straight line of this road. After a march of about fifteen miles we were within sight of the Virgin of Albert, a gilded statue poised there, by a freak of shell-fire, in a diving attitude above the church of Notre-Dame-de-Brebières, to be dislodged altogether in 1918, but eventually restored. We were but a few more added to the hundreds of thousands who had looked or would look up at it, many for the last time. We camped in tents, in low shelters, and on dusty straw-littered ground above the village of Dernancourt on the Ancre, going down in the afternoon to bathing parade under the railway arch and through the sordid ruined village to the Ancre, a swift grey-coloured stream, very cold and not deep enough for a plunge. On again, at night-fall, crossing the railway to the right of Albert and camping on a ridge near Bécordel, overlooking Fricourt, in the zone of the heavy artillery. Before, behind, all around, batteries were firing; to the left and in rear, a battery of 6-inchers; in front, in cages of netting, two 6-inch naval guns, long-nosed monsters, contrasting with the stubby uptilted howitzers whose cough was heard from Bécourt Wood on the opposite slope. In the immediate roar and reverberation of all the batteries about us we could not hear the general rumble half as clearly as when we had been farther back from the line; but sometimes in momentary lulls, we could make out the rapid firing of 18-pounders and imagined that we could distinguish the *rafale* of French 75's far away on the right.[6] The noise all around was more reassuring than the ocean-roar heard from Coisy.

Aeroplanes had been common enough at Armentières, the 'Mad Major' suicidally skimming the trenches, or groups of aeroplanes attacking some observation-balloon as small birds harry a daylight owl.[7] But this at the Somme was on an altogether different scale, a constant aerial vigilance but for which we could not have camped with such impunity on this crest, commanding a view of six-mile radius from Thiepval to Longueval. In front, on the left-hand slope of a valley, were the ruined bricks of Fricourt, badly smashed as it seemed to me then, but not nearly so much as other villages seen later. This valley rose suddenly on the right to a chalk spur named 'King George's Hill',[8] conspicuous by a great mine-crater gouged in its side; on the lower slope of this spur was the old British front line, and nearer our camp the old support and subsidiary lines, now mere ruins of tumbled sand-bags. From Fricourt a line of white road ran behind the hill to Mametz and Montauban, hidden from view. Beyond Fricourt the ground rose gradually to that far ridge on the skyline, the limit of our gains, less than five miles, in this battle of over two months. The stages were visibly marked by a rising series of woods; Fricourt Wood, overtopping Fricourt; above and some distance beyond, the larger and infamous Mametz Wood; above again and much farther away, the straggling trees of High Wood on the left and the more extensive Delville Wood on the right, where the opposing lines faced each other under the blasted tree-trunks. To our left, across the valley lying between Fricourt and Albert, the ground rose to the ridge of Thiepval-Pozières, with the wood of Bécourt in the foreground. High Wood at night was always under bursts of fiery-red shrapnel, too far away to be heard; from the region of Thiepval in the north the heavy 'crumping' never ceased.

Our neighbours on this ridge near Bécordel were the Grenadier Guards, their own area being sacrosanct—as I discovered by unknow-ingly trespassing on the smallest corner of it while making a short cut to camp. I could have wished to watch them more at leisure, for the routine, movements, and machine-like discipline of a 'crack regiment' had for me the fascination that the technique of a virtuoso violinist has for an amateur. I even took notice of the vibratory salute of the fingers, a recent innovation, in the Guards sergeant who respectfully but firmly saluted me off the hallowed area.[9] A totally negligible matter, but inter-esting as one of many differentiating features. The spirit and tradition were visible in the smallest detail, seeming, however, to rest on a history and social stratification different from our own; almost royalist, it seemed to me, as against republican. I wondered also whether the inflexibility inseparable from such a perfection was carried into action; for we ourselves had disciplined our platoons, ever since Citernes and Coisy, to a deliberate waviness and avoidance of anything regular or rectilinear in order to counter the danger of enfilade or of bunching;

and always, within the limits of schedules that were too strict, we looked for the unexpected chance. My batman, Scott (killed 27th September 1916), a serious man old enough to be my father, told me of a characteristic incident. A party of our men, hard at work on some road repairs, was sharply called to attention by an affronted Guards sergeant. Intent on the job, they had failed to hear, over hill and valley a mile and more away, the almost inaudible strains of a regimental band concluding its practice with the National Anthem. It was impossible not to admire so single-minded a worship of the god of names and forms.

Though soon to take part in an advance we supplied the usual working parties by day and night until ordered to move up to the front, and as a newly fledged subaltern I was put in part charge of several of these. The first was a night one, digging gun-pits near Bazentin-le-Grand, in advanced positions for the 18-pounders to occupy immediately after the projected great attack of mid-September. The night was 'quiet', a few spent bullets falling about but hitting no one. I recall it merely for contrast with the daylight road-repairing and road-making type of fatigue duty, such as I next shared with Thompson in Caterpillar Valley. The road to the valley was so congested with traffic and limbers that we were forced to walk along the sleepers of the railways, from which siding after siding led off into the wood on the left. Each siding had a howitzer among the trees, the largest being a 12-incher, firing off every few minutes. The road turned left at a corner and ran up to Bazentin. On this corner a German high-velocity gun registered with accuracy at five-minute intervals, and here we were amazed, not by the stoicism, but by the absolute disregard of the limber-drivers passing this point. On foot ourselves, we could make a detour, and did so, avoiding the shelling by cutting over to the right and coming down in the hollow by Caterpillar Wood. The place was bad enough still; what must it have been like in July? Evidence lay in the bed of the valley that we had to level and convert into a road, the ground pitted with craters, dud shells all about, piles of anti-aircraft shells hurriedly abandoned; up on the wooded slope, sunk deep into the chalky earth, German dug-outs, their entrances half concealed by trees, many containing machine-guns not yet cleared away, some facing so as to shoot over-precipitate attackers in the back. What a nest of ambushes must have been here! It must be a bad chapter in more than one regimental history.[10] We filled in the craters, trampled down, levelled, topped off; all the time the gun playing on the corner punctuated our work, the fragments of shell whirred over and clipped the trees, ever and again some limber was smashed to pieces and limber, dead or wounded driver, or disemboweled horse, dragged to the side; and still the riders, like the figures on the north frieze of the Parthenon,[11] went past without respite, without end, feeding the machines of destruction.

It was now 13th September, two days before the new advance. The 2nd Otago Battalion, which was to lead off in our sector by capturing Switch Trench[12] and which had been in the line learning the features of the ground, was now relieved and encamped near us. About noon a curious rumour began to circulate, of armoured cars with caterpillar wheels; such marvellous powers were attributed to these that at first the matter was dismissed without consideration. Scepticism was shaken when a few officers, N.C.O.s, and men were given permits to visit a group of these 'tanks' in a hollow half a mile to the south. My own first impression is still vivid; surprise took the form of involuntary verse:

> *Rhomboids painted on a field,*
> *Forty Brobdingnagian toads*
> *Basking in the sun!*

'You can look inside, sir', said a mechanic. I entered the oven-door, for so it seemed, rapidly scanned the bicycle-seats from which the 6-pounders or machine-guns, as the case might be, could be elevated, depressed, or traversed; imagined with no difficulty the heat during action, in spite of covered ventilator and motor-fan, and the discomfort and nausea of uneven pitching over shelled ground. The crews, for reasons of security, had been interned in England without leave for six months. A practical demonstration was given, a tank crossed trenches and ditches and knocked down and flattened portions of brick wall and other obstacles. Unfortunately, in taking a trench at too acute an angle it tilted and fell in on one side, the belt on the other side working impotently in the air. *Absit omen!* [13] It was too easy to visualize what effect such a mishap might cause two days hence! However, taken all in all, here was inventive and constructive imagination at last mobilized on our behalf, in contrast to those distant days of the Gallipoli catapult, the 'jam-tin' bomb, and the 'cricket-ball' bomb with its futile match-striker. We returned to Bécordel in good spirits. Deeper reflection might have made us ask why these Wellsian land-ships[14] were so few in number; but for the moment the novelty was everything.

19 Fricourt to Flers: 15th September 1916

Now the somme takes over, the acceleration begins. memory tightens, moves by hours, then by minutes, then by seconds. On the next afternoon, the 14th, the eve of the great attack, the 2nd Otago Battalion marched out of camp on its way up to the assembly trenches. We lined the road to watch them pass. 'Through earth and out of life the soldiers follow.'[1] I still see in my mind's eye Captain Wilson, young, freckled, sandy-haired, only two years senior to me at school, in the lead on horse, turning cheerily to wave back. He was killed next day in front of the attack.[2] They wheeled to the right at the corner by Fricourt and were seen no more.

In the evening a tank, well camouflaged in green with touches of brown against the side of King George's Hill, could be seen crawling slowly, like some pertinacious beetle, up to the line. The 1st Brigade, perhaps because it was the veteran brigade and had fought on Gallipoli, was to take no part in the opening attack, but was to be in reserve. Kits were stacked, including the violin, which now, the special care of my batman Scott, had come thus far and no farther and which, as I have mentioned, I never saw again, nor even expected to see, until it was returned to me almost two years later in New Zealand, packed and forwarded by Hawkes & Co., London, at the order of Cuthbert Parr. Here, then, is the place to return it to Ithaca and, for *envoi*,[3] to give the list of names in indelible ink that now covered the baize lining of the case: 8/2524, *Indian Ocean, Aden, Suez, Cairo (Zeitoun), Alexandria, Sarpi (Lemnos), Anzac, Apex, Mudros East, Moascar, Suez Canal, Ferry, Ismailia, Port Said, Marseille, Morbecque, Steenbecque, Estaires, Armentières, Wardrecques, Citernes, Airaines, Tirancourt, Coisy, Fricourt.* The further travels of the violin, after I had gone, are more vague; but they must certainly have included Messines and Ypres.

Leaving a few officers and N.C.O.s in camp at Bécordel as a 'base reserve', the rest of the Battalion marched up after dusk and bivouacked for the night in the plantation above Fricourt. Before 6 a.m. we were astir, lining the path by the long sparse wood.

The morning dawned sunny and cloudless. The attack[4] was to be launched at 6.20 a.m., that is, 5.20 a.m. by solar time.In the cool early air and under such a sky it was impossible to believe that at this moment, only four miles ahead, a fierce and critical battle had begun and must now be raging. Between 7 and 8 a.m., when the first bloom of the day was beginning to wear off, a limping figure, then two, then fives and sixes, and soon a continuous straggling stream of dusty, bandaged men began to come down the road, the 'walking wounded'. Wounded so soon after zero time, they could give no accurate details and were dazed and shaken and as if out of hearing, but everything seemed well so far.[5] Switch Trench was certainly ours, the Rifle Brigade were over it and away to Flers—my friend Gunn of Terdeghem must have fallen here—Scottish troops, the Black Watch, were said to have captured Martinpuich easily; at High Wood, between these villages, the position was less clear. From a remark here and there we had deduced uncut wire entanglements in front of Flers and a check in the break-out from High Wood when orders came to move ahead. In the afternoon we bivouacked in the great Mametz Wood, a mass of shattered stumps and tree-trunks; about midnight we were stirred from sleep, the last sleep of any duration for many days, and continuing farther entered a sap and zigzagged in file along it until we came to a trench on the ridge between High Wood and Delville Wood, where we stayed for an hour or two until dawn. Heavy German high-explosive shrapnel came up from the other side of the ridge to burst with terrific crashes and the familiar whorls of black or greenish-yellow smoke. A hundred yards in rear of us a battery of our own field-guns was firing continuously, and other batteries were all around. Once again, as with the limber-drivers in Caterpillar Valley three days earlier, I tried to pin down in a word the quality of what I was seeing: stoicism, unconcern, nonchalance, sang-froid, indifference, fatalism—none of these fitted the case. For example, above us and behind the nearest battery a British artilleryman was boiling some water in a mess-tin, not even looking up at the shrapnel-bursts—but, indeed, this was the spirit of the Somme, as I was soon to see in my own Platoon, even the latest-joined, the 13th Reinforcements, that same Saturday afternoon.

At midday we followed the sap right up to the assembly trenches of the day before, passing now the dead bodies of some of our 2nd Battalion, the first of them a youth of nineteen or less, a Battalion runner, as I supposed, killed before he could deliver his message. So ugly and pointless an end; but I had no time to moralize. Farther on, where the ground fell away in a downward slope, trenches were so damaged that we had to go overland in full view of the enemy, descending as we were the reverse side of that ridge that had cost two and a half months of fighting and perhaps 300,000 casualties.[6] By now the German high-explosive shrapnel was bursting thickly in its black and yellowish-green clouds, and the geysers of brown earth mixed with black smoke, thrown up by 5·9 and 4·1 shells, were spouting all around us. Hardly ever in my life was there a time less apt for absorbing impressions of beauty, yet in those few minutes, through and beyond the immediate volcano, I saw far over on the skyline by the Bapaume-Péronne road a space of green and intact country with trees and villages unspoiled. So peaceful and dreamlike it seemed, strangely unmoved, a mirage above a storm, if such a thing can be. In later days the shells reduced it to a desolation like the rest.

By this time a small but steady stream of our men was coming back past us, wounded. My lance-sergeant, Crowe (8/2422), had been hit in the side, but was able to walk; in our ignorance we wished him luck with his 'Blighty', but he died of wounds. Petrie of the 10th Otagos, my former platoon commander after Mr. Johnston was wounded in the raid, staggered back, shot in the chest; Thompson of the 8th Otagos, wounded in the side, came by, holding his hand to his hip. Here below us was a trench, Switch Trench, the first objective of the day before. Lying wounded in it were two Germans whom amid more pressing needs it had not been possible to take back; dry-lipped and unable to speak, making signs of thirst. Water—I could spare them none; my own men might be in worse case later.

It seems that our guide or guides, perhaps losing direction from the diagonal trend of Switch Trench, must have taken us too far to the right, for we now ran over a trench full of men of an English regiment, who hoped for a moment that they were being relieved and were disappointed when we inclined half-left again towards Flers in the hollow. Here the guides must have been still more at a loss, unable to locate and identify the trench assigned to us. On the exposed slope there, in full view of five German observation-balloons, we were ordered to halt and dig in; nothing was more certain than that we should be instantly sighted and shelled. We fell flat and dug for our lives; the entrenching tool, miniature pick-and-shovel hafted on one short handle, seemed exasperatingly inefficient. Over on the left of us was a long bank crested by a hedge, and in its flank a forward aid post, where medical officers could be seen working without respite among the never-ending groups of wounded who were being brought up by stretcher on the track from Flers. Stretchers with bandaged men on them lay around, waiting to be carried over the ridge into safety; but there was a shortage of bearers. At this moment I saw four Germans come up the track, a German officer following close behind. These prisoners were at once impounded for carrying service; I saw them pass with two stretchers, the officer supervising, slowly up the slope through their own black shell-bursts and out of view. Many German wounded, some severely mutilated, lay awaiting attention; each man was being taken in turn according to rota and with no favour or distinction of nationality. Truly, if I had had time to reflect upon it, an insane paradox—every energy in the one place devoted to the extermination of life, in the other to its preservation!

All this, in minute and unforgettable detail, I saw, however, as an aside, and with a curious detachment, not distracted in the least degree from the work in hand or from our own self-preservation. We were now digging hard to join shell-hole to shell-hole and gain at least a little cover—that is, the men were, the platoon commanders were walking above and supervising—when the expected 5·9's and 4·1's arrived and began to crash down much more thickly. The aid post and the inert wounded on the stretchers were being showered with earth and clods, so that I feared to see a shell land full among stretchers and doctors. And one must have done so that night; for it was here, if what I have heard is true, that Major Martin, author of *A Surgeon in Khaki*, met his death.[7] I felt then, and feel still, that we were largely responsible for drawing such fire. Howden and I had noted, down on the flat a furlong ahead, what looked like a practicable trench. We suggested to our O.C., Captain Herbert, that the Company should move down and occupy it, since it seemed to be empty and it was pointless to invite more shelling on this exposed slope. He answered that he, too, had seen the trench clearly enough, but had to stick to his orders, and so must we. None the less, Howden and I, deciding on second thoughts that this might be—as in fact it was—the very trench that we ought from the first to have been occupying, took a quick stroll down the track to survey it, with the idea of getting our men into it should the high explosives become too deadly. On the way I recognized one of the doctors, Captain P. B. Benham, of Otago University, but he was in no mood for old acquaintance. 'Who the hell's your Colonel? Can't he get his battalion off that bloody slope? Damn you, you're getting us shelled.' Then a fresh batch of stretchers arrived and exacted his whole attention.

Howden, ever quick and thorough, had already reconnoitered the trench and found it empty and in good order. We reported this and continued to supervise the digging. The Company had luck that afternoon, remembered as marvellous by all survivors I have since met, almost all being able to record one or two narrow escapes, but few being hit. The only casualty of the afternoon in my own Platoon was Crowe. Had the ground been hard and stony, had the Germans trusted to shrapnel more than high explosive, we should have suffered severely, might indeed have been annihilated. As it was, the steeply dropping howitzer shells drove deeply into soft ground and were either duds or, if they did explode, sent clods and earth but little metal vertically into the air. One burst on the Flers track four yards from me, almost knocking me over, the deluge of clods bringing me to my knees; the same shell half buried Major Rose of the Machine-Gun Company, and another a few yards farther down severely wounded him.

The latest draft to join us before the Somme had been the 13th Reinforcements. They naturally had no previous experience of being under fire. I wondered how they felt as they descended the slope and saw and heard the heavy shells landing all around. None of them flinched, so far as I could see; on that day and all through the Somme I could hardly distinguish them from the rest.

Late in the afternoon we had dug some sort of irregular trench and had become more used to the shells, or more probably had gained practice in quick aural sound-ranging at short distance. Observant and experienced infantrymen know very well that it is possible to see howitzer shells in the air near the end of their trajectory, unless they come direct. If there is any lateral component in their motion they can be heard a fraction of a second before they strike; extraordinarily slight, but enough. Not only so, but with practice—such as we were intensively having—the ear can tell by the slightest deviation of direction in the sound whether the shell is landing right or left. If there is even the finest deviation, one is safe. If the deviation is moderately wide, the change of sound gives, after some experience, a quick idea and estimate of the trajectory; and several times I saw a black object, foreshortened by some optical effect to a squat obtuse-angled triangle, fly past at perhaps a hundred yards' distance and bury itself in the earth. There was then just time to throw oneself down with the Platoon for cover. Against the direct hit, of course, such defensive reactions are useless; and shells in straight alignment with us, whether over or short, were heard only, not seen.

After nightfall we were ordered to cease digging and move down the track to Flers—in column of fours![8] In this way we at last dropped into the trench we had seen, 'Fat' Trench (as named according to some alphabetical code) to the left of Flers, where we should really have been for many hours past. Continuing along it we filed into our front line, or more exactly our outer line, for the London Regiment was still held up in front of High Wood and our left flank thus rested on air. The position was in the highest degree exposed, subject to enfilade fire of every kind and to sniping from a ridge, Grove Alley, in front. At many places, too, the trench did not exist for a space of several yards. A tank out of action, whether or not the one that had been reported in the newspapers as 'coming down the main street of Flers, with the British Army cheering behind' (a *locus classicus* in what war correspondents wrote down, and the public was led to believe!), lay like a stranded hulk just in front of the line.[9] We began at once to dig deeply into the clayey flank of the trench; it had so far no dug-outs, except a deep one that was used for Battalion H.Q., so that—as on Gallipoli—we merely cut coffin-like holes in the sides in which to curl up and sleep; if, indeed, we should have the luck to sleep, which was unlikely, since orders were to dig and to keep on digging.

Platoon commanders took turns of duty in two-hour watches, and in this way I sniffed for the first time, at midnight, the German lachrymatory or 'tear' shells, with their peculiar aromatic irritant smell, half-pineapple, half-pepper—it was also known that these might occasionally be mixed with noxious phosgene shells.[10] During a short doze in my recess before daybreak I felt the thud and quake of a shell driving through the parapet. A 5.9, it failed to explode, and so I was still alive; but it had smashed the thigh of Cotton (8/2198), one of my men, curled up in the next recess. He was carried away, but died like Harper from loss of blood.

The 17th, 18th, and 19th September were weary days and nights of digging and sentry-go[11] with hardly a wink of sleep, in constant expectation of a counter-attack on the exposed left flank. On the 18th, or perhaps the 17th—dates become a little confused at this point—the Londoners on our left attacked at 6 a.m. under a shrapnel barrage and gained their objective, straightening the line at last. They did not, it was said, suffer many casualties, a thing they could hardly afford to do, being reduced by the struggle on the fringe of High Wood to a mere fraction of their strength.[12] Later in the morning we extended our front to the left and took over their whole sector, letting a few exhausted men, so few that they seemed no more than a dozen, stumble to the rear, looking as if they had been in prison for twenty years. I did not see the subaltern, their only remaining officer, who was reported by our men on the left to have led them *around* the German barrage—a skillful modification of tactics if true, but very hard to believe. About the middle of the morning of the 19th our Battalion bombers established a 'block' on the crest of the rise, near where Flers Trench joined Grove Alley.[13] From our hollow ground we could see the rapid march of the bomb-bursts up the slope. An old schoolmate of very early years, James Marston, lost his life here.[14] The attack was led by Frank Jones, who replaced another officer at the last moment. To my great grief, not felt so much then, when death was occurring all round, as later when I was out of it, he was hit by a German stick-grenade, was carried back wounded, and died on 22nd September.[15] My old platoon sergeant, when I was a corporal, in the far-off days of Trentham, and later on Gallipoli and Lemnos, in Egypt, and France; constantly with me as we worked in co-ordination; sharer with Finlayson of our blanket and deck tarpaulin on the night we left Gallipoli; sharer of a dug-out with me at many parts of the trenches at Armentières; older than I by ten years; mature, responsible, generous, and brave—no country can afford to lose such men.

Now the weather, which had been hot and dry since the morning of the advance and earlier, fell misty and wet. The trenches, unprovided with sand-bags or duck-boards, were seen for what they were, ditches in which at every step we sank knee-deep in clay and water. Softened by rain, the overhanging sides crumbled in on the wretched make-shift dug-outs, and these continual small landslides filled the already oozy bed of the trench. Falling against the wet sides or into the pools, unable to pull our feet out of the clinging mud, we were daubed from feet to head, until it was a waste of time to bother about it. Clay in the bread—but lucky to have bread at all in an advance like this—clay in the drinking water, tasting already of petrol from petrol tins; faces with clay-masked stubble of beard, eyes pig-like in their setting of muddied eyebrow and eyelash. But that is not the chief thing I remember; such things can be endured in a life not specially feather-bedded. What I remember is the spirit of unselfish alacrity, both here and at Goose Alley later on. 'Four men to go to Flers Dump for supplies!' 'Here, sir! Here, sir!' And Flers Dump, even if 'the British Army had streamed cheering down the main street' a few days before, was not at the time a place anyone would choose to visit.

It would be late at night, 19th September, when we were relieved by the 2nd Otago Battalion. On my rounds I had just come upon a 12th Reinforcement man whose twin brother had been killed at his side by a shell; he himself was killed next year, on that bad day, 12th October 1917, at Passchendaele.[16] A little farther on, with the relieving company beginning to jump down in, a Main Body man was killed. In those days, when communication trenches either did not exist or were imprac-ticable, relieving troops walked overland by night and dropped into the trench. This man's brother, separated from him since Gallipoli, dropped in at the very spot.[17] The Somme seemed to predispose such abstract and inhuman coincidences as these.

20 Delville Wood: Longueval

O<small>N BEING RELIEVED WE WENT BACK, AGAIN IN THE INCREDIBLE</small> column of fours—a few casual shells and this record would never have been written—past the eastern fringe of High Wood. Shrapnel did burst not far off, but always a furlong to our left; perhaps there was an old communication trench over there, drawing this fire, and perhaps therefore our extraordinary formation was a justified risk. Parr and I brought up the rear with the stretcher-bearers to prevent any straggling. Once again the guides, as on the previous Saturday afternoon but now by night, must have been at a loss, for we wandered circuitously—being at one time, as I reckoned later by the lie of the land and by map-contours, close to Bazentin-le-Petit—until at length, a little before dawn, we were sleep-walking in a labyrinth of communication trenches, irritably awakened every few minutes by bumping against the back of the man in front. There were numerous halts, tempers were frayed. At daybreak the Battalion had intersected itself in a communication trench called Turk Lane.[1] Though previously in the rear of the long file, I now heard the voices of the leaders, and was ordered by the Colonel, who was close behind them, to jump out on top and locate, if possible, 'Carlton' and 'Savoy' trenches. The head of the column was in fact just about to enter them; old trenches, ironically named, on the ridge joining Bazentin to Longueval. In the drizzling dawn we occupied them, having taken about four hours to cover a distance, by straight line on the map, of about three miles. There we lay down, some in the few dug-outs that could be found, the greater number, including Parr and myself—remember Airaines!—in wet shell-holes.

This area was out of the intenser zone of shell-fire, though occasional long-range high-explosive, gas-, and tear-shells fell about at random. Flers was hidden again behind the ridge. On the right front was Delville Wood, and at its left fringe the ruins that had once been Longueval; on the side of the road a few tanks in reserve; on the left front, across a hollow and on the skyline of the farther slope, the skeleton of High Wood. The whole expanse between these woods—though *wood* in relation to them had ceased to have any meaning—a wilderness of mud and torn brown earth—was covered with batteries firing and limbers continually driving up with shells. Every half-minute green or black smoke from German high-explosive shrapnel bloomed out and drifted on the wind, followed in a second or two by the rending crash; the crest was ever exploding somewhere with the black smoke of 5·9's—tear-shells burst along it with a weak pop and a mist of white vapour. From Trônes Wood on our right rear to the wood of Bazentin-le-Petit on our left our own heavy howitzers fired continuously. It is impossible to integrate all these chaotic impressions; they are as much a part of infantry experience and recollection as any organized attack. Once, far behind the enemy lines, an enormous mushroom of smoke rose to 10,000 feet, indicating an exploded dump; but any sense of exultation was soon damped by a similar but smaller mushroom shooting up behind our own rearward lines, distracting the attention to our observation-balloons running eastward some miles behind us and marking the French salient by curving away southward.

In these Dantesque surroundings, when prolonged loss of sleep and unremitting *qui vive*[2] had made the skyline acquire a fiery edge and tree-trunks had begun to shimmer in a subjective heliotrope mirage, we received letters from New Zealand sent up from Bécordel. I had almost no inclination to read my own four letters—I felt like putting them aside meanwhile until I should be in a frame of mind to understand them. One contained some piece of old family history that at any other time would have interested me to the exclusion of everything else; I read it, tried to disengage the facts and set them in order, but the mind stubbornly refused its office, and I have now no clear notion of what those facts were.[3]

These letters had been brought up by the Q.M. department; it had also brought up the field kitchen, so that we again had the welcome taste of hot food; since Mametz Wood we had fared on bread, tinned meat, and petrol-flavoured water. There is, of course, nothing whatever to complain of in this; far from it, for in such conditions what we had was luxury; bread is unusual in the front line after an attack, on Gallipoli it had been beyond imagination. These good supplies we owed to the Company in reserve, the 14th, which up to now had suffered forty casualties. During the five days of this 'rest in reserve' the weather cleared and the ground hardened, the clay on our uniforms caking like plaster. The Q.M. department once again proved its resource by conjuring from nowhere a gross or so of scrubbing brushes. With these we removed our plaster-casts, and after shaving became once more individual and recognizable. Full psychological recovery followed. A platoon resembles a lizard with tail severed, a crab that has lost a claw, a trisected starfish; given time it will grow the missing part and function as before, though not indefinitely often.

All this time the tear-shells continued to burst along the ridge in front, the lachrymatory mist drifting white on the wind and still pungent at 400 yards. This brings to mind an unusual picture; of a party of red-tabbed staff officers, remissly unprovided with the close-fitting tear-gas goggles, passing through our lines to observe some advance from the ridge, but returning in a few minutes with streaming eyes.

While the Staff are thus in the foreground it may save time, and prevent the holding up of action later, to hazard a word or two concerning the relations between the Staff and the fighting units.

Not that, in strict truth, there is much to be said. We thought of the Staff very little, and saw them less. Major Hastings, in the front line at Armentières, two or three times; usually on some morning after the Germans, during the night, had blown up some of our barbed wire; the Brigadier-General himself twice—he had, indeed, one misty Stand-to in August, roused up the Colonel to go out into no-man's-land with him and do a tour of inspection of that same wire.[4] But for the most part the Staff were a distant and impersonal body of Olympians. For example, I never saw Field-Marshal Sir Douglas Haig or General Sir Henry Rawlinson.[5] As for their work, it was sometimes, as will be seen on 25th September, surpassingly good; equally sometimes, as on the 27th, slipshod.[6] But—I often asked myself—what was the 'Staff'? It was a vague term, ranging from remote G.H.Q. at Montreuil, Hesdin, or elsewhere to Army, to Army Corps, to Division, to Brigade, perhaps even to Battalion.[7] Consider an order, coming down this long chain, to exploit an advance that had met with initial success; it might rest with Division, I imagined, to draw a general plan, with Brigade to time-table it, with Battalion to put final touches and execute it. If this succeeded, everyone would praise it as first-class staff work; if it failed, as far too often it did, it would be hard to locate the cause of failure in the long chain from the general to the specific. For example, the Otago raid, still a bad memory. Who was to blame for its failure, that is to say, for the plan itself? Probably Division or Brigade, having chosen so large a unit as a company to go over—but surely Battalion also, for drafting so unimaginative a scheme. But all such reflections were apt to return to one consideration, that the enormous casualties of the Somme, as of Loos, were due to the combination of uncut wire and unsilenced machine-guns, especially those which, firing from either flank, sent the deadliest kind of all, the intersecting streams of 'cross-fire'. The losses incurred from these causes at the Somme, Arras, and Passchendaele later, were incalculable. They made nonsense of the theory of attrition; what was produced was a disproportionate detrition of our manpower.

On the night of the 20th our area was heavily shelled with gas-shells. I donned my gas-helmet, and in spite of the surroundings lapsed into short spells of sleep, waking from time to time to find myself breathing in the prescribed manner, inhaling through the nose and exhaling by the mouth-valve.

Our proportion of casualties was so far not excessive; in my own Platoon, exceptionally fortunate, only three, and one gone to hospital. We knew well that we had not seen the last of the Somme but were being reserved for a fresh advance; in fact its line, Grove Alley, was plotted on the map. About the 22nd we learned that the 2nd Canterbury Battalion had beaten off heavy bombing counter-attacks lasting the whole night of the 20th; and that on the 21st, under Captain Starnes, they had counter-attacked in turn and captured this very stretch of trench, Grove Alley.[8] A new objective was therefore assigned to us, like Grove Alley, and parallel to it, a 'switch' trench called Goose Alley, which will figure importantly in a day or two.

This 'rest' of ours was not unbroken, nor were we free from casualties. A species of pattern was imposed each day by the methodical searching in depth of this area by a battery of four German howitzers. Beginning by dropping four shells in a line to the left of Delville Wood, straddling the Longueval-Flers road, they would increase range by some 100 yards at each salvo until the line of explosions crossed our rectangle and passed behind; then, shortening range systematically, they would return in the same manner. This process they mechanically repeated, for hours on end. On the 24th, in part command with Howden of a road-mending party near Longueval, I marvelled again at the phlegm of the limber-drivers turning the dangerous corners of the Longueval-Flers road, the shells seeming to burst right among them, the smoke clearing away to show them riding on as before, except that every now and then a limber was smashed, with driver, horse, and freight, and dragged to the side. We passed by Longueval, or what had once been Longueval, at the north-eastern corner of Delville Wood. By the roadside the limbs of men in khaki or field-grey lay half-covered in hastily dug graves that the shells had again laid bare; at the turn leading into the village a grey hand beckoned from the ground and a splintered bone protruded from a boot and puttee.

It was here, as Lieutenant James Reid of the Gordon Highlanders told me in hospital later, that men, stupefied by loss of sleep for many days, had driven their bayonets into the ground and leaned forward sleeping with shoulder on rifle-butt, uncaring in the midst of shell-fire whether they lived or died. Longueval itself, which before the war must have been as secluded as Citernes, was now levelled, razed to the ground, hardly one stone resting on another, a ruin of charred sticks. One iron gate-post still stood, twisted out of shape by blast. The tortured trees of Delville Wood made the wood of Harpies in Doré's illustrations to Dante seem like a harmless lyric.9 Taking broken bricks and stones from the ruins, we patched the holes in the road, scattering for cover as the four shells completed their cyclic return. We met them again on the way back to our reserve trenches; one shell seemed to burst right on our Company field kitchens, and another of the same salvo fell among a group of men of the 1st Canterbury Battalion. So it continued all afternoon, ceasing only at nightfall.

21 Goose Alley:
25th September 1916

N OW IT WAS THE EVENING OF THE 24TH SEPTEMBER; WE WERE TO ATTACK some time next day. All details of the plan were known except zero time, which was usually not divulged until a few hours before action; or perhaps some later fictitious time was given out. My Platoon, Platoon 1, was to be the first wave on the left half of the Battalion sector; and if ever I prepared for an examination it was now, to learn by heart, relative to zero time, every particular of the time-table and of the ground. Maps had been run off on a duplicating machine from the official ones of scale 1 in 10,000; every officer and many of the senior N.C.O.s had one of these.[1] Small study groups had been formed, and the scheme of attack had been discussed down to its finest details; each platoon commander was responsible that every man should understand both it and his own share in it. I have still in my possession, carried with me to England in my paybook after I was wounded, a tattered Brigade map of this kind and some rough copies, penciled on small sheets, that I had made of those squares which were especially my own concern; these copies I held in my left palm, on the way across behind the barrage, to make certain of landmarks and times. In the event I had no need to consult them; they can still be deciphered well enough to reconstruct the plan.

The first German line had been broken, but on the southern part only of the front attacked, on 1st and 2nd July; the second line in the night attack at Contalmaison on the 14th; the third, the Martinpuich-Flers line, had fallen to us only lately, on 15th September. Parallel to this and about a mile farther back was the strongly fortified fourth line, from Le Sars to Eaucourt l'Abbaye and thence to Gueudecourt and Le Transloy; its code name was Gird Trench; it had still to be captured. I believe that it marked the limit of advance at the Somme in 1916. The lately captured third line, Flers Trench, was joined to the fourth line by communication trenches each about a mile long, Grove Alley and Goose Alley. At this time our outer line round Flers formed a salient, which was being widened by pushing out fanwise to the north-west, so that on our left we were capturing communication trenches instead of main lines of defence.[2] Grove Alley was ours as far as the point where it crossed the Flers-Ligny-Thilloy road; the projected new line was to run from the south-western part of the next switch trench on the west, Goose Alley, to a point on the Flers-Ligny road called Factory Corner. This whole line was the Brigade objective; our Battalion was to capture the left third or so of Goose Alley. Assembly trenches were to be in Grove Alley, to the left of the Flers-Eaucourt road. The advance would be at first downhill to a hollow, below the 120-metre contour containing a road forking into two parallel avenues; then uphill on a similar slope 300 or 400 yards to Goose Alley, on a ridge above the 130-metre contour, looking north-west to Eaucourt l'Abbaye and south-east backward to Flers. The total distance from assembly to objective was 700 yards. The plan of attack, with the addition of a few verbs, I reconstruct as follows:

> At zero time, oo, a dense barrage of shrapnel will fall 50 yards in front of assembly trenches and will continue 2 minutes. At +2 barrage will move forward; first wave will go over top. Barrage to move forward 100 yards

every 2 minutes. Later waves to follow at 50 yards interval. Barrage to remain on road in hollow and not move forward till +18. Wave will cross both roads and light ground flares beyond second; contact aeroplane will fly above with streamer and horn-blasts. Wave to continue up slope. At +25 barrage will lift from Goose Alley. Wave will double to objective. Bayonet if necessary. Barrage will remain 200 yards beyond objective as long as required. Consolidate.

This was as clear as could be desired. The rate of progress behind the barrage, fifty yards per minute, was everything. There were also to be fixed barrages playing on side-trenches, machine-gun nests, and so on; these we might take for granted. All ranks had been drilled in the plan and their own part in it; lance-corporals even, or senior privates, in extreme emergency, could have taken charge. Such thoroughness bred confidence everywhere; there seemed every chance of success.

After sunset all officers went to Captain Hargest's dug-out and had a final detailed run-through. As we were about to disperse to our companies I heard someone say, 'What about a sing-song?', which for the moment surprised me, since New Zealanders were supposed, rightly as I believe, to be laconic and undemonstrative. I recalled few songs sung on the march; one or two in Trentham, none at all in France; in Ismailia, on the home stretch of a route march, only the monotonous 'Ayalissa' or 'Saliana', copied from the Egyptian bargees of Lake Timsah. But now we sang, a little self-consciously at first; songs, already beginning to be rather out of fashion, from the *Scottish Students' Songbook*—'Riding down to Bangor', 'In a cavern, in a canyon', and others like these, and, for a close, 'Vive l'amour, vive la compagnie'.[3] We saw no irony then in these words; we might have, could we have foreseen that at the same hour three nights later almost all the singers would be lying dead or wounded in no-man's-land.

Thus ended Sunday, 24th September. At midnight we packed up, passed on the right of High Wood to the line beyond Flers and filed into the assembly trenches at Grove Alley. Zero time was duly announced for the middle of the afternoon; but this, taken for what it was worth, made no interruption in the ceaseless scouting of the ground in front. With periscope I scanned every tree in the hollow and fixed where I should go through; I practised the mental counting off of seconds, nought, *a, b, c,* one, *a, b, c,* and so on. All morning we were peppered by a casual but vicious fire of German 77-mm. shrapnel; we lost several men, killed and wounded. Captain Hargest came by, his usual calm disturbed; a senior field officer, reflecting on probable casualties, had remarked to him, 'The planter will have some work to do'. The planter!⁴ This jarred. Captain Hargest's own brother, in the ranks, had just been killed by this shrapnel.

Zero time was now announced with precision as 12.35 p.m., and since this was fairly soon it could be believed. We were thus due to drop into Goose Alley at 1 p.m. summer time, exactly midday by solar time. Once more, and finally, watches were accurately synchronized with 'Brigade time', and now every precaution, so far as we could see, had been taken. We must have had a slight meal—though meals before an attack are eaten in a kind of absentness and not remembered; we arranged ourselves in order for going over. All the platoons densely filled the assembly trench from end to end, in readiness to move out in successive waves. The men of my Platoon were extended right and left of me at intervals of eight or ten yards, with N.C.O.s uniformly spread among them, in such a way that in emergency they could take over according to seniority. Ten minutes before zero all platoons were arranged in this way, dove-tailed and interwoven. All was ready, but for these last few minutes we kept the men spacing themselves still more evenly in the congested trench, merely to keep their minds, and ours, occupied up to the last. My watch is showing 12.34. One more minute.

Zero! Crash of explosions in the best barrage yet seen, bursts of cotton-wool smoke at different heights but all in one vertical plane. The air twanging like a bow-string; seconds-hand moving round. Now, 12.37! Platoon, lifted like one man, clears parapet. Very evenly; but it must be fifty yards a minute, exactly half ordinary marching pace. Mentally count seconds, nought, *a, b, c,* one, *a, b, c,* and make a full pace at each second. The trees down there—as if I had known them always.

A glance back; that is Captain Herbert, wearing a private's tunic and carrying a rifle, as we all are, to avoid being picked out by snipers; for our own men the stars on our shoulders are enough. Grove Alley, now all platoons are out, begins to go up in air behind us. Halt here till barrage moves on—man three to my left, 13th Reinforcements, has dropped on one knee but is looking my way and will come on all right. Trees quite near now, no casualties yet, everything running wonderfully, better than at Citernes or St. Vaast. Count seconds again. Something disturbs from half left; birds, six or eight, panic-running across front, now rising, flying away half-right. My watch, my piece of paper, the barrage are everything, but—not quail, not grouse, *perdrix* of course, partridges![5] Something else also running from left—a hare, not three yards in front. Man two to my left makes mock point at it with his bayonet, grins at me in this blazing barrage! This is a green slope with only a few fresh shell-holes. Company on right, under Rutherford in first wave, seems a little too far forward. Corporal Gilmour there, keeping contact, a little too far—pass the word along to Corporal— too late! One of our own shells has exploded short, very little. Five or six men in the 8th Company fall forward; Arthur Gilmour, friend and fellow student, also. My Platoon otherwise still intact.

The trees; just as imagined always. Through here; barrage forward; 35 plus 18 equals 12.53 and everything is still right. Same man grins and jerks his bayonet upward towards a tree. Nought, *a, b, c,* hardly time to glance up, but—an owl! How in the name of all that shrapnel? Cross parallel roads, double drive, light all red flares along this ditch.[6] Horn-blasts from left, contact aeroplane above, red streamer flying low down along line of trees. Everything incredibly right so far.

Three hundred yards more, up farther slope same way. Lessening gradient, the ridge, line of thrown-up earth, Goose Alley! My watch dead on 1.00, barrage forward. 'Platoon! Rush trench with lowered bayonets and jump in!'

We met with no resistance. The Germans, seeing the unbroken lines coming at speed with fixed bayonets, fled, most of them away to the right, like the partridges and the hare, north-east along Goose

Alley to Gird Trench, a few the other way, over towards Eaucourt
l'Abbaye. I could not believe that we had been twenty-three minutes
in no-man's-land; it felt like twenty-three seconds. Ordinary time came
back the instant my feet touched trench bottom. A few machine-guns
were seized at once. A handful of prisoners, Bavarians, surrendered
and were sent to the rear; several others, including a company officer,
had been badly wounded, while dead lay in the floor of the trench
at every few yards. Most of these seemed very young, eighteen or
nineteen years old; myself only two years older, I felt a compunction.
The officer, dignified, distinguished, was bleeding from a grave wound
in the upper part of the leg. We bandaged him as soon as we could and
sent him back on a stretcher, but I fear that, wounded in the same way
as Harper and Cotton had been, he must inevitably have died like them
from loss of blood. Deathly white and in grievous pain, he made no
complaint and thanked me in French. One can have no quarrel with
such a man. As for my own Platoon, Arthur Gilmour died of wounds
later; but my roll-book showed no other casualties on 25th September.

Shell-fire and counter-attack were now to be expected. All men were
carrying pick and shovel, inserted in the braces of the web equipment behind the shoulders. They had already set to work deepening
the trench against machine-gun fire and shrapnel. Suitable sites were
chosen, facing Eaucourt l'Abbaye, for a shield of machine-gun posts.
We divided up our sector, each platoon commander making himself
responsible till night for his own quarter; mine was farthest to the
right, where we joined the 10th Company under Captain Hargest.
On the extreme left, where once again we rested on air, Sutherland
jumped up to pick a site; he was sniped fatally on the instant. Sergeants
Carnegie and Malcolm leapt up to pull him in; both were severely
wounded. Our left flank must be badly exposed; the Black Watch,[7]
who had viewed our attack from their trenches and who—so my left-
hand corporal told me—had waved us on, impatient at our slow fifty
yards per minute, must be farther back. I saw the reason next day.
We ran out T-head saps[8] with machine-guns over the crest, bearing
on Eaucourt l'Abbaye. By nightfall Goose Alley was deeper and safer,

but digging continued unremittingly. High explosive was now crashing down in enfilade from the north-east, not so much on us as on the 10th Otagos, who were suffering losses. So far there was no sign of a counter-attack; if it took any form at all it would presumably be a bombing attack straight down Goose Alley, like our own in Grove Alley on the 19th.

Darkness fell. The remaining three platoon commanders divided the night into two-hour watches and took turns on duty, those off duty not sleeping but sitting in a waking-sleeping state; the mind might try to sleep, but obscure fears would seize it the moment the head drooped, making one sit up with a start. So it passed, a 'quiet night' as nights went on the Western Front, quiet except for the kettle-drum rat-a-tat of machine-guns and the occasional howl and crash of a heavy shell. On our rounds we tramped in the dark over the dead bodies of those young Germans in the floor of the trench; once, for a few minutes, I was pillowed in broken sleep between two of them, and now and then, stumbling thus upon some dead man's head, I shook off our conditioned callousness, shook off the feeling, now taking root, that this world of arbitrary violence and random death was the real world, and that justice, mercy, peace, and love were phantasms that had never been. I thought of Brockett, now dead, and of our last conversation under a starry sky; of Paisley, the friend of William Robertson, of Captain Hargest, of Ivor Edward Champion (8/1426), all along there with the 10ths under those crashing shells to the right; Champion, that courteous and reserved Englishman, perhaps forty or even forty-five years old, of unknown background, whether born in India, as it might seem, or of public school, or Oxford; at any rate a legend of impassive courage under strafes of shrapnel, so much so that it was said no bullet or shell would ever find him. The Somme, however, had no respect for such legends; in London, in the long and terrible lists of early October, I found his name among the killed in action.

It was past midnight, I was on duty again. The sky had cleared and was now of great beauty, could I have seen it so. I noted several bright stars and identified those northern circumpolar constellations that we do not see in New Zealand. Suddenly I felt as if caught out in some neglect of duty. Had anyone ever taught the men to fix the celestial North Pole by reference to the Great Bear?[9] I could not remember, since Egypt, any such lesson; the change of hemisphere must somehow have been forgotten in our course of training. And so I made my turn of duty a tour of inspection, teaching small groups how to fix the Pole Star, making them describe it themselves, and insisting always that the Germans were to the north of us, and we to the south of them.

This was a lucky inspiration. Years afterwards, in New Zealand, I met one of my Platoon, O'Driscoll (23603), wounded like me on 27th September. He told me that this impromptu lesson, suggested by a starry sky, had without doubt saved the lives of himself and several others. He and these others of a different company were all lying out wounded on the afternoon of the 27th, waiting in shell-holes to crawl or scramble back when machine-gunning should die down. They had to wait until night, and it had rained; they had lost their bearings and were in fact making for the north, so that they would have ended on the wire of Gird Trench, when the sky cleared and O'Driscoll picked up the Pole Star. He succeeded in convincing the others; they turned completely about and the whole group at last and without further harm reached our own trenches.

Does O'Driscoll still live, I wonder, in 1962?[10] And if he does, can he ever forget those days and nights in front of Flers?

22 Goose Alley:
26th September 1916

THE NEXT DAY, 26TH SEPTEMBER, WAS AS DIFFERENT FROM THE 25TH AS both were from the 27th.

Dawn broke at last; our fears of a night attack down Goose Alley, such as had fallen five days before on the 2nd Canterbury Battalion, were for the time being dispelled. In daylight Goose Alley appeared a worse shambles than ever. On my rounds I reached the extreme left of our sector, Flers Trench, where we were now presumed to be in contact with the Black Watch. I saw none of them alive, but many of them dead. I saw, too, what cannot be described, a sergeant of the Black Watch, a powerful red-haired man with magnificent shoulders, and five Germans lying radially extended from him. They had closed in upon him and he had let off a Mills bomb. Greater horrors—if indeed there be any greater or lesser in such things—were in store next day; this compact hub-and-wheelspoke tableau was enough for me, of itself, to make nonsense all talk of the chivalresque, in the mode of Ashby de la Zouch,[1] or of the glory of war. Yet the indurated callousness returned. I set the men to collect systematically the large quantities of equipment, rations, and ammunition that had been abandoned. The greatcoats we abstracted for our own use in keeping warm by night; to judge by quality and cleanness of cloth they were a new issue, bearing the regimental number, 115, on the shoulders. Our own greatcoats and blankets had been left back in reserve. Numbers of machine-guns, complete with cartridge-belts, had been abandoned, as well as quantities of the familiar stick-grenades and hundreds of small black-lacquered bombs of a new type of the shape and size of a goose-egg. Belts lay about, inscribed *Gott mit uns*,[2] also a saw bayonet, intended of course, in spite of atrocity stories in the newspapers, to be really used as a saw; lastly, numerous rifles of Spandau make. I appropriated one of these; my own, left for a minute in the corner of a bay, was twisted and stripped of all woodwork by a shell while I was, fortunately, in the next bay. We found a few diaries—we were not allowed to keep any ourselves, and these seemed rather pathetic—and handed them in to Stuart Macdonald, the Battalion Intelligence Officer. Food in plenty was found: large numbers of white bags, containing small loaves of palatable black or brown bread, small square biscuits like our own emergency 'iron rations', and tins of *Rindfleisch*, the German equivalent of our bully beef. Dozens of small bottles of soda-water lay about, and were soon sampled.

The date 26th September 1916 was regarded as important in the history of military operations of that year. This was the day on which Thiepval fell at last, and on which British and French met at midnight in the capture of Combles.[3] For us it was an inactive interlude; from our ridge we were spectators of advances made on both sides of us. In the morning we endured accurately aimed shelling, some coming down Goose Alley on enfilade and some, as in the salient at Armentières, actually from behind, for at that time the line had an abrupt bend to the south where the French joined us at Combles. Once again the brunt of this shelling was borne not so much by us as by the 10th Company under Captain Hargest on our right. My own Platoon was exceptional in suffering only one casualty on the 25th and none on the 26th.

All day, however, for every shell arriving in Goose Alley many of ours went over in the opposite direction. The upper air was full of roaring and whining noises, long high notes, sinister descending chromatic scales. The green carpet of fields that I had seen as a mirage of peace above the smoke and dust ten days before was being torn up; the ground in and far behind the German lines was spouting in great brown geysers. The enemy were keeping so low in cover under all this that it was possible to lean over the trench-wall and make observations, even to send parties across the open to Flers Dump. Men who had been killed were now lifted over the trench, on the south-east side, and buried by their friends, the spot being marked by any spare rifle and bayonet driven into the ground.

During the morning I tried out the two types of German grenade and demonstrated the mode of throwing, in case we should be counter-attacked and should run short of our own. The stick-grenade, like a potato-masher with wire inside the handle, button-end and fuse-time eight seconds, was already fairly well known; the egg-bomb was novel but of limited effect, its chief advantage presumably being its range, perhaps sixty yards or more. Midday passed in this way; we made a meal of bread, tinned Maconochie rations[4] and pork-and-beans, which for attack fare in a captured line was wonderful to have. Battle-strain and continued loss of sleep over many days were beginning to tell, on myself at any rate, as I could not but notice; but the events of the afternoon made us forget that for the time being.

Eaucourt l'Abbaye, the village that figured so prominently—and with an apparent importance quite disproportionate to its size—in the communiqués and press reports of the next week and more, was in front of our ridge, that is, north-west; not really a village, rather an abbey with the usual outbuildings now being reduced to ruins by our shells. Every two minutes four shells of large calibre crashed down together, sending up the familiar clouds of black or brick-red dust. Sometimes they landed full in Flers Trench, to the west of the abbey, the part that held out till 3rd October; at other times they blasted a line of trees between the trench and the abbey. The whole area must have been a warren of machine-guns.

It was still early in the afternoon, about 2 p.m. Chancing to look back to the high skyline east of Delville Wood, I distinguished with binoculars (not mine but Corporal Fitt's, picked up in no-man's-land on the night of the Otago raid) what at first appeared to be a brigade or divisional staff, apparently watching a heavy shrapnel barrage which was falling a mile to the east of us, in front of Gueudecourt. Something about the staff struck me as peculiar; they seemed too many, and for a moment I thought, horsemen, but dismissed it. Now I saw men rise out of the ground before Gueudecourt in successive waves, and move steadily and evenly towards the village; an intervening fold of ground then cut off my further view. About half an hour later I saw the strangest sight. Horsemen rode at the trot in the same direction until they too disappeared behind a rise. At first I doubted my eyes. Was I hallucinated by insomnia at last? Or was this an attempt at a cavalry break-through? It did not seem to be followed up; and I saw none come back. Now from the west, in the direction of Thiepval, sounded a gigantic bombardment; simultaneously from the extreme right, far down by Combles and round towards Péronne, I fancied I heard a mightily increased roll of French 75's. North, away forward by Le Barque, not far east of the strange chalk mound called the Butte de Warlencourt, I saw movement and picked up with binoculars a line of men marching down a road, perhaps an enemy regiment thrown in to counter the advance upon Gueudecourt. Now you ring up artillery, I thought; but without lowering the binoculars I saw a fountain of earth spout at the head of the column and faint puffs of shrapnel bursting above. In less than ten seconds all the blue-grey figures had vanished.

For two hours we had been free from shell and machine-gun fire. We were sitting with impunity on the trench-wall, almost under the delusion, for a brief space, that the defence was cracking, that a breakthrough was imminent, and that at any minute orders might come to go over the top, side-step Eaucourt l'Abbaye, and rush for Ligny-Thilloy. Doubtless it was the sight of cavalry, not many it is true, but going forward at a quick trot, that made me believe this, though not for long. I heard or read, not long after, that these horsemen were merely doing patrol work; but cavalry patrol had not the faintest relation to the conditions of the Somme. On a colder analysis and in the waning afternoon I believed, and continue to believe, that on this day, 26th September 1916, there was still the hope, at the highest Staff level, of a cavalry break-through, a hope very quickly dashed.[5] But there was the further and graver thought, that if, after two years of this war, and the reiterated proofs of the role of the German machine-gun, placed as it could be in great numbers in ambushes of every kind—and I remembered those concealed dug-outs in Caterpillar Wood—'if', I thought, 'in spite of all this the Staff still believes in cavalry charges, then it has learned almost nothing, and the outlook for the infantry, ourselves, is so much the worse'.

Thinking of cavalry, by association I thought of the tanks, in some sort a grotesque type of cavalry. There were those few back at Longueval, and there was a rumour that one had been sighted away over towards Gueudecourt or Lesbœufs; but in our own sector they seemed to have vanished from the scene.[6] Their intervention, though it may have met with a small local success here and there, had therefore been a transient episode; premature disclosure in too small numbers, those bare forty in the park behind Bécordel, had wasted the element of surprise. The Germans could now at their leisure devise counter-measures; even I could imagine one or two possibilities, such as adapting to ground use the petrol-bombs used in the air for extirpating observation-balloons.

Evening came on amid these reactions and speculations. The sky must have been overcast, during my spells of duty at least; for I remember intending to give more lessons on the Pole Star but not doing so. By the early morning orders had come in for a fresh attack, to be made precise later; and now, with further loss of sleep from another night spent on this exposed ridge in expectation of counter-attack, we were beginning to feel that we had had more than enough of our small share in the first battle of the Somme. My own Platoon continued to be lucky; no casualties at all during the night, in spite of several narrow escapes; net strength, excluding men who were elsewhere on

Lewis gun, Company bomber, traffic, transport, sanitary duty, and so on, thirty-two, including myself.

The counter-attack did not materialize; the night of 26–27th September passed off for us in relative quiet. Now from headquarters came more precise details of a new objective, to be captured if possible some time during the afternoon of the 27th, time-table and barrage scheme to be communicated to all ranks about the middle of the morning.

23 Goose Alley:
27th September 1916

THIS WAS THE LAST DAY OF MY ACTIVE SERVICE IN THE LINE; ITS EFFECTS will remain for the rest of my life.

Our success of two days before must have caused a lack of thoroughness in the plans for the new attack. I simply believe that this happened over and over again at the Somme. The maps and time-tables for both attacks, still in my possession in rough draft, show a marked contrast. The objective this time was Gird Trench itself, on a frontage of about 400 yards, the very strong fourth line of the Germans, with its thick hedge of barbed wire in front and its support line, which we were also to capture, 150 yards in rear. This was, indeed, the barrier against which the Somme offensive of 1916 was checked by autumnal rains and the onset of winter, the position remaining at a deadlock until the Germans made their secretly phased retreat to the straighter and shorter Hindenburg line in February and March 1917. Gird Trench was incomparably more formidable than Goose Alley had been. For one thing, that line of crosses on the map, a thick hedge of wire; Goose Alley, a switch trench, had had no wire. Then again, Goose Alley was as yet occupied by us along half its length only; in order to attack Gird Trench we should have to file along Goose Alley to our extreme point, scramble out there on the right, and deploy into line at the double across the enemy's front, finally inclining half left to face Gird Trench and move forward in the usual waves. Those were in fact our eventual instructions; but let anyone imagine such a movement carried out under machine-gun fire! Yet again, Goose Alley was almost at right angles to Gird Trench, and half of it, several hundred yards, was still occupied by Germans, who while we were attacking would have to be dislodged by our bombers. Finally, Gird Trench was concealed from periscope scrutiny by a slight ridge, almost imperceptible but significant, along the Eaucourt-Factory Corner road; and here enters a circumstance which must have caused tens, perhaps hundreds, of thousands of casualties on the Western Front, the inadequacy of even apparently good maps. My map showed much valuable detail, but few contour lines, and those not fine enough. The only contours shown were the 120-metre one, between Grove Alley and Goose Alley, and the 130-metre one, curling round on either side of the south-western half of Goose Alley. Ten metres, thirty-three feet, of difference, and nothing in between; it is far too crude; even three metres, or ten feet, can make all the difference between having cover or being visible and shot to pieces by machine-guns. In that respect the ground, 1,000 yards in depth, that lay between the point of deployment and the Gird Support objective was a *terra incognita*; it had no contour lines at all. I feared it; it was clearly lower than 130 metres, and all of it might be visible from west and north. The fanwise-spreading pattern of our attacks, hitherto an advantage, was now a serious liability. Machine-gun fire on our uncovered left flank, 'out in the blue' once again, would come principally from the hornets' nests of Eaucourt l'Abbaye and the uncaptured trench systems all about it. These several drawbacks were apparent to everyone, officers, N.C.O.s, and men alike, before ever the detailed time-table was given out. Captain Herbert, I noticed, a quiet and reserved man, was grave and preoccupied all morning, as though he already foresaw his death in the afternoon.

The time-table, communicated later in the morning relative to an unspecified new time, was even more discouraging. The careful arrangements of the 25th had allowed twenty-three minutes for the crossing of 700 yards; these of the 27th allowed a bare eight minutes for the crossing of 1,000 yards far more exposed to fire of all kinds. We should have to move at 150 paces a minute. As for barrages, there was nothing remotely resembling the elaborate creeping and stationary barrages of the Monday; little more than the bare statement that the barrage would lift and move forward at zero time, when we should make our dash.

For this new advance the order of companies had been reversed. The 14th had come off supply duties and was to be in the lead, the 8th next, our own, the 4th, next. The 10th, having so far lost most men, was to be in reserve on supplies, and therefore—I add as a late post-script in 1962[1]—Captain Hargest was probably spared to play his noted part as Brigadier Hargest in the Second World War, to be captured by Rommel at Sidi Aziz, to be imprisoned in Italy, to escape and write *Farewell Campo 12*, but to be killed in 1945 on his way up to the French front. Yet he may have been spared even earlier; for there was more than a rumour that on the 25th, on capturing Goose Alley, we were almost immediately to be sent against Gird Trench;[2] in which case, conditions being similar but even more improvisatory, and orders from headquarters probably the same, the 4th, 8th, and 10th Companies of the 1st Otago would have been annihilated (the verb is that of the official history for 1916)[3] instead of the 4th, 8th, and 14th.

The attack being as usual by waves of platoons, I saw that I should go forward in the middle of the ninth wave. We must have had a midday meal, but I forget it. At noon zero time was given out as 2.15 p.m., watches were synchronized with Brigade time and the interval was spent in instructing N.C.O.s and men. There was little to say; no one could feel any conviction in the opening manoeuvre and the brief and apparently inadequate barrage. There was the lurking suspicion that the Staff (but which Staff—Army, Army Corps, or Division?) were counting on our making a flying dash and capturing Gird Trench by luck.

At 2.15 the barrage, which seemed a perfunctory affair, moved forward and the first two companies, in eight platoon waves, scrambled out and over to the right. My Platoon followed quickly up Goose Alley and climbed out on the right at the point where the sunken road from Flers to Eaucourt l'Abbaye crossed it. When the last man was clear we inclined left and hurried forward after the other waves. This deployment was carried out without loss, so far as I could judge from a quick survey, which gave me my last glimpse in this world of Captain Herbert at the gap, directing the next wave. Like all the other officers I was wearing a private's tunic and equipment and carrying a rifle and bayonet, the Spandau rifle I have mentioned. We had not gone a furlong when it became clear that there was something wrong ahead; the leading waves were not to be seen, except for isolated men straggling here and there. The reason became clear as we neared the road running due east and west from Factory Corner to Eaucourt.

My friend Tucker, advancing a year later with the stretcher-bearers over to Gravenstafel in front of Passchendaele at dawn on 4th October 1917, was haunted by Shakespeare's sonnet, 'Shall I compare thee to a summer's day?', and heard all round him the slow movement, *Largo e mesto* in D minor, of Beethoven's 7th Pianoforte Sonata. Such elevation was not mine; nothing extraneous or allusive distracted my deadly attention. We were about half-way across when German high explosive mixed with shrapnel, of the greenish-black kind, began to fall thickly. Not ten yards ahead a group of the 8th Company vanished in the smoke of a shell-burst, some falling where they stood, the others walking on dreamlike. I passed through the smoke. In a dim way I wondered why I had not been hit by the flying pieces, but the mind would not trouble itself with problems at that moment, the overmastering impulse being to move on. On! On! In an attack such as this, under deadly fire, one is as powerless as a man gripping strongly charged electrodes, powerless to do anything but go mechanically on; the final shield from death removed, the will is fixed like the last thought taken into an anaesthetic, which is the first thought taken out of it. Only safety, or the shock of a wound, will destroy such auto-hypnosis. At the same time all normal emotion is numbed utterly. Close upon this road now, I heard a voice abusing the Germans; crossing the road, I realized that it had been my own.

As I took the bank I looked left and saw Private Nelson, one of my men, fall forward on his knees and elbows, his head between his hands. I mentally registered 23598, Nelson, W. P., and the terrific electromagnetic force pulled me on. He was dead.

Now from two directions, half-right, half-left, came the hissing of many bullets, the herring-bone weave of machine-gun cross-fire. I saw some cut long straight scores in the ground, sending up dust; some, as I found later, cut my tunic, frayed the equipment, and made rents in the cloth cover of my shrapnel helmet; many seemed to whizz past my ear, some to bury themselves under my feet as I walked. Again these things are remembered as sometimes a deeply submerged dream may be recaptured in waking moments; at the time I took account of them only dimly, and certainly did not think of death for a single moment— no merit in this, we are not responsible for what we do in dream or hypnosis. Suddenly at my left side my platoon sergeant, Livingston, dropped on one knee and looked up at me in a curious doubtful gaze. 'Come on, sergeant!' I said, stepping forward myself. He was killed, I think, the next instant; I never saw him again.

All this occurred within a few yards of crossing the road. I glanced right and left and saw the Platoon, thirty of them, crumple and fall, only two going on, widely apart, and no N.C.O. A few yards farther on I was nearly knocked down by a tremendous blow in the upper right arm and spun sideways; simultaneously the right hand unclenched and the Spandau rifle and bayonet fell to the ground. Even then no thought of death came, only some phrase like 'sledgehammer blow', from a serial read years before in a boys' magazine. Pain came the next moment; the spurious self-hypnotism vanished and gave way to an overwhelming desire to run, anywhere. Of three men—as I heard later—crouching wounded in a shell-hole that afternoon, one tried to keep the other two in safety, but they broke away and made a wild dash in no particular direction, both being killed by machine-gun fire within a few yards. I had the same wild wish, but it was crossed and quelled by the resurgent rhythm of the first impulse, so that I found myself walking on mechanically, yet wondering what I should do, disarmed now, if I reached Gird Trench. A second wound dismissed the question. As the right foot was coming to the ground a bullet passed through in front of the ankle and fractured the several tarsal bones. I crumpled and fell sideways to the right into a providential shell-hole, curling up like a hedgehog.

Sleeve sopping, boot oozing blood through the holes, I settled in as compactly as I could, lying back with head towards the enemy, tilting the shrapnel helmet in the direction of the bullets and waiting for the hours to pass. It was 2.23 p.m. summer time; the attack had begun only eight minutes before; firing could not be expected to cease before nightfall at least. The wounds, numb at first, soon throbbed recurrently. I drank very little water, reserving it for emergency. At one stage I wondered for a few seconds whether the arm-wound would affect the bowing of the violin, supposing I should ever get out of this; it seemed a foolish and unimportant thought. The hours seemed to pass very slowly; I wondered again whether any of us had reached Gird Trench— twelve had, to find it empty—and whether any officers were with them—there was one only, Cuthbert Parr; from the moment of going over the top I had not seen a single officer ahead of me. As I learned later in hospital in Chelsea, all the officers who had gone before, and all except Parr who had followed, had been killed or wounded; this, in the three companies. Bain, Howden,[4] Rallinshaw, and Captain Herbert were among the killed. Of the thirty-two in my platoon, five were killed outright, twenty-five were wounded, two remained unwounded at the end of the day.[5] A like proportion held in each of the twelve attacking platoons, and all those casualties must have been sustained in the first ten minutes. The communiqué, I remember, was terse, suggesting a successful advance; the front, it said—and it might be legally true—had been brought to a point in line with the east side of Eaucourt l'Abbaye. This might pass for home consumption; I should rather have put it that unimaginative staff work at some level had extinguished three companies. As usual, the German communiqué filled in with truth the censored evasions of our own: '. . . after the sanguinary repulse of the enemy attacks of September 27th, the Somme battle yesterday slackened considerably. . . .'

Bullets still hissed above my shell-hole, a raised hand would have been perforated at once; it was out of the question to think of crawling back. I saw the head and shoulders, and once or twice the hands also, of a field telephonist running forward from shell-hole to shell-hole and unrolling his wire; he was still unwounded as he drew level with my crater and passed behind me towards the front, but I fear he could not long have remained so.

Soon afterwards I was myself forced to move, by noticing amid the uproar a regularity, a periodicity, in a particular type of explosion. I watched carefully, and saw that shells from a 5·9 or 4·1 howitzer were coming closer every two minutes, apparently in a straight line. When first seen, their burst seemed close to the part of Goose Alley, perhaps 500 yards back, where we had emerged and strung out. I visualized the German gunners lowering their howitzers by a fraction of angle each time; I reckoned that in about ten minutes one of these shells would fall near my crater, possibly on it. Being blown to pieces or killed by blast seemed worse than the machine-guns. Using what cover I could, I crawled from my shell-hole over to our original right, now my left, out of the line of fire. This brought me in a few minutes to the Factory Corner road again, at a point some 200 yards to the original right of Goose Alley, which I could trace by its thrown-up earth at that distance down the road. It was a narrow country road with very little camber—even so slight a detail meant life or death at such a moment—and with a low bank eighteen inches high on the side towards Gird Trench; not much protection in itself, not enough even for explicit mention on the map, but enough for me. Under the lip of the bank was a fresh shallow crater. I fitted myself into it. The road here and the ground to either side were strewn with bodies, some motionless, some not. Cries and groans, prayers, imprecations, reached me. I leave it to the sensitive imagination; I once wrote it all down, only to discover that horror, truthfully described, weakens to the merely clinical. A few yards back from the road a man lay forward supported on his elbows, not letting his body touch ground; one could but surmise why he did this. He remains vivid, indissociable from the place. This was the Otago raid again, but by daylight and magnified. Yet there is something to be confessed. Under the strictest eye of truth, my sympathy for these men at that moment was abstract almost to vanishing-point. I deduced their pain, I knew I should feel it as grievous beyond measure; but I was still wholly mathematical, absorbed in the one problem, whether pairs of consecutive explosions of those howitzer shells showed the slightest difference in direction. It seemed to me that they did. Soon two successive bursts straddled the road. I could not raise my head to look, but judged that the later one must have landed very close to the shell-hole I had first occupied.

Relieved for the time being, I attended to things near at hand and saw—how had I failed to notice him earlier?—a man lying flat on his face almost within reach on the road, his eyes shut but his face twitching. I studied him; wounded in the arm, able to move elbows and knees. While I looked his eyes opened and looked back at me, but their gaze was unfocused; he was in a state of shock and fear. But suppose—I thought—suppose he could manage to crawl on his stomach under the lee of this slight bank as far as Goose Alley, then drop in, turn left, and make a dash for it! It was what I should have done in his place. I spoke peremptorily and ordered him to do this. 'No, no,' he almost gibbered, 'they nearly got me, they'll get me.' I threatened him; he was of another company but I knew his face. I said, 'You know me. When you get back, say that when last seen Mr. Aitken was on this road, but all right. Now, off you go!' He crawled five yards and flattened down quivering. He plucked up courage and crawled a few more; then after a while the same. I watched his disappearing heels. Down towards Goose Alley I lost him for some time in a hollow, then suddenly I saw him throw himself in, turn left, and run; his shrapnel helmet appeared for a moment flying past a gap farther down. The Germans had not yet begun to shell Goose

Alley as heavily as they did later; and I learned when I myself got in that he was safe and had delivered his message.

About 4 p.m. the sky clouded over and drizzle fell. I angled for a German waterproof sheet a yard away, and this, though riddled with bullet-holes, gave me some shelter. I did not have my own waterproof sheet, for at the former shell-hole I had discarded everything except my water-bottle and Fitt's binoculars, a present from New Zealand which held a personal sentiment for him. The rain was fortunately not heavy, the ground became wet and greasy but the craters did not fill with water. I had thought of crawling like that other man down the road to Goose Alley, but now a dense barrage of green-black shrapnel mixed with heavy shells fell on the junction of trench and road; the trench was in bad repair and the shrapnel swept it on enfilade. There was nothing for it but to wait until dark, when, if machine-gun fire should die down, I might hope to crawl back overland to somewhere near the starting-point of our attack, where the trench would be occupied by the 10th Company and would be in better repair. The distance would be about 500 yards.

As for the attack, I had long decided that it had failed, and had set it out arithmetically: twelve platoons of some thirty men each, say 360 to go across; probably 330 wounded or killed near this road; the rest have at the very least a further 400 yards to go and there is the unbroken wire protecting Gird Trench; also the exposed left flank, as open as a park from Eaucourt l'Abbaye. Add to all this the brief and perfunctory barrage. Thus when, many years after, I read in the official history of '3 companies of 1/Otago almost annihilated by shell-fire and streams of machine-gun bullets after reaching the forward slope beyond the Factory-Corner-Eaucourt l'Abbaye road', I had the feeling of a dream, known to me beforehand, in ancient times along that very road.*[6] But let us notice the objectivity of official accounts; one might almost

---

* A similar annihilation, under similar auspices but on a sevenfold scale, was virtually ordered a year later, on 12th Oct. 1917, at the Ravebeek stream, Passchendaele. Casualties: 100 officers, 2,635 other ranks.

suppose that those shells and bullets were an unexpected meteorological phenomenon, instead of having been foreseen hours before by everyone who took part.

About 8 p.m. the rain had stopped, the sky had cleared; in the dusk I could just distinguish our observation-balloons. The stars shone in a moonless night, the Great Bear swinging low with the Pole Star above. I turned my back on them, fixed south by other constellations and began the long crawl, leaving behind the water-bottle but hanging Fitt's binoculars (which I later returned to him in 1st London General Hospital, Camberwell) round my neck.

It was thus that I ended my active service, so slight, unimportant, and uneventful compared with that of hundreds of thousands of others who went through such things over and over again, who saw three or four years where I had seen less than one. From shell-hole to shell-hole I side-crawled on left elbow and knee; perhaps taking three or four hours—though I had ceased to consult the luminous wrist-watch, now daubed with mud. Many times I was tempted to curl up and wait for the stretcher-bearers, but I crawled the few yards farther, rested, and crawled again. The accurate memory that I have retained of my active service flags and blurs a little here, but at length I saw outlined, in black against the rain-washed night sky, the figures of two men on a mound, digging. I recognized them, Alf Ellis of my old section and Lou Mylchreest, a Manxman, also of the 10th Company, which had evidently come up from supplies to hold the line. Both men were killed next day.[7] I called 'Alf!' Instantly the figures vanished. Three or four minutes passed, and then I felt a prod in the rear with a bayonet, a foot pressed into the hollow of my back and 'Who's this? Speak!' 'Your old corporal, Alf,' I said; 'steady with that bayonet.' They bent down, recognized me, and returned to the trench for a stretcher; but all stretchers must have been in use. Here the picture fades still more, but since the next thing I remembered is the earthy parapet, I had evidently crawled the last fifteen yards. I fell in; suddenly I was back on the top of the hill at Hallencourt;[8] then much farther away, with an impression of something beautiful, music or the stars, perhaps the star Canopus, the warmer Sirius of the southern hemisphere.

An indefinite time later, after midnight, I came to and found myself propped up on a ledge cut in the side of the trench, no longer troubling to identify the constellations above; they had served their turn. My mind was at rest; the long responsibility had ended. Somewhere not far away was a soft Scottish voice, of David Sibbald, making me think for a moment of the hill Maungatua and the Taieri Plain, where my father had been born; Sibbald came from that part, and after Messines would not return. About 1 a.m. the regimental doctor, Captain Prior, M.C., his hands more than full even with the wounded who had been able to bring themselves in, bandaged the arm and foot; but stretcher-bearers had so much to do with more urgent cases that they could not come until just before daybreak. Several had already been killed at their stretcher-bearing. At length two came; one, felicitously, was K. C. Finlayson (8/918), who had shared the tarpaulin on deck with Frank Jones and me on the night of our leaving Gallipoli; the other was a man with a reddish moustache and the build of a farmer, a silent smiling man whom I had not seen before and whose name I never knew. But the memory of him is very clear to me, and will always be so. I do know, however, that both he and Finlayson were killed, no doubt at their stretcher-bearing, afterwards on that same day, the 28th.[9] As the first grey light began to drive away the stars they carried me, taking turn about at either end, so that I looked into the one face and then into the other, down Grove Alley and Flers Support trench to the advanced aid post in the bank by the track from Flers, then farther back to another post behind the crest of the High Wood ridge. Then stretcher and ambulance and hospital train took me far away from the guns, which I never heard again in the Great War.

Epilogue

T HE VIOLIN, WHICH I HAD IMAGINED LOST AT THE SOMME, CAME BACK
to me some eighteen months later in New Zealand. It had been
picked up, had trundled round with the Company field kitchens, and
must at various times have been near Messines and Ypres. Cuthbert
Parr, going on leave to London in 1918, had it packed for me by Hawkes
& Co., the music firm, and forwarded to Dunedin.

In 1952 Mr. H. P. Kidson, former Rector of the Otago Boys' High
School, visiting me in Edinburgh, took it back to New Zealand, and
presented it on my behalf to the school on 3rd August 1953, the nine-
tieth anniversary of the foundation. It now reposes in a glass case in
the front hall, with a suitably brief inscription. It will outlive me; but it
will be a reminder to all who see it, of the service and sacrifice of New
Zealanders in the First World War.

Appendix

LEMNOS, October, 1915.

J— and I have had leave to visit Castro, the ancient Myrina, a port on the west of the island. At 5.30 a.m. we put on our haversacks and set out across country. Soon we were in Arcadian scenes, translated away into the past. I saw those antiquated wooden ploughs, drawn by slow oxen, far more interesting to me now than when I read of them in Virgil. J— has a good sense of direction; we cut off several kilometres and emerged on the high road near Therma, where there are hot springs. After breakfasting there, we struck out briskly, making each 'borne kilometrique' in ten minutes or less, and reached Castro about 10 a.m. It is not a large nor an interesting place, some 10,000 odd people, perhaps. The boats in the harbour were all Aegean fishing smacks. We had dinner at a place where, on hearing our order, they ran out of the back of the shop to buy the necessary meat and vegetables, which they cooked while we waited impatiently. Then we examined the town. J—, a sometime student of Greek, found a bookshop (J— has a special 'flair' in that direction), and invested a few 'lepta' in books, one a kind of prayer book, one a 'penny horrible' translating for Greek boys the doings of 'Nat Pinkerton, Detective'; these he has posted to a professor of Greek in New Zealand.

In the afternoon we explored the citadel, the most interesting part. A high rock promontory divides a stretch of sandy coast into two curving bays. Steps have been cut up this rock, leading to a huge iron gate, studded with bolts. Through it we entered a steepish cutting, with numerous trap-doors to right and left and a well-shaft at the summit. Here was a plateau, a fort, with barracks and outbuildings, surrounded on the edge of the cliff by crenelated battlements. We climbed around these; at one part there is a shore platform two or three hundred feet below, where, doubtless, in mediaeval times, they hurled any enemy that had gained entrance. An old brass cannon reposes on a heap of round rusted cannon-balls, many of which have rolled down the cutting, and even to the base of the promontory. It was a clear day; to the south we saw other Aegean islands, wood-crowned, their coasts descending sheer to the sea. It has been well worth while to have a day free from camp surroundings.

GALLIPOLI, November, 1915.

The New Zealanders are back on the Peninsula again. On November 9th we marched from Sarpi to Mudros West, and embarked on that vile boat, the 'Osmanieh'. The usual wild rumours said we were bound for Salonika, but after dark we came near to a coast gleaming with lights, and across the calm waters sounded clearly the crackle of machine-gun fire, dying down every now and then into a silence pierced by a desultory shot. To the south a warship was firing; to the north the green line of lights and the red cross of a hospital ship undulated with the gentle swell. Old hands recognised the contours and pointed out this and that post; new hands said little, but were very thoughtful. A lighter came from the dark shore and received us, packed like sardines, on its bare iron deck. We headed shorewards and passed through a zone where dropping bullets kept 'plipping' into the water unpleasantly near. Landing at a pier, we marched around the beach to the left and up a valley, on the right side of which we 'dossed down' for the night.

LEMNOS, December, 1915.

The Peninsula is abandoned once and for all. There had been strange rumours. Fatigue parties sent to the beach had brought back word of great numbers of Australians embarking by night. It was thought that there was to be a period of training on Imbros, and a fresh landing at Suvla Bay. No one dreamed of an evacuation. On December 13th, before dark, the Battalion had sudden orders to pack; after dark we marched from our gulley down the long sap to the beach. There must have been a hitch in the embarking, for there were frequent halts, more tiring than continuous marching. We fell dozing during these halts, and were aroused afresh to go—ten yards, and another halt. Towards dawn it was plain that there was no embarking for us that night, and we had to hurry back up Waterfall Valley, where we spent the day, lying low and sleeping mostly. Next night we set out earlier; there was no hitch this time, and soon we were aboard a lighter and passing through that zone of 'plipping' bullets; two or three men were slightly wounded. A transport took us on board at midnight. The sea was choppy, and a bleak wind chilled us to the bone as we 'dossed down' on deck where we could. My bed was a tarpaulin that covered some angular pieces of coal. As dawn broke we were speeding past Imbros; it was now known that we had left the Peninsula finally. Soon that rugged coast was left far astern, and we looked our last on the land that was the grave of many a good comrade.

MOASCAR, February, 1916.

The desert here has witnessed a strange scene, the ceremony with which the First Maori Contingent greeted the coming of the Second. The latter was due to arrive one Saturday afternoon; the old Maoris prepared to give the newcomers a real tribal welcome. Between the foremost long row of tents that belongs to the several Battalion Headquarters of our Brigade and the slope of sand that forms this side of the railway cutting there is a strip of desert, a thoroughfare some hundred yards or more wide. Along it, from Ismailia, the column would arrive on the march. Half an hour before the appointed time the veterans, stripped to the waist and clad as in the days of 'pa' and 'taua', holding improvised 'meres', squatted in circle in the middle of this sandy road. A line of scouts at intervals, crouching on the alert, extended towards Ismailia. Himia, a well-known Maori, son of a chieftain, was the leading scout. He held a spear, which he was to let fall in the path of the strangers, as though to find out whether they were hostile or friendly; if hostile, they would pick it up in challenge; if friendly, they would pass over it. This was the make-believe, the gist of the ceremony. The Maoris entered fully into the spirit of it, and I think some of the old ancestral blood stirred in their veins.

A tenseness, as of an animal that sees prey, came over the scouts. In the distance a brown line came into view, from which rose like steam the clouds of fine sand from the marching feet. A wave of excitement passed from Himia through the scouts to the squatting party, but the silence was unbroken. Now we could see the faces of the new-comers, and could hear the soft swish of the sand as they marched. Himia threw down the spear and all the scouts leaped back several paces. The head of the column came to the weapon and passed over it. With a ringing shout up sprang the 'taua' and delivered a thunderous 'haka' of welcome.

All then sat down, and a Maori orator, advancing into the centre, addressed the new contingent in an impassioned speech. We 'pakeha' onlookers were not familiar with the tongue, but, from the pathos of his inflection and the effect of his words on his Maori audience, we knew that he was speaking of their brave dead on Gallipoli; we knew from the fire of his peroration that he was exhorting the strangers to emulate the glorious deeds of their Anzac brothers.

To this address a Maori chaplain replied, and the ceremonies continued with fresh 'hakas' and pantomime. The Brigadier spoke briefly to the contingent, his words being interpreted into Maori without hesitation by the orator who had first spoken. After this the First Contingent filed along the ranks of the Second, and every Maori of the one shook hands with every Maori of the other. Thus the assembly broke up. It was a memorable scene, framed as it was in the setting of an Egyptian desert; surely a splendid vindication of our Empire.

FRANCE, April, 1916.

We are in 'billets'. We had heard much of this 'billeting', and had fondly dreamed of being guests at private houses, no less. The vanity of human wishes! This is a barn; it has a high thatched roof, and there are holes in the walls. A path, bounded on each side by a breast-high partition wall, divides it into two compartments, in which we are stabled in straw.

We have had a slight encounter with 'Madame', who owns the barn. There was not enough straw for all, and some had recourse to a little stack that seemed to be going to waste. 'Madame' observed this, and, reinforced by another Flemish lady, bore down on us. It was after nine o'clock, and we were disrobing for sleep, in the dim light of candles, when those who could be put to confusion were put to confusion by the sound of excited female voices and the sight of two angry dames leaning over our partition. I caught the word 'paille' and understood their grievance. No one else knew any French, and someone had to speak in the defence. Accordingly I arose from the straw, draped in a blanket, and addressed to them a few soothing words of the most suave and courteous French I could muster up at the moment. They seemed quite surprised, and, after a short dialogue between themselves, left us to our slumbers.

ARMENTIÈRES, June, 1916.

What a peaceful morning after the night! This nightly programme becomes wearing. There are raids sometimes, and bombardments always. Often, at any late hour, the dark outlines of the town behind us, indistinguishable from the horizon, spring suddenly into sharp silhouette in the light of many white flashes; in a few moments follow the scream of shells passing overhead, and the rumble of the guns that have sent them. We have begun a bombardment. The din increases as the Germans retaliate, and the darkness leaps with the distant white flashes of the guns, and the nearer red ones of the bursting shells. Flare-rockets draw white parabolas against the black sky, and, drooping at their highest like slender flower-stems, bloom into flame. Constantly we hear the 'crump, crump!' of the heavy shells, and the terrific rending reports of the 'minenwerfers' bombs. Gas is sometimes discharged by either side; it is a hateful time when the wind blows gently from the east, for then we must be on the alert with eyes, ear, and nose—eyes for prowling enemy patrols, ears for the hiss of gas escaping from pressure cylinders, and nose for its acrid smell. Sometimes an alarm comes from a flank, and the night is made hideous with the long-drawn doleful hoots of 'stromboshorns', the tapping and clanging of the suspended shell-cases that serve as gongs, and the tolling of bells in the town.

But this is a peaceful Sunday morning. How beautiful the country must be away from the line! Even here Nature is trying to cover the wounds of the Earth. Long, luxuriant creepers, trailing golden flowers, overgrow the winding saps and spangle the ground between our trench-lines; tall grass conceals the rusty and unsightly entanglements of our rear defences; dark red poppies bloom in the wire of No Man's Land. In the gardens of ruined houses there are flowers amid the weeds and blossoms on the unpruned fruit-trees. A delicate blue haze softens everything, like a veil of gossamer. Through this haze comes the faint tolling of church bells, memory-compelling. But at intervals a German battery is firing single shots and salvoes into the outskirts of the town. What poets! kultur!

WARDRECQUES, August, 1916.

We have left Armentières and are bound for some offensive. Some suppose that we are to take part in the Somme Battle, others that we are to begin a new offensive between Ypres and Armentières. This village is some miles from St. Omer. It is on high ground; south-eastward we look across the plain of the Lys toward Neuve Chapelle and Bethune.

On clear days the observation balloons are visible as faint black dots, and by night we hear the dull rumble of the guns and see the flashes. There are many fields of crops here, over-ripe and standing uncut for lack of reapers. A military order has said that wherever possible we are to assist the French to cut their crops, but how can we if bayonet-drill occupies us all day?

CITERNES, August, 1916.

We are at a small village, inland from Abbeville, and south of the Somme. It seems plain that we are going to take part in the Somme offensive. We marched from Wardrecques to Arques, near St. Omer, entrained there and arrived at Abbeville late at night. After a short rest in a field we set out again about midnight, and after a most exhausting march reached this village between six and seven o'clock in the morning. Our billets are in the usual barns and deserted buildings.

There is an old-world feeling in this village that I have not noticed to such a degree in any other. One would think it had strayed long ago from bustling highways and had lost its way in this secluded forest. From here the plain falls gently to a railway that is a violent anachronism, and rises as gently to other villages in their clumps of trees. There is many a droning old windmill; at the cross-roads, many a crucifix. This then is Picardy. I prefer it to Flanders. There it was all flat plain, dotted with many villages clustered sociably together. It was beautiful, but with a homely kind of beauty that seemed more like what we imagine Holland to be than France. Picardy is different. It is rolling country here, and the villages, besides being widely separated, have quite a distinct character. They remind one of those castles of romance, charmed to sleep for a hundred years; alone of all wakeful, the tall church spire stands sentinel above the trees and keeps watch over the wide landscape, but nods drowsily itself the while.

At night I went up to the high ground toward Hallencourt, and looked eastward. There was no sound, but on the dark horizon a single flash winked like a beacon-light, and again, after an interval, and again. The sleepless guns were sending death.

COISY, September, 1916.

We are much nearer the line. Today we passed Amiens on the right. The Cathedral towers high above the town. My bed tonight is to be a table in a deserted shop. As dusk fell, I stood in an apple-garden with an old Frenchman, the only man I saw in the village, listening to the guns. The noise is not quite like thunder; rather is it like the boom of rollers on a long beach, even and continuous, except where a louder burst than the rest stabs the smooth curtain of sound like a sword-blade. It continually suggests new visual images; now it is a plain of sound, with pinnacles. Tonight it is rising high, like a storm on a coast; there must be an attack there. The old Frenchman listened with me, but all he could say, in his Picard dialect, was 'la guerre! ke malheur! ke malheur!' We have all become serious; none can escape from the reminder of that sound. But the suspense will not be long; we are marching on every day, and soon shall be in the thick of whatever hell it is.

Otago University Review, October 1918, pp. 47–51.

Editor's Notes

Introduction

1 Aitken's fullest account of his reconstruction of the missing platoon book is in a letter of autobiography to R. P. Kania, quoted in ch. 16, note 5.

2 'Intolerably nameless names': from Siegfried Sassoon's sonnet 'On Passing the New Menin Gate' (1927), which derides the Memorial to the Missing at Ypres as a 'pile of peace-complacent stone'.

3 Alexander Aitken, *To Catch the Spirit*, ed. Peter Fenton, Dunedin: University of Otago Press, 1995, p. 103.

4 Alexander Aitken to Jean Morris, 8 December 1945. Misc-MS-0900, Hocken Library.

5 Winifred Aitken to H. P. Kidson, 24 April 1967. MS-0690/001, Hocken Library.

6 Winifred Aitken to Derek Hudson, 3 January 1963. PB/ED/008476, Box OP 1146, Oxford University Press Archives.

7 Alexander Aitken to R. P. Kania, 23 May 1956. MS-0690/002, Hocken Library.

8 Peter Fenton, 'Biographical Introduction', in Aitken, *To Catch the Spirit*, p. 42.

9 Winifred Aitken to Derek Hudson, 3 January 1963 (see note 6).

10 'He once told my wife that for seventy-five per cent of his time he was thinking of music. He must have employed the other twenty-five per cent to very great purpose.' Letter from E. T. Compson to Arthur Erdélyi, 8 November 1965, in R. Schlapp (ed.), 'Obituary: A. C. Aitken, D.Sc. F.R.S.', *Proceedings of the Edinburgh Mathematical Society*, 16 (1968–69), p. 156 (151–76).

11 Sarah Shieff, 'Time out of Mind: Musical Patterning and Retrospective Coherence in Alexander Aitken's *Gallipoli to the Somme.' Journal of New Zealand Literature*, 33 (2015), pp. 124–41.

12 Alexander Aitken to Les Aitken, 17 June 1946. MS-0690/002, Hocken Library.

13 From an address to the Educational Institute of Scotland, Mathematics Section, 'Some Further Observations on Arithmetic', 27 November 1948. MS-2484, Hocken Library.

14 Winifred Aitken to H. P. Kidson, 24 April 1967 (see note 5).

15 Paul Fussell, *The Great War and Modern Memory* (Oxford University Press, 2013; 1st edn 1975), p. 8.

16 Cited ibid., p. 31.

17 According to Fussell, the major impact of the Great War on modern memory has been the way those who write about it filter the past through paradigms of ironic action. 'A slaughter by itself is too commonplace for notice. When it makes an ironic point, it becomes memorable' (ibid., p. 33).

18 In Hugh Sebag-Montefiore's *Somme: Into the Breach* (London: Viking, 2016), the chapter covering the New Zealand contribution is entitled 'Bloodlust'. While war crimes were certainly committed by individual New Zealand soldiers (Starkie in *Passport to Hell* among them), one would need more evidence before concluding that our troops had a worse record than comparable units such as the Australians

or Canadians, who, like the New Zealanders, were regularly used to spearhead an attack.

19 L. M. L Hunter, 'An Exceptional Talent for Calculative Thinking', *British Journal of Psychology*, 53 (1962), 243–58. Other details in this paragraph are taken from 'As Fast as Thought', a transcript of a BBC Radio programme hosted by Bertram Bowden, with guests Prof. Alexander Aitken, Mr Wim Klein and Sir Cyril Burt. Recorded 6 Oct. 1954; broadcast 29 Oct. 1954.

20 For details of Aitken's career as a schoolmaster, I am indebted to Fenton, pp. 55–57 (see note 8).

21 J. M. Whittaker, 'Aitken, Alexander Craig (1895–1967), rev. Anita McConnell, *Oxford Dictionary of National Biography* online edn (Oxford University Press, 2004–). McConnell's revised entry contains an error serious enough for me to remain uncertain about the Bletchley connection until firmer evidence appears (she wrongly states that Aitken was awarded the Hawthornden prize in 1963).

22 Christopher Smith, *The Hidden History of Bletchley Park* (London: Palgrave 2015). Aitken's name appears in a table of personnel as a 'Foreign Office Civilian working in Hut 6' (p. 178).

23 'I have very little leisure, being a statistical adviser to the East of Scotland College of Agriculture, which involves analysing experimental results in many fields and suggesting design and lay-out for future experiments. It is very interesting work, and involves much more theoretical mathematics than might be supposed'. Alexander Aitken to Les Aitken, 6 November 1943. MS-2477, Hocken Library.

24 Winifred Aitken to Arthur Erdélyi, 28 November 1963. E2005.24, Alexander Aitken Papers, University of Edinburgh Library.

25 The notebooks are in the Hocken Library, MS-0717. See Illustration 1b for the first page. Rather than use the library identification number, I will refer to them in the editorial notes as the 1961 notebooks or MS-1961. Winifred explained the old title in a letter to Alec's brother, Les Aitken, 1 April 1963: 'We had put as the title "An Anzac Remembers", because it is partly a great feat of memory, but when we saw in the Radio Times announcements of items such as "Bud Flanagan Remembers" and numerous other ". . . Remembers" we realized that the title was quite unsuitable, as OUP agreed. I suggested several alternatives & they selected "Gallipoli to the Somme".' E2005.24 Alexander Aitken Papers, University of Edinburgh Library.

26 Winifred Aitken to Arthur Erdélyi, 28 November 1963 (see note 24).

27 Davin gives an account of his meeting with Fergusson in a letter to the Secretary of the Clarendon Press, 24 May 1963. PB/ED/008476, Box OP 1146, Oxford University Press Archives.

28 A. J. P. Taylor, *Observer*, 'Books of the Year' column, December 1963. Cuttings of this and other book reviews cited are preserved in E2005.24, Alexander Aitken Papers, University of Edinburgh Library (the cuttings usually have a date but no pagination).

29 Sir John Elliot, 'Frontline Fighter', *Daily Telegraph*, 15 November 1963.

30 Cecil Malthus, *Armentières and the Somme* (Auckland: Reed, 2002), p. 16.

31 Back cover blurb, *Somme: Into the Breach*. I should point out that Sebag-Montefiore's book is one of the few general military histories of the Somme published in the centenary year to extensively incorporate the perspectives of Canadian, Australian, and New Zealand combatants—including Aitken. But I sense the tide is turning

against the revisionists. Peter Barton's impressive television documentary, *The Somme* 1916: *From Both Sides of the Wire* (BBC, 2016), for example, concludes that while the Allies eventually achieved most of their objectives, they did so at such cost that the battle must be regarded as a German defensive victory.

32 'A Tribute from Major-General Sir A. H. Russell, K.C.B., K.C.M.G.' In A. E. Byrne, *Official History of the Otago Regiment, N.Z.E.F. in the Great War* 1914–1918 (Dunedin: J. Wilkie & Co., 1921) pp. iii–iv.

33 Anon., *Church Times,* Review of *Gallipoli to the Somme,* 25 October 1963.

34 Anon., 'Lest We Forget', *Times Educational Supplement,* 18 October 1963.

35 Lorna Rhind, 'Figures Come Easy to Edinburgh Professor', *Evening Dispatch,* Edinburgh, 8 May 1948, p. 3.

36 Letter to Sidney Newman, 4 August 1941. E2005.24, Alexander Aitken Papers, University of Edinburgh Library.

37 Letter to Sidney Newman, 19 April 1950. E2005.24, Alexander Aitken Papers, University of Edinburgh Library.

1 Egypt to Lemnos

1 Those 'first six weeks': the first of Aitken's 1961 MS notebooks concludes with 'Some Notes, for Recollection Only'—these include a section on the voyage on the *Willochra*.

> Left Wellington, 14th August 1915. On morning of 15th the ship's band saluted the vanishing *Farewell Spit.*
>
> Flinders Island in Bass Strait, about 21st August.
>
> The whales and the molly- mawks.
>
> Albany in Western Australia about 28th August.
>
> A great storm, two days out from Cape Leeuwin; the companion vessel, S.S. *Tofua,* lost for several hours. No one on deck for a day and a half.
>
> Flying fish appear; we enter the warm waters of the Indian Ocean.
>
> The violin is raffled, and R. J. Maunsell draws the lucky ticket. H. L. Smith the journalist is in our cabin.
>
> Indian Ocean. On guard in full kit on a still sultry night. During some late watch I see the Southern Cross sprawled on the rim of the ocean, like the mast and spars of a foundered ship.
>
> Evening 11th September. A glimpse, in rusty sunset, of a high coast to the west; rumoured to be Cape Guardafui, on the eastern horn of Africa.
>
> Midnight, 12th September. Must have infringed some rule in running into Aden. A concentration of searchlights turned on us, and a shot fired across our bows.
>
> 13th September. Wakened at an early hour by Arab voices and the splash of oars through the porthole. Arabs have rowed out from Aden to sell cigarettes,

trinkets, silks, pomegranates, which they throw up on lassoos. Deafening babel and, at first, great over-charging. They soon row back.

No shore leave. We are mile or two out from the Rock. Near us there rises a tall yellow fang, sheer out of the sea, a sun-stricken, shadowless and birdless rock, like nothing on earth; aorian, a landscape from Mercury.

14th September. We enter the Red Sea, seeing numberless fish below us. We pass Perim. The heat in the Red Sea. A photograph is taken, under awnings (which we have had since entering the Indian Ocean), of a group of men from Otago University. On being printed it looks as if taken in blazing sunlight. All brass on deck burns the touch.

The sea in places is indeed red, from holding countless millions of infusoria.

We pass very close to the chocolate-coloured cliffs of the Sinai Peninsula, and are now in the Gulf of Suez.

19th September. We draw up at the quay, Suez. A motley crowd on the quay, from light brown, in flowing garments, to Nubian black and pure nakedness. An old man, rather like an orangutang, dives for coins. A policeman in tarboosh every now and then makes spasmodic rushes at no one in particular, laying about him with his baton; this must be purely to keep up prestige. All this time the train is drawn up at the station opposite, but it is hours before we go across to it. Meanwhile, in the early afternoon, wounded and invalided from Gallipoli are brought on board, but they are obviously nerveless and exhausted, and not disposed to talk of their experiences; so we leave them alone. One tells me just a little about the August advance, and the topography of Anzac. The train sets off late in the afternoon, about 17.00. I lean with my back to the partition between two compartments, playing on the violin and watching the attentive faces in the haze of cigarette smoke; the two Arthurs, Moreton and others destined to die at Armentières, the Somme or Passchendaele. Outside, in falling dark, an Arab is seen toiling home with his camel. The lights of Cairo after midnight, warm and soft on the gardens of residential suburbs. At 2 a.m. the snappy voice of a staff officer, doubtless grudging his sleep. We have reached the sandy camp of Ezbet-el-Zeitoun, and settle into the long huts. It is the early morning of 20th September, five weeks and two days since we marched out of Trentham.

2   *Tectis bipatentibus*: see *Aeneid* 10:5. The Council of the Gods meets to consider the war between the Trojans and the Italians in 'a hall with doors open at each end' —like an army hut, but more splendid. Aitken knew Virgil's epic poem by heart.

3   Yashmak: a veil worn by Muslim women, leaving the eyes exposed.

4   Robin Hyde gives an account of the brothels of Cairo in *Passport to Hell*, pp. 87–103.

5   Aitken's MS wording, 'both feet', is more accurate. According to his medical notes, Singleton 'lost toes both feet' in the accident.

6   12th October 1917: at Passchendaele, in the space of a few hours, 846 New Zealand soldiers were killed and 3,000 wounded in an attack on Bellevue Spur, heavily defended by German pillboxes, machine guns, and uncut wire. It remains New Zealand's worst military disaster.

7 Alexander Kinglake's impressions of the Pyramids are in Chapter 19 of *Eothen*
   (1844). Aitken left an account of his own visit to the Pyramids in 'Some Notes,
   for Recollection Only' (MS-1961). These are more fully composed than the notes on
   the voyage and were probably cut from an earlier version.

   > On the 22nd, I think it was, Frank Tucker, having leave from 11.00 until a
   > guard at 17.00, came and proposed a visit to the Pyramids. (I had met him at
   > Trentham, over a coffee and pie in a canteen; an excellent pianist, playing early
   > Beethoven sonatas on a piano in the Y.M.C.A. hut.) We began to walk across
   > towards Helmieh, when an Egyptian, Mohammed, rose from the sand as if he
   > had known our intention, offered to be a guide to the Pyramids, would pay all
   > expenses and make a reasonable charge for himself later on. We fell in with
   > this simple plan, and he took us across Cairo, north to southwest, it must be
   > at least 12 miles. We lunched, sipping iced pomegranade, at a Café or Hôtel
   > des Pyramides, in sight of them, then proceeded to the Pyramids of Cheops,
   > pestered on the way by a rabble offering to hire out camels or donkeys, to sell
   > statuettes of the Pyramids or Sphinx, or to tell our fortunes. Mohammed
   > dispelled them with apt words. He handed us over to a special guide, a tall
   > one-eyed and ill-featured Arab. This one took us up the steps—where another
   > rabble called for us to take off our boots, and led us into the interior, down the
   > first sloping tunnel. The surface is worn and slippery and it would have been
   > well to take off our boots. He led us spirally upward, and from time to time lit
   > a piece of magnesium wire at the entrance of some King's or Queen's chamber,
   > toward which he waved a vague hand. It was intolerably hot and stifling;
   > his one eye looked more and more malevolent in the glare of the magnesium.
   > At length Frank touched him on the sleeve and indicated that we had seen
   > enough and were satisfied; and so we descended and came out, never so glad
   > to see the blue sky and breathe unpolluted air.
   >   Money passed between this ill-favoured guide and our own urbane
   > Mohammed, who next took us to the Sphinx, then being excavated among
   > its foundations; indicated the smaller pyramids of Sakhara on the other side
   > of the Nile, spoke of the flat-boats which had brought stone for the Pyramids
   > from 560 miles up Nile (I think he said), perhaps somewhere about Wady
   > Halfa; showed some sort of temple with a monkey-statue of shiny black
   > marble; and an account of it which we both failed to understand; and so back
   > to the tram terminus, parting from us somewhere in mid-Cairo. I think all this
   > cost no more than five or six shillings.
   >   For me all this threw much light on Kinglake's description in *Eothen*, of how
   > he had similarly 'seen the Pyramids' in 1835.

8 Melrose Abbey is a picturesque ruin in the Scottish Borders; Aitken is recalling
   Sir Walter Scott's lines: 'If thou wouldst view fair Melrose aright / Go visit it by the
   pale moonlight.'

9 Sand colic is caused by the ingestion of sand with food.

10 The places named in this sentence are now known as: Banha, Tanta, and Lake
   Mariout.

11 Number Nine pill: a laxative indiscriminately handed out by medical officers (hence
   the Bingo call: doctor's orders, number nine).

12 The charming melody of Dvorak's 'Humoresque' Op. 101, no. 7 in G-flat major, originally for piano, became well known in arrangements for violin. A columnist in *Etude* (August 1910) captures the appeal of this short piece: 'it is used in recitals by the world's greatest violinists, and never fails to make a telling hit with even the most uncultured audience'.

13 Maxwell was General Officer Commanding British Troops in Egypt. He later gained notoriety as the military governor who ordered the executions after the 1916 Easter Rising in Ireland.

14 The Sari Bair offensive of early August 1915, which included the capture, defence, and eventual loss of the heights at Chunuk Bair, was followed later in the month by an assault on Hill 60. Around 42 per cent of all NZEF deaths at Gallipoli occurred in that one month, most in the failed attacks. 1,124 deaths are recorded for August, compared with 54 in November and 51 in December, the months of Aitken's active service on the peninsula. Pugsley, *Gallipoli: The New Zealand Story*, p. 363.

15 Brobdignagian: of colossal size. Lilliputian: tiny, miniature. Both adjectives are derived from places visited in Jonathan Swift's *Gullliver's Travels*.

16 O.C.: Officer Commanding.

17 Those landing on Gallipoli with the Main Body up to and including the Fifth Reinforcements numbered 12,256—of which 900 returned to the camp on Lemnos. Pugsley, *Gallipoli: The New Zealand Story*, p. 327.

18 N.C.O.: non-commissioned officer. A Company of about 250 men would normally have had eight sergeants (senior N.C.O.s), two per platoon.

19 Sir Ian Hamilton was Commander-in-Chief of the Mediterranean Expeditionary Force. His dispatches to the War Office were published as supplements to *The London Gazette* during 1915–16. Aspinall-Oglander's two-volume official history, *Military Operations: Gallipoli,* appeared in 1929 and 1932. Neither of these works is as critical as C. E. W. Bean's Gallipoli volumes of the Australian *Official History* (1921, 1924)—works Aitken seems not to have encountered. John Masefield's *Gallipoli* (1916), by contrast, is exculpatory propaganda. It is written as if Masefield had first-hand knowledge of the campaign, but the future poet-laureate was merely putting the results of an inquiry into lively prose. A sample of his excerpts from *The Song of Roland* reads: 'Then said Roland, "Oliver companion . . . we shall have a strong and tough battle, such as man never saw fought. But I shall strike with my sword, and you, comrade, shall strike with yours."'

20 Mustafa Kemal was the resolute front-line commander of the Turkish 19th Division at Gallipoli. He became first president of the Republic of Turkey.

21 Like Tennyson's 'Charge of the Light Brigade' (1854), G. K. Chesterton's 'Lepanto' (1911) celebrates feats of arms in a bombastic style.

22 The Hellespont is an older name for the Dardanelles, the narrow strait dividing the Gallipoli Peninsula from mainland Turkey, swum in legend by Leander to meet his lover Hero, and by Lord Byron in 1810 to prove it could be done. Ancient Troy is on the Turkish coast at Hisarlik, close to the southern entrance to the Dardanelles. Cape Helles is at the northern entrance; Suvla Bay and Anzac are further up the coast. Samothrace, Tenedos (Bozcaada) and Imbros (Gökçeada) are offshore islands.

23 One furlong is about 200 metres.

2   Lemnos: Sarpi, Kastro

1   Aitken was on Lemnos from 29 September until 9 November 1915.
2   The monastery is in the village of Tsimandria. At Mount Athos, women are still barred from visiting the twenty monasteries of the peninsula. A tenth-century edict also bars female animals (a prohibition long since ignored by the cats of the district).
3   Picket: sentry duty.
4   The second of Holst's '4 Songs, for voice and violin' (Op. 35, no. 2) was composed in 1917 and features a spare, drone-like accompaniment in the Phrygian mode— i.e. using the white notes from E to E on a keyboard.
5   Hagios or Ayios: either word means 'saint' when used as the preface to a name.
6   Boreas: god of the North Wind in Greek mythology.
7   Pelasgic: Pelasgians were the pre-Hellenic indigenous inhabitants of the Aegean islands and parts of mainland Greece.
8   *Koniak*: the local brandy.
9   'Nuts in May' is a variant of 'Here we go round the mulberry bush'. The call, 'Who will you have for nuts in May, nuts in May?' is followed by the response: 'We'll have (name) for nuts in May, nuts in May', each chorus concluding with the line 'On a cold and frosty morning'.
10   O. A. S. envelope: a standard military envelope with the heading, 'On Active Service'.
11   The poet Rupert Brooke died of blood poisoning in April 1915 en route to Gallipoli.
12   J. 'Cicero' Johnston: a list of former Otago University students on active service up to February 1916 offers two possible identifications. One is A. T. Johnston 24/480, the other is John Johnson, 8/2630. The latter is clearly 'Cicero'. In 'Notes on the 'Varsity in Egypt', published in the *Otago University Review*, October 1916, Sergeant Ewan Pilling recalls meeting his fellow students after the Gallipoli evacuation. 'One saw many 'Varsity faces. There was "Swotty" Aitken, whom one always pictures with a battered violin, which he has carried over the fields of Lemnos, up the gullies of Gallipoli, and over the sands of Egypt. Perhaps you might see a disgracefully untidy sentry slouching along on his beat. Look closer and you will recognise the bony form and features of "Cicero" Johnstone, M.A.'
13   Aitken's reference to Elgar's visit to Lemnos tells us a little about the compositional layers of the book and casts a sidelight on the author's memory. Elgar visited Mudros briefly on 23 September 1905, while on a cruise. In his travel diary, he mentions expecting a telegram which, to his relief, 'came from Kistro, eight miles on a donkey' (p. 151). Extracts from the diary first appeared in an edition of *Letters and Other Writings* in 1956. In the 1961 notebooks, Aitken has correctly recalled the misspelling of Kistro, but has conflated the story of the donkey with the composer's visit ashore at Mudros.
14   See 'Scraps from a Diary, 1915–16' (Appendix) for Aitken's original 1917 account of the visit to Kastro. It is notable for the absence of the many classical allusions Aitken incorporates in subsequent versions. As Tim Leadbeater (2014) has suggested, Aitken's memory is busily fetching information from his store of classical and musical knowledge, while warding off the more difficult recollections of Gallipoli to come.

15 Virgil gives instructions on ploughs and ploughing in the *Georgics*—his poem about farming.

16 For *Morgenstimmung*: for a morning mood. The 'Hunter's Chorus' from Carl Maria von Weber's *Der Freischütz* has the 'valderi! valdera!' qualities of a good hiking song.

17 The map is plate 89 of Ortelius's *Theatrum Orbis Terrarum* (London, 1606). MS-1961 includes a further sentence: 'The Maoris imagine that the hot springs and fumaroles of Rotorua have been caused by fire-bolts flung to the mainland by the goddess of fire on White Island. Even so it was pleasant to imagine . . .'

18 Milton, *Paradise Lost*, Book 1, 744–45. Milton tells us that Mulciber is the name the Ausonians (Italians) knew Satan by. Aitken then notes the parallel fate of Hephaestus, god of metallurgy, who was thrown down from heaven by Zeus, also to land on Lemnos. The village of Haephaistos is associated with his cult.

19 Myrina is the more common name for the town, with Kastro designating the castle or citadel that Aitken describes later. The two names have often been used interchangeably.

20 Mons Meg: a large medieval siege cannon on display at Edinburgh Castle.

21 'Wine-dark sea': an epithet associated with Homer.

22 The island is now commonly known as Agios Efstratios.

23 Since Chryse disappeared beneath the waves much as Atlantis did, the map would have had to have been very ancient.

24 Saint Eustratios—the name means straight path—was an abbot who was exiled to the island in the ninth century. Aitken has been remembering arcane points about Lemnos; he now anticipates finding more such information to remember at a future date. Again, we sense the memoirist's reluctance to leave this time and place for Gallipoli.

25 The 'great blizzard' took place 27–28 November 1915.

26 Godley was a British officer appointed by the New Zealand government before the war to organize and train the nation's army. He went on to command the New Zealand Expeditionary Force and the Second Anzac Corps.

27 The Battle of Loos, the so-called 'big push' of September 1915, was an attempt to break through the German trench system. Combined Allied casualties approached a quarter of a million for little gain.

3 Lemnos to Gallipoli

1 See 'Scraps from a Diary' for his 1917 account of the departure from Lemnos and the arrival at Gallipoli.

2 For these and other Gallipoli place-names, see the interactive 'Gallipoli Places Map' maintained by the New Zealand Ministry for Culture and Heritage. It has glosses as well as informative photographic views taken from many locations of interest. https://nzhistory.govt.nz/map/gallipoli-places-map

3 Vermiculations: worm-like lines.

4 Bauchop's Hill was taken by the Canterbury and Otago Mounted Rifles on 7 August. Along with Table Top and Destroyer's Hill, it was one of the key foothills captured early in the August offensive, clearing the way for the attack on Chunuk

Bair the next day. It is named after the Commanding Officer of the Otago Mounted Rifles who was mortally wounded in the attack.

5   The dying man was Private Kenneth McDonald, 10/1891.

6   For a view from a point near Aitken's location, see the 360-degree photographic panorama from Table Top on the interactive 'Gallipoli Places Map' (see note 2 above). Aitken is in fact looking seaward from the Apex, further up from Table Top, not far below the summit of Chunuk Bair, and to the right of Farm Cemetery. The panorama taken from Chunuk Bair is also informative, as Farm Cemetery is visible from the summit, but the Apex is hidden from view. For views of Imbros and Samothrace, see the panoramas taken from Walker's Ridge or Ari Burnu Point.

7   In the *Iliad*, Poseidon watches the Trojan War unfold from the heights of Samothrace. Kinglake had thought Homer guilty of a geographical infelicity until he himself looked westward from the ostensible site of the Greek camp. He writes: 'I knew that Homer had PASSED ALONG HERE, that this vision of Samothrace over-towering the nearer island was common to him and to me' (*Eothen*, ch. 4).

8   British troops landed at Suvla Bay on 7 August in support of a planned breakout from the Anzac bridgehead towards the Sari Bair ridge. The poorly led British units ought to have secured the lightly defended Tekke Tepe hills quickly, but dithered until the 9th, by which time the Turks (the term Aitken uses in referring to troops of the Ottoman Empire) had sent in reinforcements. Their failure to secure these heights made the hand-hold gained by the Wellington Battalion at Chunuk Bair untenable. The implication, developed later in this chapter, is that had the Anzacs not been let down, they would have secured the high ground, and Churchill's plan of rolling forward to Constantinople might have become practicable. It would be more accurate to say that the campaign was doomed from the start. As so often in the Great War, military planners underestimated the tactical difficulties of attacking entrenched positions defended with machine-guns and wire, and were apt to overestimate the strategic significance of an advance. Even had Chunuk Bair been held, the Allies had no large guns to put there, and would have faced a difficult fight through to the Narrows. The Turks, controlling the heights since the landings, had for months failed in their attempts to drive the invaders into the sea; had the positions been reversed, another stalemate would in all likelihood have ensued.

9   Fire-step: a ledge running a couple of feet above the trench floor, from which soldiers can fire through or over the parapet.

10 C.S.M: Company Sergeant-Major; Ship's SM: Ship's Sergeant-Major. Brodie was killed on 24 November 1915.

11 There were indeed drownings in the flash-floods that rushed down the deres to the lower trenches. From the 29th Division, Captain R. Gee of the 2nd Royal Fusiliers reports: 'Within half an hour the trenches had a foot of water running so quickly that it was difficult to stand. At 7 pm the Barricade gave way and a solid wall of water 7 ft high swept the trench carrying everything and everyone before it . . . . To add to our comforts it began to freeze hard and a snow blizzard came down and the whole of the place was soon covered by snow; many of the survivors of the flood died from exposure. With the help of the Sgt Major I counted the Company and of the 139, only 69 remained'. By the 30th, his Company's strength was down to 27. National Archives [Ref CAB 43/224].

12   Aspinall-Oglander's account of the Suvla Landings emphasizes muddle and confu-
      sion. The footnote Aitken has in mind is drawn from an eyewitness report and
      reads: 'A peaceful scene greeted us. Hardly any shells. No Turks. Very occasional
      musketry. Bathing parties round the shore. An entire absence of the expected bustle
      of a great disembarkation. There seemed to be no realization of the overwhelming
      necessity for a rapid offensive, or the tremendous issues depending on the next few
      hours' (vol. 2, p. 277).

13   Aitken's view of the August offensive was widely shared by Anzac veterans who
      knew nothing more could have been asked of their comrades who had fought
      superbly at places like Lone Pine and Chunuk Bair. Later, in the 1980s, the notion
      that incompetent British generals far from the action were responsible for the
      failures at Gallipoli became an orthodoxy with the popular success of Peter Weir's
      Gallipoli (1981) and Maurice Shadbolt's *Once on Chunuk Bair* (1982). While this view
      is not without foundation, the scapegoating assists a sentimentally redemptive
      'birth of a nation' interpretation of the sacrifice made by our soldiers. Among the
      many factors contributing to the failure of the Sari Bair offensive, military historians
      have identified faults in the time-tabling and coherence of the Anzac plan, as well
      as poor judgement by several senior Anzac staff, including Colonel F. E. Johnston,
      the commander of the New Zealand Infantry Brigade, who had inadvertently made
      himself drunk by sipping water laced with rum.

14   The Farm, a flat plateau just below the ridge of Chunuk Bair, was then a portion
      of no-man's-land overlooked by New Zealand machine-guns at the Apex. It had
      earlier been the scene of the some of the heaviest fighting in the August campaign.
      The position was originally taken by a Gurkha regiment, then held by British and
      some Maori troops. At dawn on 10 August, before a strong defensive position
      could be established, a massive counter-attack led by Mustafa Kemal swept over
      the summit and overran the area. Casualties were so high the Turks were unable to
      consolidate the position and withdrew to Chunuk Bair.

15   Latin phrases often appearing as military epitaphs. Henry Newbolt's poem 'Clifton
      Chapel' (1908) ends with the words, 'Qui ante diem perit / Sed miles, sed pro
      patria'—'who died before his time, but a soldier, but for his country'. The line 'Dulce
      et decorum est pro patria mori'—'it is sweet and fitting to die for one's country'—
      is from Horace (and used ironically in Wilfred Owen's well-known poem of that
      title).

16   Owing to Bulgaria's entry into the war in September 1915, the Turkish Army
      could be directly supplied with advanced new weaponry brought in by train
      from Germany.

17   H.E. Shelters: high-explosive shelters.

18   Parados: a defensive mound of earth (or sandbags) above the rear wall of a trench.

19   Either man's shot may have killed, wounded, or missed the enemy soldier.
      The three fatal possibilities are a kill and a kill, a wound and a kill, a miss and a kill.

20   Louis Raemakers: a Dutch propaganda artist who drew many cartoons featuring
      brutish German military figures. Tales of atrocity: while the German Army was
      responsible for numerous war crimes against the citizens of neutral Belgium, these
      reports were magnified in Allied propaganda as the 'Rape of Belgium'.

21   Psalm 91:5: 'Thou shalt not be afraid for the terror by night; nor for the arrow that
      flieth by day.'

4 Gallipoli to Lemnos

1. Bulair, on the Gulf of Saros, had been the site of a feigned landing at the beginning of the campaign. Bernard Freyburg earned a D.S.O. after swimming ashore and lighting flares to confuse the enemy.
2. See 'Scraps from a Diary, 1915–16' (Appendix) for Aitken's 1917 account of the evacuation.
3. Although several soldiers from the Main Body named Page were killed earlier at Gallipoli, none were killed in December 1915. The only Otago soldier to be killed in action on 13 December 1915 was Albert John James 8/2436, a member of the 5th reinforcements. This is almost certainly the person to whom Aitken refers. It is possible he is misremembering, but it seems more likely that he is recalling misinformation generated at the time.
4. Pistol is a swaggering rogue in the army of Henry V. In several other plays, he is a drinking companion of the tubby knight, Sir John Falstaff. We meet Aitken's Ancient Pistol, Private Kelly, again in France (ch. 9 n. 3), where he is spokesperson for a protest concerning lack of pay and other grievances.
5. 'In sight [of Troy] lies Tenedos, an island widely famed' (*Aeneid* 2:20). Aeneas is describing how the Greeks set sail for Tenedos, apparently giving up the war, but leaving behind a band of warriors concealed inside a huge wooden horse.
6. Achi Baba is the highest hill in vicinity of Cape Helles, the southern foot of the peninsula, where British had made landings on 25 April.
7. Orpheus laments Eurydice on the banks of the Strymon, a river associated with cranes by Virgil in the *Georgics* (1:118–20) and the *Aeneid* (10:264–66, 11:578–80).
8. A standard atlas is unlikely to feature the name Gallipoli. It may show the location of Gelibolu, the largest town on the peninsula.

5 Lemnos to Egypt

1. A film of the landings run backwards would show three phases: troops moving about in comparative safety, sustained combat on the hills, heavy casualties on the beach.
2. Ormond Burton says of Alderman's rear-guard: 'Scores of men begged for a place in this little band. Main Body men who had been right through the adventure demanded a place as of right; others begged and cajoled and even attempted to bribe. Everything that could be done they did to secure a place in this fellowship of sacrifice. None expected them to come through alive. . . . It was a supreme act, made without fuss or show of emotion in a manner typically New Zealand' (*Silent Division,* pp. 109–10).
3. Following the word 'now', MS-1961 has the date: '(1920)'.
4. Alderman had a post-war career in the Australian Imperial Force.
5. The Senussi were Libyan Islamists. In November 1915 they came to the aid of the Ottoman Empire by launching a jihad against British-controlled Egypt from the west, with the hope of sparking a general insurgency and weakening the defence of the Suez Canal. A battle near Mersa Matruh on the Egyptian coast, on 25 December 1915, was one of several that removed the Senussi as a military threat. New Zealand's 1st Rifle Battalion fought in this campaign.

6   Egypt: Ismailia

1   The Sporades and Cyclades lie south of Lemnos, Salonika (now Thessaloniki) to the north-east. The recent entry of Bulgaria into the war had made Salonika a centre for operations on the Balkan front.

2   Alexandretta (now Iskenderun) is a city on the southern part of Turkey's Mediterranean coast.

3   Ismailia, on the Suez Canal at Lake Timsah, is the junction of railway lines to Port Said, Suez, and Cairo.

4   A separate New Zealand Infantry Division was created on 1 March 1916. Aitken briefly describes the reorganization of units later in the chapter.

5   Hesperides: a legendary garden famous for its golden apples and gorgeous nymphs.

6   'Square dinkum': a less common variant of 'fair dinkum'. Aitken may not have made his implication clear. The Riflemen, who had seen light action in the Western Desert, took pride in their punctiliousness and military bearing. To veterans of Gallipoli, they seemed inordinately fond of themselves—hence the ironic view that these lads were the genuine article, the square dinkums, or dinks. The nickname stuck and would later come a badge of pride.

7   The following account of the arrival of the 2nd Maori Contingent is closely based on the 1917 'Scraps from a Diary'. Te Rangi Hiroa is not there identified as the orator, and the most significant alteration is the deletion of a concluding sentence: 'It was a memorable scene, framed as it was in the setting of an Egyptian desert; surely a splendid vindication of our Empire.'

8   *Pa* and *taua*: 'fort' and 'war party'.

9   The name Himia does not appear as a surname or forename in the Nominal Roll of the 1st Maori Contingent, leaving too many possible variants for identification. The clause concerning the 'crown-and-anchor board'—on which a popular gambling game would have been played—is not present in MS-1961.

10 Regarding Aitken's footnote: by 'the Maori part of New Zealand' he means Rotorua, where the Queen received a traditional welcome—a highlight featured in newsreels of the tour.

11 The chaplain was the Rev. Henare Wepiha Te Wainohu.

12 A surprising error for Aitken to make. Brigadier-General Johnston was away sick in England during the Battle of Messines in June, but was killed by sniper fire on 7 August 1917. It is one of several details that suggest Aitken's lack of reliance on published accounts.

13 Te Rangi Hiroa died in December 1951. Aitken's list of his achievements could be much extended, but it is worth mentioning that, like Aitken, Te Rangi Hiroa went on to pursue a distinguished academic career abroad and, alongside his professional anthropological research, wrote *The Coming of the Maori* and *Vikings of the Sunrise*—works that have lasting value as non-fiction.

14 According to Masefield, soldiers about to embark for the Gallipoli landings 'felt a gladness of exultation that their young courage was to be used. They went like kings in a pageant to the imminent death' (pp. 34–35). Aitken may also have in mind an earlier paean to the men of Anzac: 'For physical beauty and nobility of bearing they surpassed any men I have ever seen; they walked and looked like kings in the old poems . . .' (p. 19).

7 Ismailia and the Suez Canal

1   The Sweetwater Canal, now known as the Ismailia canal, was built to provide fresh water from Lake Timsah to the region bordering the Suez Canal. Tel-el-Kebir is a town 50 km inland and due west of Ismailia.
2   Baksees: usually spelled 'baksheesh'—a small donation of money.
3   Gustave Doré's illustration shows Arachne in the moment of transformation, her head and torso arching backwards, with spider legs behind.
4   *Ei-ouk-nem*: the 'yo-heave-ho' refrain from 'The Song of the Volga Boatmen'.
5   Nullah: a dry river valley or ravine.
6   The battles of Neuve Chapelle (March-April 1915), Aubers Ridge (May 1915), and Loos (September-October 1915) were successive costly failures.
7   *The Pleasant Land of France* (1908) is a collection of essays on French topics written by an English peer with strong interests in the history of farm management. One chapter is devoted to 'boycotting and other forms of agrarian outrage'. It must have seemed an unlikely choice of gift.

8 Egypt to France: Hazebrouck

1   No troopships were sunk, but in the first two weeks of April 1916, eight cargo ships were torpedoed by U-boats operating in the Mediterranean.
2   'Every man has two countries—his own and France'. This much-repeated sentiment derives from *La Fille de Roland,* a play by Henri de Bornier.
3   A notice stating the capacity of the carriage: 40 Men or 15 horses lengthways or 12 horses sideways.
4   *Dame de la Croix Rouge*: a woman of the Red Cross.
5   The French explorers who wrote about New Zealand did so early, before the term Maori came into use. For them, and for their readers, 'New Zealanders' were the indigenous people of the country.
6   *Cafard*: depression, funk.
7   The Battle of Verdun, fought largely between the French and German armies, commenced in February 1916 and continued through to December of that year. Its demands and priorities had knock-on effects all along the front—including the Somme offensive, which was intended to relieve pressure on the French. By the end of May 1916, the French had already suffered 185,000 casualties, the Germans 200,000. The Ypres Salient was the site of major battles throughout the war. The New Zealand Division suffered heavy casualties in the Third Battle of Ypres (31 July to 10 November 1917), particularly at Passchendaele on 12 October.
8   In Aitken's text, Le Grand Hasard is between Morbecque and Steenbecque. It is in fact in the opposite direction: between Morbecque and Hazebrouck. Subsequent corrections are made silently.
9   Ortelius made several maps of 'Flandria' showing these villages. The earliest is in *Theatrum oder Schauplatz des Erdbodens* (1572).
10 Captain Leopold McLaglen, a Boer War veteran and fairground athlete, claimed to be jiu-jitsu champion of the world. On visiting New Zealand in 1915, he talked his way into instructing New Zealand troops in an elaborate system of bayonet-fighting.

His pamphlet about the system claimed '30,000 Australian and New Zealand troops' were using his system with 'deadly effect in the Dardanelles'. Aitken is confusing Leopold with his brother, Victor, the noted boxer and Hollywood film star—a misapprehension Leopold was known to encourage.

11 La Bassée was captured by the Central Powers during the so-called 'Race to the Sea' in October 1914. It is about 30 km from Allied-held Hazebrouck.

9 Hazebrouck to Estaires

1 M.O.: medical officer
2 There is a fuller account of billets and the affair of the straw (*la paille*) in 'Scraps from a Diary, 1915–16' (Appendix).
3 When last observed, 'Ancient Pistol' was making unofficial disbursements of rum (ch. 4, n. 4). In one of 'Some Notes, for Recollection Only' appended to MS-1961, Aitken adds: 'Private Kelly: ribbons worn were Chitral, Boxer Rebellion, Boer War. It was doubtful whether he had served in these campaigns.' Kelly was born in Queenstown in 1882. He would have been an implausible fifteen years old at the time of the siege and relief of Chitral, in what is now Pakistan, in 1895. The Boxer Rebellion in China (1900) overlaps with the Boer War (1889–1902); despite Aitken's scepticism, it would have been possible for him to have served in both. Kelly's attestation form claims the following prior military service: 'South Africa 2 yrs China Fleet, Main Exped. Infantry'. In June 1916, Kelly was wounded by a bomb from an aircraft. His medical records indicate that he was hospitalized in England with a broken knee and diagnosed with shell-shock ('strain and stress of service'). He was returned to New Zealand for a rest of six months in March 1918.
4 The 1st Otago Battalion marched from Morbecque to Estaires on 9 May 1916.
5 'Alas, how changed from what he was' (Virgil, *Aeneid,* 2:274).
6 74 lb. is 33.5 kg; 62 lb. is 28 kg. The 'statutory' weight would have been set in 1914 or earlier, before the introduction of specialized equipment such as the steel helmet, gas helmets, grenades, etc.
7 Thirteen and a half miles is 'only' 21.7 km.
8 The Chaconne from Bach's Partita No. 2 in D minor (BWV 1004), one of the greatest works in the solo violin repertoire, would represent a significant challenge for the amateur musician. In the circumstances, it seems likely Aitken was playing from memory.
9 'Now the young lady will carry a baby.'
10 Sergeant B—. Probably Sergeant James Bree, who is named as Aitken's former platoon sergeant in the account of the raid of 14 July 1916.

10 Estaires to Armentières

1 The 1st Otago Battalion reached Armentières on 13 May 1916.
2 In 1916, the front line near the French-Belgian border skirted two towns in Allied hands: Ypres and Armentières. At these places, the front line pushed forwards, creating a salient in which the German front line lay to each side as well as directly

ahead of the Allied lines. Very lights were shot into the air from a flare-pistol for signalling or to illuminate the battlefield.

3   'Quatrième Classe': fourth grade.

4   Aitken is describing a 'Strombos Horn': a cylinder of compressed air connected to a powerful horn that would sound in the event of a cloud gas attack. There was one such horn for every 400 yards of trench.

5   Asile des Aliénés: psychiatric asylum.

6   *Pauvre vieux*: poor old chap.

7   Although the map showing trenches near Armentières (Illustration 9) is correct for 24 September 1917 and the trench-numbering system described by Aitken is no longer in use, the front line in this area was essentially unchanged from 1915 until April 1918. The sector Aitken describes is at the join of squares 10 and 11, across which runs the Armentières-Lille railway line. The bulge of the 'Mushroom'—trench 69—is visible below the railway line. Epinette, in square 5 above, marks the junction of trenches 76 and 77.

8   Polar coordinates identify location by measuring distance and direction from a central point: a farmhouse, for example, is 200 yards away at an angle of 45 degrees. A mathematical diagram of polar coordinates might show a number of concentric circles radiating outwards from a central point, with particular points plotted by their distance from the centre (the radius of a circle) and their angle (radian) measured from a fixed 'horizontal' line of zero degrees.

9   On 1 July 1916, the first day of the Battle of the Somme, there were 57,470 British casualties, 19,240 of whom were killed.

10   Carlyle's *Sartor Resartus* ('the tailor re-tailored', 1836) is a spoof philosophical consideration of the views of Professor Teufelsdröckh, author of 'Clothes: their Origin and Influence'. Aitken's anecdote prompted a friendly note from a reader: 'You describe the finding of Carlyle's "Sartor Resartus"—"left there, no doubt (to quote you) by some metaphysically minded Scots private or corporal, whose fate might be doubtful". No Scotsman this, I am sure. In fact, I am convinced that I left that book in the dugout you describe. I was a corporal signaller attached to the 61st Division, which held the line between Laventie and Armentières, before you arrived.' Hubert Tetley to Alexander Aitken, 9 March 1964. E 2005.24, University of Edinburgh Library.

11 Armentières Salient: The Front Line

1   Aitken's 10th Company relieved the 4th on 26 May 1916.

2   Letters written by Aitken to his family during the war have not come to light.

3   'Stand-to' was a period when troops were required to stand on the fire-step fully equipped and with bayonets fixed, ready to repel an enemy advance. As attacks were generally made around dusk or dawn, the daily routine was punctuated by a stand-to at each of these times. The evening stand-to would more commonly last for an hour or so, after which troops with no special duty were permitted to rest at their battle stations—so long as they could do so in full kit.

4   Lieutenant Hall was shot in the head three weeks later, on 13 June 1916, dying later that same day. Aitken is probably confusing Hall with the Otago Battalion's first

casualty at Armentières, Lieutenant A. C. Boyes, of the 4th Company, who was killed by a sniper on 16 May 1916.

5 Erich Maria Remarque's novel *All Quiet on the Western Front* (1929) takes its title from a concluding irony: the traumatized protagonist is killed on a day when there is nothing to report from the front.

6 Aitken gives the correct date.

7 *Minenwerfer*: a heavy trench mortar. According to Ormond Burton, the projectile was visible in flight, making a sound like 'Where's your bivvy, where's your bivvy', before landing with a massive explosion. Burton, *Silent Division*, p. 130.

8 'Pineapple' bombs: round or oval grenades with a dimpled pattern. The German version, the *Kugelhandgranate,* was too heavy for long throws but could be fired into the air by rifle—a less than accurate method of delivery.

9 *Sforzando*: musical term meaning 'with force', or played with a sudden loud emphasis.

10 The main square of Ypres was dominated by the tower of the Cloth Hall and the nearby Cathedral. Both were obliterated by artillery shelling in 1915. Photographs of these imposing ruins are among the stock images of the war.

11 'Der Wegweiser'— 'The Signpost'—is part of Schubert's song cycle *Winterreise* (1827). When the traveller on his winter's journey comes across a signpost, he has a sense of foreboding: 'I must travel a road from which no man has ever returned.'

12 Canto 3 of Dante's *Inferno* begins with an inscription over the Gates of Hell: 'Through me the way to the city of woe'.

13 *Ostinato*: a persistently repeating musical pattern.

14 The Battle of Mount Sorrel (2–13 June 1916) began with a successful German attack on the only high point in the Ypres salient still in Allied hands. The Canadian Divisions suffered a crushing bombardment on the morning of 2 June and were subsequently overrun by German infantry. Two generals were among the immediate front-line casualties. Battle ranged to and fro until, on 13 June, a counter-attack by the Canadians regained most of the lost ground. Casualties were around 8,000 on each side.

15 Buterne Farm, the distillery, and Willow Walk are on squares 28 and 29 of Illustration 9.

12 Armentières: The Crescendo

1 *Scharfschützen*: snipers.

13 Terdeghem: A Grenade School

1 According to Sergeant Robert Gunn's personnel file, he and Aitken left for the grenade school on 19 June 1916 and returned to their units on the 26th.

2 Robert Gunn was killed two weeks later on 1 October 1916.

3 See Ch. 11, n. 14.

4 In the British Army, a grenadier is a soldier serving in the Grenadier Guards—one of the elite regiments.

5   *Dies infanda*: dreadful day.
6   When the statue of the Virgin and Child atop the spire of the steeple of Notre-
     Dame-de-Brebières was hit by shell-fire in 1915, it was secured by engineers into a
     gravity-defying downward-slanting position (Anzacs dubbed her Fanny Durack,
     after the Australian Olympic swimmer). It was often said the war would end when
     the statue fell.

14 Armentières: The Raids Begin

1   Aitken's journey from the rail junction near the Asylum, past the brickworks and
     the houses of Chapelle d'Armentières towards Lothian Avenue (square 10), can
     be traced on Illustration 9. Neither Square Farm nor the cemetery is identified by
     name on the map.
2   Pérenchies ridge, a couple of kilometres from the New Zealand lines, is not shown
     on Illustration 9, but the Armentières-Lille railway line runs through the village of
     that name.
3   Private William Nimot was born in New Zealand to parents who had emigrated
     from Germany. On 29 June 1916, when he was on sentry duty at the Mushroom,
     Nimot went across to the German lines, only about 60 yards away. Aitken's account
     of the hostile treatment of Nimot's parents back in New Zealand is largely correct,
     but bullying and teasing by fellow soldiers on account of his origins seems to have
     been the more significant motivation for his desertion. Cecil Malthus recalls:
     'we knew him by the name of Marshall. He was a malcontent who always had a
     grievance, and he had recently been punished for insubordination. In any case he
     was said to be of German blood' (*Armentières and the Somme*, p. 63). Nimot became
     a POW, survived the war, and in 1919 was found to be working in a cheese factory
     near Frankfurt. He never faced a court-martial.
4   Official communiqués concerning these places reported successes. La Boiselle and
     Fricourt were heavily defended villages, with deep bomb-proof cellars and well-
     sited machine-gun posts, incorporated into the front section of the German line.
     Both villages were in British hands by 4 July—but at immense cost. Further south,
     in the French sector, the villages of Curlu and Hem were first-day objectives secured
     with relative ease.
5   Aitken's 'Some Notes, for Recollection only' (MS-1961, vol. 2) offers the following
     examples by way substantiation.

> For fatuity: 'There's no doubt in mind but that if Master Boche had no
> machine-guns he would have stood no chance at all.' Wounded officer's
> remark: reported in *Scotsman*, 6 July 1916. (The Germans at one point waited
> until attackers were within 150 yards: then with machine-guns caused 5,274
> casualties to a single Division.)

> For pure evasion and misdirection: 'The proportion of our losses in the early
> stages of this battle due to rifle fire will be found to be very small. The greatest
> factor has been machine-guns, and next to that the heavy artillery.' *The Times*,
> 13 July 1916, p. 7, col. 3.

6 Better known as the 'Battle of the Boar's Head', this diversionary attack north of the Somme battlefields on 30 June was preceded by an intense bombardment that failed to dislodge machine-gun positions or cut wire. Three 'pals' Battalions of the Royal Sussex Regiment were committed to the attack: within hours 1,100 men were killed or wounded—a casualty rate of 60 per cent. Edmund Blunden, who was nearby, gives an account of the disaster in *Undertones of War* (1928). Aitken may be recalling the following passage: 'The communiqué that morning . . . referred to the Boar's Head massacre thus: "East of Richebourg a strong raiding party penetrated the enemy's third line"' (*Undertones,* p. 48).

7 'Highland Jessie' appears in a popular tale of the Indian Mutiny. During the Siege of Lucknow, when all hope seems to be lost, Jessie hears the bagpipes of the relieving force long before they are audible to anyone else.

8 The Aucklanders endured an especially ferocious bombardment, but it took place on the night of 3 July. Ormond Burton writes: 'At 10.30 p.m. hell suddenly broke loose. Every kind of missile rained down upon the front line. The parapet was blown in, dug-outs smashed, men killed, wounded and buried alive. For an hour the noise continued, the detonations filling the night with a roar of sound, and sheets of vivid flame' (*Silent Division,* p. 131).

9 According to Burton, five men on outpost duty were caught between the barrage and their own line. When the German raid commenced, they 'made a most gallant resistance, and were not taken until their supply of bombs was exhausted and every man wounded' (*Auckland Regiment,* 96). He makes no reference to any of the attackers remaining behind in a hidden position but does note that a dazed German raider was captured the next morning.

10 Bruce Bairnsfather's 'That "Out Wiring" Sensation' appeared in *The Bystander* Christmas Number, 1916. The cartoon shows a soldier, noisily hammering in a wiring-post in the darkness—his hair standing on end as a German searchlight fastens onto the scene.

11 MS-1961 has a paragraph subsequently deleted at this point:

> Wiring, trench-digging and the cyclic routine of our days and nights must seem dull to those who were not there, may even seem dull to me long hence, except insofar as they bring back what I then was, and the men about me. And this is relative too, for an archaeologist of A.D. 4000, all written records of A.D. 2000 being known to have been destroyed in the suicidal wars of that era, might be excited to find some evidence, an entrenching tool lacking the haft but bullet-pitted, some shattered bones, bullets, shell-shards. This is, alas, not wholly fantasy; but at the moment we are speaking of 7th July 1916.

12 Aitken means the night of 8/9 July. Cecil Malthus of the 1st Canterbury Battalion, who was for a time buried alive by a shell bursting on the parapet above him, gives an account of the bombardment and raid in *Armentières and the Somme,* pp. 77–80.

13 Whizz-bangs: shells fired from a German light field-gun. One heard the whizz of their flight an instant before the bang.

14 The official *History of the Canterbury Regiment* gives total casualties for the month only. Malthus reckons 'well over a hundred, out of a strength in the line of about 300' (*Armentières and the Somme,* p. 80); Peter Pederson says 'all told the Canterburys suffered 116 casualties' (*Anzacs on the Western Front,* p. 9).

15 A box barrage is laid down on three sides of a given area, either to box in the enemy and prevent reinforcement, or to support friendly troops by supplying a tight pattern of cover on attack.

16 Aitken cites the full text in 'Some Notes, for Recollection only' (MS-1961, vol. 2):

> Communiqué concerning the raid on the Canterbury Battalion, 9 July 1916:
>
> Further north, after a heavy bombardment of a sector held by the New Zealanders, a strong hostile local attack succeeded in entering our trenches at one point. After half an hour's fighting the enemy were ejected by the New Zealanders, leaving German dead in our trenches. No incident of importance on the rest of the front.
>
> *The Times*, 10 July 1916, p. 8.

17 In 'Some Notes, for Recollection only' (MS-1961, vol. 2) Aitken writes: 'See German report, *Times*, 17 July, p. 8.' The contrasting report reads:

> Berlin, July 18.—German official communiqué:—
> The British attack, which was continued after its first sanguinary failure, has developed into a severe battle.
>   Between Pozieres and Longueval concentrated enemy masses succeeded, in spite of the heaviest losses, in penetrating our line and, for the present, in gaining ground and establishing themselves in the Trônes Wood. The attack has been checked and is proceeding today.

15 Armentières: The Raid of the 4th Otagos

1 'Greater love hath no man than this, that a man lay down his life for his friends.' John 15: 13.

2 Pioneer battalions consisted of trained infantry soldiers who specialized in engineering and construction. The term has no special colonial inflection: every division in the British Army had their pioneers. On the Western Front in 1916, the New Zealand Division's pioneer battalion consisted of the Maori contingents, the remnant of the Otago Mounted Rifles, and soldiers from the Pacific Islands. In practice, the distinction between infantry and pioneer battalions was less marked: all soldiers dug and repaired trenches, and pioneers undertaking such work were just as vulnerable to artillery bombardment as other front-line troops. Nonetheless, the implication that pioneers took a less active role in the fighting rankled, and Maori were especially keen to contribute to the raids taking place in the Armentières sector. Cowan's *Maori in the Great War* mentions raids on 3, 9, and 11 July, before noting that raids took place frequently after that (pp. 85–91).

3 *Morgengruß*—Morning Greeting—is the eighth song in Schubert's *Die schöne Müllerin* (Op. 25, D795). It is a tender lilting folk-song capturing some of the delusions of the protagonist's unrequited love for the young maid of the mill.

4 The solemn 'Dead March' from the third act of Handel's oratorio *Saul* (HWV 53) might well have the taunting quality Aitken describes.

5 Germany, having sunk more ships and killed more men, immediately hailed the Battle of Jutland as a victory. (It turned out to be a strategic victory for the Allies:

the Royal Navy continued its blockade and the German capital ships stayed in port for the remainder of the war.) The news reached the front in the first week of June, soon to be followed by news of the almost total loss of those aboard H.M.S. *Hampshire*, sunk by a mine on 5 June, while conveying Lord Kitchener and his staff to Russia.

6   In Illustration 9, Aitken's 'section 74' is on square 11 of the trench-map, between the railway line and the border of square 5 above. On a present-day map, the starting-off point of the raid is near the junction of the Chemin de l'Épinette and the Ruelle de la Blanche. The German lines lay ahead of this T-intersection.

7   Allington was killed a week later on 14 June. Aitken is gathering those he knows to have died at Messines under the date of the main assault on the ridge: 7 June 1917.

8   Howden's military file ambiguously states that he was 'Reported missing now supposed killed in action 30 September 1917'. Aitken's date could well be the correct one. Following the disastrous attack at Goose Alley on the 27th—in which Aitken himself was wounded—Howden may have been reported missing then supposed dead in an entry made on the 30th.

9   Second Lieutenant Claude Hall Clarke; his name is also misspelled as Clark in the *Official History of the Otago Regiment,* p. 103.

10   Private Douglas Stark, better known as Starkie, is the subject of Robin Hyde's documentary novel, *Passport to Hell.* Her reconstruction of the raid of 14 June is in Chapter 11, pp. 165–74. Prior to the raid, Stark had been sentenced to five years in prison with hard labour; following his conspicuous gallantry in repeatedly bringing back the wounded under fire, the sentence was remitted.

11   Cecil Malthus was under the impression that the raid carried out by the 4th Otagos on 14 July involved a small number of men and had resulted in no casualties—a view he maintained until reading *Gallipoli to the Somme* in 1963. After summarizing the catastrophe, he writes: 'I repeat, incredulously, that this raid took place right along-side our company, yet we had no inkling of the truth. The morning following a raid, things would return to something like normality, and there would be contact and communication along the line. We knew well enough that *suppressio veri* was usual in the official communiqués, but here was an extraordinary instance of our own failure to communicate at all' (*Armentières and the Somme,* p. 81).

16 Armentières: After the Raid

1   Both were undergraduates. Brockett had enlisted as a law student at Victoria University, Wellington, while Aitken had been a student of languages and mathe-matics at the University of Otago. Aitken wanted to join up in 1914, but his father insisted on his waiting until he turned twenty. Unusually for a war memoir, Aitken says nothing about his reasons for enlisting, but the conversation with Brockett is one of several passages that the reader may find suggestive.

2   Moloch: a pagan god to whom children were sacrificed. In *Paradise Lost,* he is one of Satan's generals: a 'horrid king besmeared with blood of human sacrifice, and parents' tears' (1:392–93).

3   The 'war to end war': the catch-phrase has its origin in propaganda pieces by H. G. Wells. On 14 August 1914, he argued: 'For this is now a war for peace. It aims

straight at disarmament. It aims at a settlement that shall stop this sort of thing for ever. Every soldier who fights against Germany now is a crusader against war. This, the greatest of all wars, is not just another war—it is the last war!' *The War That Will End War*, p. 11.

4   Tennysonian aspiration: Aitken may be thinking of the last lines of 'Ulysses'—'To strive, to seek, to find, and not to yield'.

5   On 23 May 1956, Aitken gave a fuller account in a biographical letter to R. P. Kania (MS-0690/002, Hocken Library).

> Now begins the material of the legend. Captain Hargest, with his character-istic consideration, told me to come to the dug-out that served as Company HQ and try and snatch some sleep there. I lay down on the cocoanut matting, but could not sleep; the noise of the bombs was still in my ears, and the flashes before my mental eyes. I was then aware, from voices behind me, that Captain Hargest and his 2nd in command, Mr. Duncan Rae, were in a difficulty; they seemed to have a list of surnames of the platoon that had gone out, almost all listed as wounded or dead, whereas Battalion, ringing up from HQ further back, were demanding complete details. In fact the platoon roll-book, with all its details, was not to be found. (My belief has always been that it was in the pocket of the platoon sergeant, Bree, lying dead at that moment in No Man's Land). Now strictly speaking I was not then in the 10th platoon but had been given on loan for the night from the 8th; it had however been my old platoon and I had no trouble in remembering all the required details, full Christian names, regimental number, and—I am not perfectly sure of this, but at any rate I knew these details—next of kin in New Zealand, and address. I dictated these, still lying on the mat, and I presume Mr. Rae wrote them down. I thought this at the time a slight affair, and do still. . . . That platoon roll, I had seen it often; and I knew the men.

The platoon roll listed details for a total of fifty-six men. I am indebted to Garry Tee, Emeritus Professor of Mathematics at the University of Auckland, for the actual number of men in the platoon. Tee obtained the figure from Professor Aris Rutherford, who taught with Aitken at Edinburgh in the early 1950s.

6   At Fromelles, the 5th Australian Division lost 5,533 casualties in one night, of whom 1,917 were killed—the worst disaster in Australian history. The British 61st Division suffered 1,547 casualties. Aitken's account of the debacle is accurate; he perhaps did not know that British Generals Haking and Haig insisted on the attack despite protests made by the Australian divisional commander, General Elliott, who foresaw the outcome.

7   Since *l'épinette* is a conifer—in fact a spruce—the pub-sign of the local *estaminet* would doubtless have featured a tree.

8   Concertina wire: barbed wire in coils that expanded like a concertina. Corkscrew pickets: also known as silent pickets, had a loop at the top of the post through which a piece of wood was inserted and twisted like a corkscrew. They were an improve-ment on posts that needed to be hammered into the ground.

9   The tunnel warfare units of the Royal New Zealand Electrical and Mechanical Engineers were involved in mining the enemy front at Messines. Their enduring

monument is the Carrière Wellington—a complex of tunnels extending from Arras.

10 The two strongpoints are on square 4 of Illustration 9.

11 Gommecourt was the scene of a costly diversionary attack on 1 July; Thiepval, Beaumont Hamel, and Serre were part of the heavily defended system of fortified villages in the northern section of the Somme battlefield. The British advance on 1 July collapsed totally in these places—which is why the names seemed 'to be hushed up'. The direction of attack then turned to the south, where German defences were less secure and some early advances had been made. Bazentin (14–17 July), High Wood (20–25 July), Delville Wood (12 July to 3 September), and Pozières (23 July to 3 September)—all first day objectives—represent a sequence of battles, and two or three miles of territory incrementally gained, as the Allied troops moved against the German second and third lines. This middle of phase of the Somme offensive was marked by the introduction of the German tactic of 'defence-in-depth'. Earlier, the priority had been to hold the front line at all cost, but now the Germans were prepared to yield ground in order to follow up with a strong counter-attack.

12 The New Zealand Division was relieved at Armentières by the 51st Highland Division.

13 Kelly was wounded on 16 June. See ch. 9, n. 3.

17 Flanders to Picardy: Citernes

1 W. O.: Warrant Officer. The slag-heaps are reminders that Flanders is coalmining country.

2 'And hopes were none, that back again / Herald should come from Terouenne, / Where England's king in leaguer lay, / Before decisive battle-day'. *Marmion* (1808), Canto 6 ('The Battle'), 7–10.

3 After winning a great victory, Henry IV of France wrote to his friend, General Crillon: 'Hang yourself, brave Crillon. We fought at Arques, and you were not there.' The remark became a popular saying.

4 After the failures of July 1916, Major-General Henry Horne promoted the use of a creeping barrage. Troops would advance behind a shifting curtain of artillery fire and arrive at their objective before enemy machine-gunners could take up their positions. On the Somme, the New Zealand Division was part of Horne's XV Corps.

5 Edmund Blunden and Siegfried Sassoon also attended Major Ronald Campbell's lecture on 'The Spirit of the Bayonet'. Sassoon recalls the flavour of Campbell's instruction: 'Stick him between the eyes, in the throat, in the chest, or round the thighs. If he's on the run, there's only one place; get your bayonet into his kidneys; it'll go in as easy as butter. . . . Don't waste good steel. Six inches are enough. What's the use of a foot of steel sticking out at the back of a man's neck? Three inches will do for him; when he coughs, go find another' (*Diaries*, 25 April, p. 60; also *Memoirs of an Infantry Officer*, pp. 7–8). Blunden found the lecture 'more disgusting than inspiring' (*Undertones*, p. 70).

6 *Schrecklichkeit*: frightfulness.

7 *Vergangenheit*: the past. In Thomas Hardy's *Jude the Obscure*, when Jude wanders

through an old University town at night, the ancient buildings exert a spell that makes the past seem more real than the present (Part 2, ch. 1).

8 Brigadier-General F. E. Johnston, commanding the 1st New Zealand Infantry Brigade.

9 R. Q. M. [S]: Regimental Quarter Master Sergeant.

10 Pascoe, who was awarded the Military Cross in 1918, survived the war.

11 Thomas Hobbes's description of mankind in a state of nature concludes: 'In such condition there is . . . no arts, no letters, no society, and, which is worst of all, continual fear and danger of violent death, and the life of man solitary, poor, nasty, brutish, and short.' *Leviathan* (1651), ch. 13.

12 Lieut.-Colonel A. B. Charters, commanding the 1st Battalion of the Otago Infantry Regiment.

13 'Piano Teacher, Piano Sales and Rentals, Music and Instruments'.

14 'We are happy to know you are back home able to once again play your violin with your second bow from Abbeville; we remember the incident perfectly . . . the Huns came to within twenty kilometres of our home and every night for six months we had bombs and torpedoes with each visit by their menacing birds . . . finally, the war is over and now the Huns have gone home . . . let us hope that they stay there . . . despite our 70 years, Madame Picquet and I are happy to send you our very best wishes.'

15 From a passage in the *Aeneid*: 'sunt lacrimae rerum et mentem mortalia tangunt' (1:462). 'There is a world of tears and the burdens of mortality touch the heart' (trans. Robert Fagles).

16 Buvez: drink!

17 Aitken is near the site of the Battle of Crécy, fought between the English and the French in 1346.

18 'We who are about to die salute you'—as spoken by gladiators in ancient Rome.

19 Paderewski was a Polish nationalist and composer, widely known as a virtuoso concert pianist in the manner of Chopin and Liszt.

20 'Ching Chong Chinaman': a racist chant with many variations, often beginning, 'Ching Chong Chinaman sitting on a fence, trying to make a dollar out of fifteen cents'. 'The Village Pump': a music hall number beginning 'There's a pretty little village far away, Where they grows new potaters, corn and 'ay . . .'

21 In Kipling's poem, Gunga Din is a lowly Indian water-carrier, someone to be ordered about with contempt—yet he risks his life to bring water to a badly wounded British soldier. The last line is: 'You're a better man than I am Gunga Din.' To Aitken, the poem would have seemed complacent about empire and clueless about war.

18 Citernes to Fricourt

1 Q.M.: Quartermaster.

2 On 25 September, as leader of the first platoon in the first wave of an attack, Aitken would be responsible for setting the correct pace for troops advancing closely behind a creeping barrage (see ch. 21).

3 '. . . wounded in the war and, like you, he has returned'.

4 The villages of Guillemont and Ginchy, south of Delville Wood, had been pulverized

by artillery since mid-July. But under the rubble were tunnels, dug-outs, and machine-gun emplacements, against which successive British attacks had disintegrated. The strong-points were finally taken in early September, clearing the way for the big push of 15 September.

5 'What a pity! . . . What a shame about the war!'

6 *Rafale:* burst. The field-guns were upwards of 7 km away 'to the right'—beyond Maricourt, where the front line passed to the French Army.

7 'Mad Major': a sobriquet often associated with the English ace, Christopher Draper. He may not have been the pilot Aitken observed as any flying stunts seen from the trenches were likely to be ascribed to the 'Mad Major'.

8 King George's Hill: due east of Bécordel and about 1 km south of Fricourt. Also known as Hill 110, it was from this point that King George surveyed the Somme battlefield on 10 August 1916.

9 MS-1961 has a crossed-out sentence at this point: 'In our own practice of this gesture of respect—not uniformly resorted to, it must be admitted—the hand, brought above the right eyebrow, became at once motionless; whereas with the sergeant it continued to perform "damped vibrations", of which I could have written down the mathematical equation.'

10 Caterpillar Valley: a long caterpillar-shaped valley extending eastward from Mametz Wood towards Trônes Wood and Ginchy, between Montauban to the south and Longueval to the north (squares 20–24 of Illustration 10a). After fierce fighting, the Germans abandoned their positions in the valley on 14 July 1914. Their dug-outs and fortifications were then taken over by British units, who were subject to frequent shelling from German guns overlooking the valley from Ginchy. The cemetery at Caterpillar Valley, one of the largest on the Somme, has the graves of 214 identified New Zealand soldiers and is the site of the New Zealand Memorial to the Missing of the Somme, recording 1,205 names of 'those whose graves are known only to God'.

11 The north frieze of the Parthenon (part of which is at the British Museum) shows a procession of horsemen and chariots.

12 Switch Trench: when a section of front-line trench comes under threat, a new connecting trench—a switch trench—is quickly dug, diverting the front line to a defensive line in the rear. The Germans made a trench of this sort to link their second defensive line to their third when it seemed they would lose High Wood. Switch Trench, as it was named, ran through the north of High Wood and crossed the Longueval-Flers road north of Delville Wood. A section of Switch Trench immediately to the left of this road, referred to as 'the green line' in planning documents, was the New Zealand Division's first objective in the offensive beginning 15 September (see Illustration 10b).

13 *Absit omen:* an invocation (like 'Heaven forbid!') expressing the hope that what is about to be said will not turn out to be true.

14 Aitken may be thinking of the Martian machines in *The War of the Worlds,* but Wells had come even closer to the idea of the tank in his 1903 story, 'The Land Ironclads'. The New Zealand Division were allotted four of the fifty-four tanks introduced on the Somme in September 1916. Haig was subsequently criticized for deploying them prematurely, before there were machines in sufficient numbers to give a decisive advantage.

19 Fricourt to Flers: 15th September 1916

1 'Behind the drum and fife, / Past hawthornwood and hollow, / Through earth and out of life / The soldiers follow'. A. E. Housman, 'In Valleys Green and Still', *Last Poems*, VII.

2 Captain Louis Wilson may have survived the day. He was reported missing two weeks later and presumed killed in action on or about 2 October 1916.

3 The allusion is to the long journey of Odysseus from the Trojan War to his home in Ithaca. *Envoi*: in poetry, a stanza of concluding words, commending a message to the reader or summarizing what has gone before.

4 The Division's plan of attack for 15 September (see Illustration 10b) involved an advance of about 2 miles along a 1,000-yard front. Four colour-coded objectives were to be taken. From their starting point in Wood Lane and Otago Trench, the 2nd Otago and 2nd Auckland Battalions were to advance uphill, overrun Crest Trench, and, just over the brow of the ridge, take the formidable Switch Trench—the Green Line. The 3rd Rifles Brigade, supported by the 2nd Canterbury and 2nd Wellington Battalions, would then leapfrog forward to the brown and blue lines extending just before and just beyond the village of Flers. Between these two lines, Flers trench and Flers support trench had to be taken. Once the blue line was reached, the direction of attack then pivoted a full 90 degrees to face Grove Alley—a communication trench linking the Flers system to the Gird system of trenches. The final objective, the red line, would be reached once Grove Alley was taken; it was a defensive line joining Abbey Road to a point near Factory Corner, parallel to the North Road.

5 Supported by a creeping barrage, the 2nd Otagos and 2nd Aucklanders succeeded in taking Switch Trench on time at 6.50 am and the 4th Rifles were in control of the Brown Line trenches an hour later. The advance had gone well so far—but not everything had gone according to plan. To the left of the New Zealanders, the advance of the British 47th Division had been checked at High Wood. Consequently, as the 2nd Otago Battalion pushed ahead, their flank was exposed to enfilading machine-gun fire from the Wood. Within minutes, the leftmost company was reduced from 180 men to just 36. In front of Flers, the bombardment had failed to cut wire, and the attackers were pinned down by machine-gun fire, but with the help of the Division's tanks, the Blue Line was gained by mid-morning. Although Grove Alley was briefly occupied on 15 September, the Red Line was still in German hands at the end of the day.

6 The recently captured ridge-line was of primary importance in the Somme campaign. It extends north through High Wood towards Pozières all the way to Thiepval. The gently undulating countryside of the Somme is seemingly uniform, yet for two and half months, from the British lines, this low-lying ridge was as far as the eye could see; from the ridge, there is a commanding view in the other direction. Aitken can see as far the Bapaume-Péronne road: this is beyond Gird trench, and beyond the front line on 30 November 1916, when winter brought the Somme offensive to a close. The New Zealand Battlefield Memorial at Longueval is on this ridge (close to where Aitken is standing) between Crest and Switch Trenches.

7 Major Martin was mortally wounded at Bogle's Post by a shell-blast but not until the next day, on the afternoon of 17 September. He died later that same night. Carbery, *New Zealand Medical Services in the Great War*, pp. 208–9.

8 The idiocy of this order is underlined by a passage in the Somme section of Blunden's *Undertones of War*: 'we accepted with joy a story that one battalion has marched in solid column of fours to Mesnil Church, and was not barraged: this incident, which we refused to consider a fiction, was to us the sublimation of the impossible which happens' (p. 94).

9 *Locus classicus:* classic example. A tank did in fact rumble down Flers main street with infantry sheltering behind, but the tank (D17) was barely operational and the village was still in enemy hands. The action was observed by an RFC flyer whose report led to a widely circulated but misleading headline: 'A tank is walking down the High Street of Flers with the British Army cheering behind.'

10 A pineapple-and-pepper smell is associated with chlorine gas. In low doses, chlorine is irritating to the eyes, much like a tear gas, but at higher concentrations it reacts with water to produce hydrochloric acid in the lungs. Phosgene was deadlier still, causing 85 per cent of gas casualties during the war. It was often used in combination with chlorine gas.

11 Sentry-go: sentry duty.

12 The Londoners' attack on Drop Alley on the 18th involved remnants of two of the battalions that had fought to clear High Wood: the Post Office Rifles (down to 220 men) and the Civil Service Rifles (down to 100 men).

13 The German strongpoint attacked on the 19th was in fact at the junction of Flers Trench and Goose Alley (Grove Alley had been captured earlier on the 16th). German bombers had been infiltrating down the communication trench towards Drop Alley. They were driven back by a 'block'—a counter-bombing party closing off enemy access to the trench. The word 'block' can mean either the men engaged in this action or a physical barrier formed by filling in a section of trench.

14 In fact James Marston was killed at Armentières on 14 July 1916.

15 Frank Jones died of his wounds a day later on 23 September.

16 Not identified. There are sets of brothers who died on or about these dates but I have found no record of twins.

17 Andrew Macdonald identifies the brothers as Leslie (killed) and Ernie Watson. *On My Way to the Somme*, p. 151.

20 Delville Wood: Longueval

1 Turk Lane was a vital communication trench dug by the New Zealand Pioneer Battalion, running from Tea trench to Flers trench. British units dubbed the soldiers 'diggers'—a term that would soon apply to Anzac soldiers generally.

2 *Qui vive*: alertness (the expression is derived from a sentry's challenge).

3 On 29 March 1958, Aitken wrote to his sister Pearl: 'When I was at the front in France in 1916, you wrote me a letter telling something about the birth of our mother. The letter reached me about Sept 22, 1916, when we had been taken out of the line for a brief spell (we were in again for an attack on the 25th when I led the first wave on the left half of the Battalion front). I had been under fire and with almost no sleep for about a week, and simply could not take in the information given in your letter. We went back in, as I say, on the 25th. That attack was successful. They put us into another on the 27th, in which 30 out of 33 of my platoon were outed, included myself.

I got out of it, after the wounds were seen to, with nothing but my identification disc, my paybook, and a dead German's pyjamas. In this state I reached the hospital in Chelsea. Well, at odd times I wondered what you had written in that old letter that had gone west.' E.2005.24, Edinburgh University Library.

4   Brigadier-General Johnston; Lieutenant-Colonel Charters.

5   Haig was supreme commander of the British Expeditionary Force. Below him, General Rawlinson commanded the British Fourth Army, overseeing three Army Corps (III, XIV, XV) and—the next organizational level down—eighteen of the twenty-three Divisions involved in the September phase of the Somme campaign.

6   MS-1961 has: 'deplorably slip-shod'.

7   The pyramid of command runs from GHQ to Army (4th), to Army Corps (XV), to Division (NZ), to Brigade (1st NZ Infantry), to Battalion (1st Otago Infantry), to Company (4th), to Platoon (1). Complicating the picture are regiments: a regiment has a number of battalions, but these are split between brigades. For example, the Otago Regiment has two battalions: Aitken's 1st Otago Infantry Battalion is part of the 1st NZ Infantry Brigade, while the 2nd Otago Infantry Battalion is part of the 2nd NZ Infantry Brigade.

8   Aitken's internal war-map is a little out of step with the published war histories at this point. Both Goose Alley and Grove Alley were long communication trenches linking the Flers trenches to the Gird trench system. A section of Grove Alley had been in Allied hands since the 16th—which suggests Aitken is again mistaking Grove for Goose—but it needs to be remembered that the further part of Grove Alley was still held by the Germans, as was that part of the Flers system extending beyond Goose Alley to the north-west. The vital point on the ground was a spur at the junction of Goose Alley, Drop Alley, and the Flers trench network. Heavily defended and tactically crucial, it had to be taken before further advances along Goose and Grove towards Gird were possible. On the night of 20 September, in a combined operation, the 1st Battalion of the Black Watch attacked from Drop Alley while the 2nd Canterbury Battalion advanced along Flers and Flers support. They took the position and established blocks further along on Flers and Flers support trenches. Over the next 24 hours, the position was lost to a counter-attack, regained, and threatened again. It was here that Captain Starnes showed the outstanding leadership and tenacity for which he was awarded a DSO.

9   Doré's illustration to *Inferno* XIII: 'The Wood of Suicides' shows human forms imprisoned in a forest of writhing trees, on whose branches sit the harpies, vulture-like birds with cruel faces.

21 Goose Alley: 25th September 1916

1   The 1:10,000 trench map Aitken refers to is 'Gueudecourt, 57c S.W.1 ed. 1A' which can be viewed or downloaded from the Chasseaud Collection, Digital Archives, McMaster University Library. Illustration 14 is based on Aitken's hand-drawn section of this map in MS-1961.

2   The planned attack across no-man's-land would result in an extension of the Division's line from just beyond the junction of the Flers trenches and Goose Alley on the left, to Factory Corner on the right. In terms of the larger history of the

Somme, 25 September is the first day of the Battle of Morval. The larger objectives in this sector were to take the Gird trenches and the villages of Gueudecourt, Lesboeufs, and Morval.

3   The *Scottish Students' Songbook* is a compilation of popular numbers put together by a committee of students from the University of St Andrews, first published in 1891, with many successive editions. 'Riding down to Bangor' is a comic song involving courtship 'on an Eastern Train'; 'In a cavern, in a canyon' is better known as 'Oh, my darling Clementine'; 'Vive l'amour' has a repetitive chorus ('vive la, vive la, vive l'amour . . .') affirming love and good fellowship.

4   Planter: someone who puts bodies in the ground.

5   *Perdrix:* (Fr.) partridge.

6   Double drive: go twice as fast (to compensate for the time taken to light the flares).

7   Two Companies of the 1st Battalion of the Black Watch were on the left of the 1st Otagos in the Flers and Flers support trenches. Having repelled bombing counter-attacks in the morning, their objective on the 25th was to extend control of the Flers trenches in support of the New Zealand advance.

8   T-head sap: a defensive position in which a communication trench runs out to a short section of trench dug parallel to the front line.

9   The Great Bear, Ursa Major, is also known as the Big Dipper. A line drawn from the outer two stars of the Dipper's bowl towards the Pole Star indicates the direction of true north.

10 O'Driscoll did not even survive the war. He died of a heart condition in Dunedin Hospital on 26 August 1918.

22 Goose Alley: 26th September 1916

1   Ashby de la Zouch: an English town with a ruined medieval castle. It is the setting for Sir Walter Scott's *Ivanhoe*—a romantic novel with jousting knights and fair maidens.

2   *Gott mit uns*: God with us. The phrase, originating in Prussian heraldry, was regularly used by the German military, appearing on helmets, belt buckles, and the like.

3   Thiepval fell almost three months after it was meant to be taken in the first hour of the first day of the Battle of the Somme.

4   According to label, Maconochie's tinned army rations contained beef and vegetables. Meant to be served hot, the canned meal was invariably eaten cold—and with congealed fat the most conspicuous ingredient, would be unappetizing in normal circumstances.

5   Haig's plan for 1 July was for the infantry to break the German line and allow his cavalry to sweep through. General Rawlinson's orders on 16 September were for the attack to be renewed to enable 'Cavalry Corps to push through and complete the enemy defeat' (cited, Prior and Wilson, *The Somme*, p. 239)—an expectation still in evidence when cavalry units were brought forward to Gueudecourt on 26 September. Haig was still anticipating that cavalry would play a decisive role at Passchendaele the following year.

6   General Horne, XV Corps commander, planned to continue using the tanks in this sector, but Haig and Rawlinson overruled him. They were right to do so: in a daylight attack across open ground, tanks could be picked off by enemy artillery.

23 Goose Alley: 27th September 1916

1 MS-1961 has '1951' as the date of this postscript.

2 On the afternoon of the 25th, the Division's senior officers received notice that, if the situation were favourable, they should expect orders to immediately push on and overrun Gird Trench. A delay in capturing the village of Gueudecourt on their right flank meant this phase of the attack could not proceed until the 27th.

3 Aitken is referring to the British official history, Miles, *Military Operations: France and Belgium,* 1916, p. 387.

4 In *Passport to Hell,* Howden is 'Bill Howard'—'a young lieutenant from Invercargill and a good boy' (p. 187). In Hyde's rather free reconstruction of Starkie's war experiences, Howden is killed in the late afternoon while leading a desperate charge on Gird trench: 'Suddenly there was a shout, and Starkie saw that Lieutenant Howard's left eye had been shot out of its socket and hung hideously against his cheek. With one magnificent and terrible gesture, the young officer tore off the hanging eyeball and flung it on the ground. He shouted, "Come on!"—and a second later dropped on all fours, shot through the stomach' (p. 187).

5 A few pages torn from a small notebook containing hand-drawn maps, bombardment schedules, along with names and numbers of his platoon came back from the front inside Aitken's pay book (War Souvenirs/Maps: E 2005.24, Edinburgh University Library). Thirteen of the names have subsequently been struck out—presumably because the men were elsewhere on 27 September; others are annotated as killed, wounded, or safe. The annotations seem to have been made soon after the events (perhaps from a hospital bed in London)—hence, there some are disparities with the text as well as with service records. Those listed as killed were: Geary, Paton, Nelson, Livingston, and Scott. Listed as wounded were: Aitken, Drew, Crowe, Ferguson, Gilmour, Huxtable, Ingrey, Jenkins, Kirk, Leake, Lindsay, Miller W. B., Miller F., Naylor W. D., Naylor W. B. B., O'Neill, O'Driscoll, Park, Simpson, Symonds, Tweedie B., Tweedie G. L., Veitch, and Walker. Only one name, that of Leaper, is marked safe. Of these names, I have added those not otherwise mentioned to the commemorative index.

6 See note 3 above.

7 Mylchreest was killed on the night of 27/28 September but Ellis was wounded—and killed in the last year of the war.

8 Where he had cycled 'in the mood of a summer holiday' only three weeks earlier (ch. 17).

9 Finlayson's date of death is uncertain. Reported as missing, a witness recalls seeing him killed by a shell on or about the 25th—and that is the date entered on his service record. But I do not believe that Aitken, even with his wounds, would have hallucinated the faces of the men carrying him to safety.

Bibliography

Aitken, Alexander. *To Catch the Spirit,* ed. P. C. Fenton. Dunedin: University of Otago, 1995.

Aspinall-Oglander, C. F. *Military Operations: Gallipoli.* 2 vols. London: Macmillan, 1938.

Austin, Ronald J. *Gallipoli: An Australian Encyclopaedia of the 1915 Dardanelles Campaign.* Macrae: Slouch Hat, 2005.

Bean, C. E. W. *The Story of Anzac.* 2 vols. Sydney: Angus & Robertson, 1921–24.

Blunden, Edmund. *Undertones of War,* ed. John Greening. Oxford University Press, 2015.

Brown, Malcolm. *The Imperial War Museum Book of the Somme.* London: Pan, 1997.

Burton, O. E. *The Auckland Regiment.* Auckland: Whitcombe & Tombs, 1922.

——,*The Silent Division & Concerning One Man's War,* ed. John H. Gray. Christchurch: John Douglas, 2014.

Byrne, A. E. *Official History of the Otago Regiment in the Great War.* Dunedin: J. Wilkie, 1921.

Cameron, David W. *Gallipoli: The Final Battles and Evacuation of Anzac.* Newport, NSW: Big Sky Publishing, 2011.

Carbery, A. D. *The New Zealand Medical Services in the Great War.* Auckland: Whitcombe & Tombs, 1924.

Chambers, Stephen. *Anzac: Sari Bair.* Barnsley: Pen and Sword, 2014.

Chesterton, G. K. *Collected Poems.* London: Methuen, 1937.

Cowan, James. *Maori in the Great War.* Christchurch: Willsonscott, 2011.

Dante Alighieri. *The Inferno: Definitive Illustrated Edition.* New York: Dover, 2016.

Dyer, Geoff. *The Missing of the Somme.* Edinburgh: Canongate, 2016.

Elgar, Edward. *Letters of Edward Elgar and Other Writings,* ed. Percy M. Young. London: Bles, 1956.

Fenton, Damian. *New Zealand and the First World War 1914–1919.* Auckland: Penguin, 2013.

Ferguson, David. *The History of the Canterbury Regiment, N.Z.E.F., 1914–1919.* Auckland: Whitcombe & Tombs, 1921.

Fussell, Paul. *The Great War and Modern Memory* (1975). Oxford University Press, 2013.

Gliddon, Gerald. *When the Barrage Lifts: A Topographical History of the Battle of the Somme.* Dover, NH: Alan Sutton, 1994.

Graves, Robert. *Goodbye to All That.* London, Penguin, 2000.

Gray, John H. *From the Uttermost Ends of the Earth.* Christchurch: Willson Scott, 2010.

Harper, Glyn. *Johnny Enzed: The New Zealand Soldier in the First World War.* Auckland: Exisle, 2015.

——, *Letters from Gallipoli: New Zealand Soldiers Write Home.* Auckland University Press, 2011.

Hart, Herbert. *The Devil's Own War,* ed. John Crawford. Auckland: Exisle, 2008.

Hyde, Robin. *Passport to Hell,* ed. D. I. B. Smith. Auckland University Press, 2015.

Hynes, Samuel. *A War Imagined: The First World War and English Culture.* London: Bodley Head, 1990.

Keegan, John. *The First World War.* London: Hutchinson, 1998.

Kinglake, Alexander. *Eothen.* New York: Wiley & Putnam, 1845.

Kipling, Rudyard. *Selected Poems.* London: Methuen 1931.

Bibliography

Leadbeater, Tim. 'Aitken's Lemnos: a transformative memory of the Aegean war.'
    100 Years of Trenches, 25 August 2014. http://100yearsoftrenches.blogspot.
    co.nz/2014/08/aitkens-lemnos-transformative-memory-of.html.
Macdonald, Andrew. *On My Way to the Somme*. Auckland: Harper Collins, 2005.
Malthus, Cecil. *Anzac: A Retrospect*. Auckland: Reed, 2002.
——, *Armentières and the Somme*. Auckland: Reed, 2002.
Masefield, John. *Gallipoli*. Toronto: S. B. Gundy, 1916.
McGibbon, Ian. *New Zealand's Western Front Campaign*. Auckland: Bateman, 2016.
——, *The Western Front: A Guide to New Zealand Battlefields and Memorials*. Auckland:
    Penguin, 2015.
McLoughlin, Kate. *Authoring War: The Literary Representation of War from the Iliad to Iraq*.
    Cambridge University Press, 2011.
Miles, Wilfred. *Military Operations: France and Belgium, 1916*. vol. 2. London:
    Macmillan, 1938.
Milton, John. *Paradise Lost*, ed. Philip Pullman. Oxford University Press, 2005.
Pederson, Peter. *Anzacs on the Western Front*. Melbourne: Wiley, 2012.
Pillling, E. G. *An Anzac Memory: Extracts from the Rough Diary of Lieutenant E. G. Pilling*.
    Dunedin: Stanton Bros., 1933.
——, 'Notes on the "Varsity in Egypt"',*Otago University Review*, October 1916, 36–37.
Prior, Robin and Trevor Wilson. *The Somme*. New Haven: Yale University Press, 2016.
Protheroe, R. E. *The Pleasant Land of France*. London: John Murray, 1908.
Pugsley Christopher. *Gallipoli: The New Zealand Story*. Auckland: Reed, 1999.
——, *Te Hokowhitu A Tu: The Maori Pioneer Battalion in the First World War*. Auckland:
    Libro International, 2015.
Pugsley, Christopher and Charles Ferral. *Remembering Gallipoli: Interviews with
    New Zealand Gallipoli Veterans*. Wellington: Victoria University Press, 2015.
Remarque, Erich Maria. *All Quiet on the Western Front*, trans. Brian Murdoch. London:
    Vintage, 1996.
Sassoon, Siegfried. *Diaries 1915–1918*, ed. R. Hart-Davis. London: Faber, 1983.
——, *Memoirs of a Fox-Hunting Man*. London: Faber, 1965.
——, *Memoirs of an Infantry Officer*. New York: Penguin, 2013.
Scott, Keith Douglas. *Before ANZAC, Beyond Armistice*. Auckland: Activity Press, 2009.
Scott, Walter. *The Poetical Works of Sir Walter Scott*. Edinburgh: Robert Cadell, 1841.
Sebag-Montefiore, Hugh. *Somme: Into the Breach*. London: Viking, 2016.
Stevens, Philip. *The Great War Explained*. Barnsley: Pen and Sword, 2012.
Stevenson, David. *1914–1918*. London: Penguin, 2012.
Stewart, H. *The New Zealand Division 1916–1919*. Auckland: Whitcombe & Tombs, 1921.
Strachan, Hew. *The First World War*. London: Simon & Schuster, 2003.
Tennyson, Alfred. *Poems*. Harmondsworth: Penguin, 1985.
Tolerton, Jane. *An Awfully Big Adventure*. Auckland: Penguin, 2013.
Virgil, *The Aeneid*, trans. Robert Fagles. New York: Viking, 2006.
Waite, Fred. *The New Zealanders at Gallipoli*. Auckland: Whitcombe & Tombs, 1921.
Wells, H. G. *The War That Will End War*. London: Frank and Cecil Palmer, 1914.
Wright, Matthew. *The New Zealand Experience at Gallipoli and the Western Front*. Auckland:
    Oratia, 2017.
——, *Western Front: The New Zealand Division in the First World War, 1916–1918*.
    Auckland: Reed, 2005.

Commemorative Index of Names

This index traces all New Zealand Army personnel mentioned in this edition. Where a soldier is listed as sick or wounded with no further comment, it can be assumed that the incident was serious enough to require hospitalization and that the soldier eventually returned to active service and survived the war. Where wounds or sickness brought an end to a soldier's service, I note that he was given a medical discharge. I have not attempted to distinguish between those killed in action, missing, or who died of wounds—all are listed as killed—nor have I tracked those who returned to New Zealand only to die prematurely as a result of their service. Readers wishing to know more about any particular individual's war experiences should enter the soldier's regimental number on the 'Online Cenotaph' maintained by the Auckland War Memorial Museum. The 'Online Cenotaph' provides links to military personnel files, embarkation rolls, photographs, the records of the Commonwealth War Graves Commission, and other documents.

Aitken, Alexander Craig: 8/2524, wounded 27 Sept. 1916, med. discharge, *passim.*
Alderman, Walter William: 5/15, wounded 25 April 1915, 40, 43, 44, 189.
Allan, Malcolm Robert: 8/2525, wounded, 25 Sept. 1916, med. discharge, 37.
Allington, George Ernest: 8/2402, killed 14 June 1917, 98–100, 198.
Alloo, Howard Cecil: 8/3149, wounded 29 Aug. 1918, 83.

Bain, William Alexander: 8/2251, killed 28 Sept. 1916, 102, 116, 162.
Bartlett, Frederick Henry: 8/2509, killed 8 Dec. 1915, 37.
Benham, Philip Blaxland: 3/1122, 132.
Black, George Harry: 11/2392, killed 14 July 1916, 102.
Boyes, Andrew Colquhoun: 8/1092, killed 16 May 1916, 194.
Bree, James: 8/13, wounded Aug. 1915, killed 14 July 1916, 65, 99–101, 105, 107, 192.
Brockett, Archibald Geoffrey: 1/286, 10/3151, sick Jan. 1915, med. discharge; re-enlisted, killed 15 July 1916, 103–104, 149, 198.
Brodie, Gordon: 10/2488, killed 24 Nov. 1915, 31, 187.
Buck, Peter (Te Rangi Hiroa): 16/593, 50, 190.
Buddle, Dudley Harcourt Sheppard: 8/1418, sick Aug. 1915, med. discharge, 63, 75.
Burnett, James: (7th Cameronians), 83, 89.
Burt, Richard Henry: 8/2410, wounded 22 Oct. 1917, 94.
Burton, Ormond: 3/483, wounded three times, xxiv, 189, 194, 196.

Carnegie, Joseph Kenn: 8/1209, wounded 25 Sept. 1916, med. discharge, 148.
Carruthers, William Thomas: 8/738, killed 12 Oct. 1917, xxiv, 74, 101.
Chadwick, Joseph: 12/1913, sick, med. discharge Aug. 1916, 39, 44.
Champion, Ivor Edward: 8/1426, killed 27 Sept. 1916, 149.